الصحابيات الجليلات

Great Women of Islam

Who Were Given The Good News Of Paradise

ALL RIGHTS RESERVED © جميع حقوق الطبع محفوظة

No part of this book may be reproduced or utilized in any form or by any means, electronic or mechanical, including photocopying and recording or by any information storage and retrieval system, without the written permission of the publisher.

2nd Edition: September 2009
Supervised by:
Abdul Malik Mujahid

HEAD OFFICE
P.O. Box: 22743, Riyadh 11416 K.S.A.Tel: 00966-1-4033962/4043432 Fax: 4021659
E-mail: darussalam@awalnet.net.sa, riyadh@dar-us-salam.com Website: www.dar-us-salam.com

K.S.A. Darussalam Showrooms:
Riyadh
Olaya branch: Tel 00966-1-4614483 Fax: 4644945
Malaz branch: Tel: 00966-1-4735220 Fax: 4735221
Suwailam branch: Tel & Fax-1-2860422
- **Jeddah**
  Tel: 00966-2-6879254 Fax: 6336270
- **Madinah**
  Tel: 00966-04-8234446, 8230038
  Fax: 04-8151121
- **Al-Khobar**
  Tel: 00966-3-8692900 Fax: 8691551
- **Khamis Mushayt**
  Tel & Fax: 00966-072207055
- **Yanbu Al-Bahr** Tel: 0500887341 Fax: 04-3908027
- **Al-Buraida** Tel: 0503417156 Fax: 06-3696124

U.A.E
- **Darussalam, Sharjah U.A.E**
  Tel: 00971-6-5632623 Fax: 5632624
  Sharjah@dar-us-salam.com.

PAKISTAN
- **Darussalam,** 36 B Lower Mall, Lahore
  Tel: 0092-42-724 0024 Fax: 7354072
- **Rahman Market, Ghazni Street,**Urdu Bazar Lahore
  Tel: 0092-42-7120054 Fax: 7320703
- **Karachi,** Tel: 0092-21-4393936 Fax: 4393937
- **Islamabad,** Tel: 0092-51-2500237 Fax: 512281513

U.S.A
- **Darussalam, Houston**
  P.O Box: 79194 Tx 77279
  Tel: 001-713-722 0419 Fax: 001-713-722 0431
  E-mail: houston @dar-us-salam.com
- **Darussalam, New York** 486 Atlantic Ave, Brooklyn
  New York-11217, Tel: 001-718-625 5925
  Fax: 718-625 1511
  E-mail: darussalamny@hotmail.com

U.K
- **Darussalam International Publications Ltd.**
  Leyton Business Centre
  Unit-17, Etloe Road, Leyton, London, E10 7BT
  Tel: 0044 20 8539 4885 Fax:0044 20 8539 4889
  Website: www.darussalam.com
  Email: info@darussalam.com
- **Darussalam International Publications Limited**
  Regents Park Mosque, 146 Park Road
  London NW8 7RG Tel: 0044- 207 725 2246
  Fax: 0044 20 8539 4889

AUSTRALIA
- **Darussalam:** 153, Haldon St, Lakemba (Sydney)
  NSW 2195, Australia
  Tel: 0061-2-97407188 Fax: 0061-2-97407199
  Mobile: 0061-414580813 Res: 0061-2-97580190
  Email: abumuaaz@hotamail.com

CANADA
- **Nasser Khattab**
  2-3415 Dixie Rd, Unit # 505
  Mississauga
  Ontario L4Y 4J6, Canada
  Tel: 001-416-418 6619
- **Islamic Book Service**
  2200 South Sheridan way Mississauga, On
  L5J 2M4
  Tel: 001-905-403-8406 Ext. 218 Fax: 905-8409

MALAYSIA
- **Darussalam**
  Int'l Publishing & Distribution SDN BHD
  D-2-12, Setiawangsa 11, Taman Setiawangsa
  54200 Kuala Lumpur
  Tel: 03-42528200 Fax: 03-42529200
  Email: darussalam@streamyx.com
  Website: www.darussalam.com.my

FRANCE
- **Editions & Librairie Essalam**
  135, Bd de Ménilmontant- 75011 Paris
  Tél: 0033-01- 43 38 19 56/ 44 83
  Fax: 0033-01-43 57 44 31
  E-mail: essalam@essalam com·

SINGAPORE
- **Muslim Converts Association of Singapore**
  32 Onan Road The Galaxy
  Singapore- 424484
  Tel: 0065-440 6924, 348 8344 Fax: 440 6724

SRI LANKA
- Darul Kitab 6, Nimal Road, Colombo-4
  Tel: 0094 115 358712 Fax: 115-358713

INDIA
- **Islamic Books International**
  54, Tandel Street (North)
  Dongri, Mumbai 4000 09, INDIA
  Tel: 0091-22-2373 4180
  E-mail: ibi@irf.net

SOUTH AFRICA
- **Islamic Da'wah Movement (IDM)**
  48009 Qualbert 4078 Durban,South Africa
  Tel: 0027-31-304-6883 Fax: 0027-31-305-1292
  E-mail: idm@ion.co.za

الصحابيات الجليلات

Great Women of Islam

Who Were Given The Good News Of Paradise

By
Mahmood Ahmad Ghadanfar

Translated by
Jamila Muhammad Qawi

Revised by
Sheikh Safiur-Rahman Al-Mubarakpuri

Edited by
Muhammad Ayub Sapra
Muhammad Farooq

DARUSSALAM
Publishers & Distributors
Riyadh, Saudi Arabia

بِسْمِ اللَّهِ الرَّحْمَٰنِ الرَّحِيمِ

In the Name of Allâh, the Most Gracious, the Most Merciful

"Verily, the Muslims (those who submit to Allâh in Islâm) men and women, the believers men and women (who believe in Islâmic Monotheism), the men and the women who are obedient (to Allâh), the men and women who are truthful (in their speech and deeds), the men and women who are patient (in performing all the duties which Allâh has ordered and in abstaining from all that Allâh has forbidden), the men and the women who are humble (before their Lord — Allâh), the men and the women who give *Sadaqât* (i.e. *Zakât* and alms), the men and the women who observe *Saum* (fast) (the obligatory fasting during the month of *Ramadhân*, and the optional *Nawâfil* fasting), the men and the women who guard their chastity (from illegal sexual acts) and the men and the women who remember Allâh much with their hearts and tongues. Allâh has prepared for them forgiveness and a great reward (i.e. Paradise)." (33:35)

Table of Contents

Publisher's Note 07

Exploits and Achievements of the *Sahâbiyât* 09

Khadîjah bint Khuwaylid رضي الله عنها 19

Saudah bint Zam'ah رضي الله عنها 31

'A'ishah bint Abu Bakr رضي الله عنها 41

Hafsah bint 'Umar رضي الله عنها 59

Zainab bint Khuzaymah رضي الله عنها 71

Umm Salamah رضي الله عنها 77

Zainab bint Jahsh رضي الله عنها 93

Juwayriyah bint Hârith رضي الله عنها 105

Safiyyah bint Huyayy رضي الله عنها 113

Umm Habîbah Ramlah bint Abi Sufyân رضي الله عنها 123

Maimûnah bint Hârith Al-Hilâliyah رضي الله عنها 135

Fâtimah bint Muhammad رضي الله عنها 145

Fâtimah bint Asad رضي الله عنها 161

Umm Rummân رضي الله عنها 169

Sumayyah bint Khabbât رضي الله عنها 177

Umm Harâm bint Milhân رضي الله عنها 183

Asmâ' bint Abu Bakr Siddeeq رضي الله عنها 189
Umm Sulaim bint Milhân Al-Ansâriyah رضي الله عنها 199
Umm 'Ammârah Nusaybah رضي الله عنها 207
Ar-Rubai' bint Mu'awwith رضي الله عنها 215
Faree'ah bint Mâlik رضي الله عنها 223
Umm Hishâm bint Hârithah bin Nu'mân رضي الله عنها 229
Umm Salamah Asmâ' bint Yazîd bin Sakan Al-Ansâriyah رضي الله عنها 235
Umm Sa'd Kabshah bint Râfi' Al-Ansâriyah رضي الله عنها 243
Umm Munthir Salmâ bint Qais رضي الله عنها 251
Umm Waraqah bint 'Abdullâh bin Hârith Al-Ansâriyah رضي الله عنها 257
Umm Aiman رضي الله عنها 263

Publisher's Note

All praises are due to Allâh the Almighty, the Lord of all that exists. May Allâh's peace and blessings be upon His final Prophet and Messenger, Muhammad, his noble family and his Companions.

Darussalam is pleased to present this valuable book, *'Great Women of Islâm, Who Were Given the Good News of Paradise'*. It was compiled in the Urdu language by a great scholar and a compiler of Islâmic books, Mahmood Ahmad Ghadanfar, and translated by our Muslim sister Jamila Muhammad Qawi.

This book is about the life stories of the Mothers of the Believers and sixteen women Companions of the Prophet ﷺ. They were those pure and virtuous women of Islâm who were honored during the very lifetime of the Prophet ﷺ with the prediction that they would live forever in Paradise in the hereafter.

All the Mothers of the Believers were of very noble character and conduct and pleased Allâh so much that He sent special greetings for Khadîjah رضي الله عنها. 'A'ishah رضي الله عنها had a brilliant mind and a remarkable memory, and had the distinction of being the source of many *Ahâdîth* (Prophetic narrations) because of her long association with the Prophet ﷺ. Her knowledge of the many branches of religion like *Tafsîr* (Qur'anic exegesis), *Hadîth* (Prophetic narrations), *Fiqh* (Islâmic jurisprudence) and *Sharî'ah* (Islâmic legislation), her wisdom in interpretation, her mastery of the teachings of the Prophet ﷺ – all these qualities made her one of the most remarkable personalities of the time.

Women Companions were very active in religion as well as in politics and business. They were courageous in the battlefield and provided services like giving medical aid to the soldiers, nursing the wounded, and providing food and water to the needy in a manner which has no parallel in history. They spread the message of Islâm and it is proved by many instances that their conduct converted many disbelievers to Islâm.

There are many more stories like this that will encourage our Muslim sisters to acquire more knowledge about such great women. I hope that they will study this book thoroughly and try their best to follow these noble women of Islâm.

I pray to Allâh the Almighty that He grants them all – the writer, translator and editor and everyone else who participated by any means – the best reward in this world and in the hereafter, for their support in the completion of such a valuable book. *Âmeen*

Abdul Malik Mujahid
General Manager
Darussalam

Exploits and Achievements of the *Sahâbiyât* (Women Companions)

Exploits and Achievements of the Sahâbiyât (Women Companions)

The *Sahâbiyât* (Women Companions) were the noble women who were the contemporaries of the Prophet Muhammad ﷺ. They were the pure, virtuous crusaders of Islâm, and were honored during the very lifetime of Prophet Muhammad ﷺ with the prediction that they would live forever in Paradise in the hereafter. Their achievements and influence are found in every sphere of that momentous period in the history of the world, which transformed the whole of humanity forever. They were as active in religion as in politics, as courageous in war as in the peaceful and persuasive propagation of the teachings of Islâm. These noble, selfless women could be found in the battlefields among the foremost ranks of those taking part in *Jihâd*. They were to be found in the political arena, in the field of education, in the courts of Islâmic jurisprudence, in the interpretation of *Sharî'ah*,[1] in trade and commerce, in agriculture, in medicine and in nursing. In short, there was no sphere that did not benefit from their intellect, their wisdom and their gentle yet firm strength of character.

Religious Achievements

Among the many services that one can render to Islâm, is to fight in

---

[1] The collective body of laws as revealed by Allâh ﷻ.

the battlefields. Few, if any, examples of such zeal, determination, perseverance and courage can be found in history. When the disbelievers attacked the Muslims during the Battle of Uhud, only a few devoted followers were left to fight with the Prophet ﷺ. At this critical stage, the woman Companion Umm 'Ammârah رضي الله عنها shielded him with her body and warded off the enemy with her sword as well as her bow and arrows. When one of the disbelievers of the Quraish, Ibn Qamiah, got within striking distance of Prophet Muhammad ﷺ, it was she who bore the brunt of his attack. She had a deep wound on her shoulder, yet she continued to attack him with her sword. But he was well protected and she could not make a dent in his armor. Later, she fought so courageously against Musailamah Al-Kaththâb that she suffered a dozen wounds and lost an arm.

In the Battle of Ahzâb (Battle of the Trench), the Companion Safiyyah رضي الله عنها displayed brilliant military strategy in handling the Jewish attack, and slew one of the Jews. In the Battle of Hunain, Umm Sulaim رضي الله عنها set out to attack the enemy with her dagger.

In the Battle of Yarmook, Asmâ' bint Abu Bakr, Umm Abân, Umm Hakeem, Khawlah, Hind and the Mother of the Believers Juwairiyah رضي الله عنهن displayed extraordinary valor. Asmâ' bint Yazîd رضي الله عنها killed nine enemy soldiers. In the year 28 AH, Umm Harâm رضي الله عنها took part in the attack on Cyprus.

The Mother of the Believers 'A'ishah, Umm Sulaim and Umm Salit رضي الله عنهن were among those who were very proficient at nursing the wounded.

The *Sahâbiyât* رضي الله عنهن usually accompanied the Prophet ﷺ on his military expeditions and took part in battles both on land and at sea. Standing side by side with the soldiers they would hand them arrows, and generally help to keep up the morale of the army. They also helped to carry the martyred and the wounded back to Madinah. Umm 'Atiyah رضي الله عنها took part in seven battles, and fought during the rule of the Caliph 'Umar Farooq ﷺ, the women and even the children helped to bury the dead.

They spread the message of the new religion and through example converted many of the disbelievers to Islâm. It was Fâtimah bint al-

Khattâb رضي الله عنها who converted her brother 'Umar bin al-Khattâb ؓ; he was to become one of the bravest and most faithful of the Companions of the Prophet Muhammad ﷺ. It was Umm Sulaim رضي الله عنها who influenced Abu Talhah ؓ, and it was Umm Hakim رضي الله عنها who convinced her husband, 'Ikrimah to accept Islâm. Umm Shareek al-Dawsiyah رضي الله عنها very discreetly worked among the women of the tribe of Quraish to spread Islâm.

Another aspect of missionary work is to preserve the religion in its pristine form, and protect it from any modifications, impurities and innovations that may creep in because of cultural or traditional practices already prevalent in society. This very important work of preserving the purity of Islâm was performed by many of the *Sahâbiyât*; most prominent among them was 'A'ishah رضي الله عنها.

In the year 35 AH, when Caliph 'Uthmân ؓ was martyred and there was chaos and confusion over who was next in the line of succession, it was she who brought unity into the ranks by influencing the Muslims of Basrah (Iraq) and Makkah.

Leading the prayers and calling the *Adhân*, or the call for prayer, is another important aspect of religious life. Although women cannot lead men in prayers, they can do so with assemblies of women. Many women contemporaries of Prophet Muhammad ﷺ performed this task as well. 'A'ishah, Umm Sulaim, Umm Waraqah and Sa'dah bint Qamâmah رضي الله عنهن were some of the most prominent among these. In fact, Umm Waraqah رضي الله عنها turned her house into a place of prayer for women; the *Adhân*[1] was given there by a lady *Mu'adhdhin*[2] for the women's congregation, and Umm Waraqah رضي الله عنها performed the duties of the *Imâm* in leading the prayers.

Political Achievements

The *Sahâbiyât* (Women Companions) played a prominent role in politics as well. Caliph 'Umar ؓ so valued Shifa' bint 'Abdullâh رضي الله عنها for her political intelligence and insight that he very often consulted with her. He often gave her the responsibility of running the affairs of state

---

[1] The call to prayer given 5 times during the day.
[2] The *Mu'adhdhin's* duty is to give the *Adhân*.

relating to trade and commerce. Before the *Hijrah* (migration) of Prophet Muhammad ﷺ to Madinah, the disbelievers wanted to lay siege to his house, it was Ruqayyah bint Saifee رضي الله عنها who warned him. The Prophet Muhammad ﷺ then secretly left for Madinah, leaving 'Ali ؓ asleep in his place. Vast political rights are granted to women in Islâm. A woman even has the right to grant shelter to an enemy, if she so wishes. A historian, Abu Dawood relates that Umm Hâni رضي الله عنها, the sister of 'Ali ؓ, had given refuge to an enemy disbeliever and the Prophet ﷺ said:

> "If you have guaranteed sanctuary and safety to a person, then we stand by you."

This is the law of Islâm that the *Imâm*[1] or leader has to stand by the guarantee offered by the woman.

Education, Knowledge and the Fine Arts

There are various subjects, an understanding of which are essential for a thorough knowledge of Islâm and its tenets. *Qirâ'at,*[2] interpretation and commentary, *Sharî'ah, Fiqh,* study of *Hadîth,* all are important aspects of Islâmic studies. Many of the women Companions were experts in these fields. 'A'ishah رضي الله عنها memorized the Qur'ân as did Hafsah, Umm Salamah, Umm Waraqah رضي الله عنهن. Hind bint Usaid, Umm Hishâm bint Harithah, Zaidah bint Hayyân; Umm Sa'ad bint Sa'ad رضي الله عنهن all knew portions of the Qur'ân by heart. The latter used to regularly lecture on the Qur'ân. In the sensitive sphere of interpretation of *Hadîth,* all were experts, but 'A'ishah and Umm Salamah رضي الله عنهما were exceptional masters of interpretation and commentary. With the former, 2,210 *Ahâdîth* are associated and 378 with the latter.

'A'ishah رضي الله عنها was an expert on interpretation and commentary due to her close association with the Prophet ﷺ. Much of the *Book of Tafsîr* in *Sahîh Muslim* contains narrations from her.

Asmâ' bint Abu Bakr, Umm 'Atiyah, Umm Hâni and Fâtimah bint Qais رضي الله عنهن also had extensive knowledge of *Ahâdîth.*

---

[1] The *Imam* leads the prayer in the congregation.
[2] The correct way of reading the Qur'ân – elocution and enunciation.

Exploits and Achievements of the 'Sahâbiyât'

In Islâmic jurisprudence or *Fiqh* 'A'ishah's verdicts could fill several volumes. The same could be said of Umm Salmah's recorded verdicts.

The invaluable verdicts of Safiyyah, Hafsah, Umm Habîbah, Juwairiyah, Fâtimah (the Prophet's daughter), Umm Shareek, Umm 'Atiyah, Asmâ' bint Abu Bakr, Laila bint Qâi'f , Khawlah bint Tuyait, Umm Dardâ, 'Atikah bint Zaid, Sahlah bint Suhail, Fâtimah bint Qais, Zainab bint Jahsh, Umm Salamah, Umm Aiman, Umm Yusuf رضي الله عنهن could fill several volumes.

'A'ishah رضي الله عنها was also well versed in the law of inheritance and many renowned and respected Companions consulted her on the finer points of the law.

Besides being masters of Islâmic law and of the finer points of *Fiqh*, the women Companions had skill and ability in other branches of knowledge. Asmâ' bint Yazîd bin Sakan رضي الله عنها was an expert in making speeches; Asmâ' bint 'Umais رضي الله عنها was famous for her interpretation of dreams. Several Companions were noted for their skill in medicine and surgery. Aslamiyah Umm Mattâ'a, Umm Kabshah , Hamnah bint Jahsh, Mu'aâthah, Ammaimah, Umm Ziad, Rubai' bint Mu'awwith, Umm 'Atiyah, Umm Sulaim رضي الله عنهن were some of them, well known for their skills. Rufaidah Aslamiyah's tent, set up as a surgery station with all the necessary instruments, was situated close to the Prophet's Mosque at Madinah. The arts were not neglected by any means. Some of the most noted poetesses were, Sa'adi, Safiyah, 'Atikah bint Zaid, Hind bint Athâthah, Umm Aiman, Kabashah bint Râfi'a, Umâmah Maridiah, Hind bint Hârith, Zainab bint 'Awwâm Azdi, Maimoonah and Ruqayyah رضي الله عنهن. A book of verses by Khansâ' رضي الله عنها, the best known among them has been published.

Industry, Trade and Commerce

The women Companions also practiced the practical or survival skills as we know them today. Agriculture, business, trade and commerce, writing, editing, cottage industries like weaving, manufacture and designing of clothes — all these are mentioned in the *Musnad* (collection of *Ahâdîth*) of Imâm Ahmad. Agriculture was not so common, but was mainly practiced in the rural fertile areas around Madinah, especially by the women of the *Ansâr*. Among the immigrants, or *Muhâjir* as they were known, Asmâ' also practiced farming. The era before the advent of the Prophet ﷺ was known as the age of illiteracy, but some of these worthy women were highly educated and skilled in the arts of penmanship and calligraphy. Shifâ' bint 'Abdullâh رضي الله عنها learned to read and write even during these dark ages and was celebrated for her skill in this art. Hafsah, Umm Kulthum bint 'Uqbah and Karimah bint Miqdâd رضي الله عنهن were all literate. 'A'ishah and Umm Salamah رضي الله عنهما could not write but they could read. Both of them were blessed with remarkable memories and inquiring minds; and because of their close association with the Prophet ﷺ many of the authentic *Ahâdîth* originated from them.

Some of the *Sahâbiyât* also ran businesses. Khadîjah رضي الله عنها was a very successful businesswoman and used to send trading caravans to different countries. Khawlah, Maleekah, Thaqafiyah, and Bint Fakhariyah رضي الله عنهن used to trade in the oriental oil-based perfumes known as *'Itr*. Saudah رضي الله عنها operated a leather tanning industry. The daughters of the *Ansâr* would compose verses and poems for festive occasions and sing. According to a *Hadîth* narrated by Rubai' bint Mu'awwith رضي الله عنها, they recited their poems in the presence of the Prophet ﷺ, who appreciated their literary skills.

Umm Salamah رضي الله عنها used to recite the Qur'ân with *Tajweed*, which is a difficult skill and much appreciated.

Thus there was no sphere of activity – social or cultural – that was not influenced and assisted by the presence of these great ladies. May Allâh ﷻ have mercy on their souls!

May Allâh be pleased with them and they with Him.

امهات المؤمنين

Mothers
of the Believers

Khadîjah bint Khuwaylid رضي الله عنها

Narrated Abu Hurairah ﷺ: Jibrîl (Gabriel) came to the Prophet ﷺ and said: "O Allâh's Messenger! This is Khadîjah, coming to you with a dish having meat soup (or some food or drink). When she reaches you, greet her on behalf of her Lord (Allâh) and on my behalf, and give her the glad tidings of having a palace made of Qasab in Paradise, wherein there will be neither any noise nor any toil (fatigue, trouble, etc.)." (Al-Bukhâri)

Khadîjah bint Khuwaylid رضي الله عنها

The strength of character and noble qualities of Khadîjah رضي الله عنها earned her the honor of being greeted by Allâh ﷻ through His Angel Jibrîl ﷺ.

The epitome of faithfulness, integrity, truth, modesty, good manners and nobility; generous, wise and understanding, nurtured in an atmosphere of wealth and luxury, she was the first person to have an abiding faith in the utterances of the Prophet ﷺ and to accept Islâm as her religion and her way of life. She was blessed with the distinction of having been greeted with *Salâm* by Allâh ﷻ and the Angel Jibrîl ﷺ. She was the first lady ever to be so honored. She was the first wife of the Prophet ﷺ, and he did not marry again during her lifetime. They lived together in peace and harmony for more than 24 years. It was in her house that the Prophet ﷺ received the revelations of Allâh ﷻ, through the Angel Jibrîl ﷺ. During the siege that the Prophet ﷺ underwent in Makkah, in the Shi'b Abi Tâlib, she was there by his side, constantly supportive and sacrificing all the comforts of life.

When she passed away, the Prophet ﷺ was heartbroken at the loss of a dedicated companion who stood by him during the most difficult period of his life. He personally supervised the preparation of her grave, and climbed down into it to ensure it was well-prepared. He then lowered her body into the grave himself. Thus ended the life of the lady who was the greatest supporter of Islâm in its earliest days. She, who was the mother of Fâtimah رضي الله عنها, the First Lady of Paradise, the grandmother of the beloved grandchildren of the Prophet ﷺ, Hasan and Hussain رضي الله عنهما who are to be the foremost of the youths in Paradise.

'Abdullâh bin 'Abbâs ؓ narrated that one day the Prophet ﷺ drew four lines on the earth and asked his Companions if they understood what these lines stood for. They respectfully replied that he knew better. He then told them that these lines stood for the four foremost ladies of the universe. They were Khadîjah bint Khuwaylid, Fâtimah bint Muhammad, Maryam bint Imrân, the mother of Prophet Isa علیہ السلام, and 'Âsiyah bint Mazâhim رضي الله عنهن (the wife of the Pharaoh).

The first named has the distinction of being the mother of all the believers, or practicing Muslims; the second Fâtimah, the daughter of the Prophet ﷺ was given the glad tidings that she would be the leader among the women of Paradise. Maryam علیها السلام, the Pure and Chaste is the only woman to have given birth to 'Isa علیہ السلام, a Prophet of Allâh without having been touched by any man.

'Âsiyah, the long suffering and righteous wife of the evil Pharaoh, had advised her husband to adopt the infant Mûsa (Moses) علیہ السلام. This was at a time when infanticide was the law of the land. All the newborn boys of the tribe of Israel were being murdered because of the prediction that one of them would finally overthrow the Pharaoh and destroy him. She not only nurtured him in the very palace of Pharaoh, but also was one of the first to accept Islâm, as preached by Mûsa علیہ السلام.

'A'ishah رضي الله عنها narrates that whenever the Prophet ﷺ talked about Khadîjah رضي الله عنها, it was in terms of the highest praise. One day her innate feminine envy overtook her sense of decorum and she spoke in disparaging terms of her, wondering why the Prophet ﷺ missed her when he was blessed with a better, younger wife by Allâh ﷻ. This displeased him, but forbearing as he was, he just sighed and answered:

> "I have not yet found a better wife than her. She had faith in me when everyone, even members of my own family and tribe did not believe me, and accepted that I was truly a Prophet and a Messenger of Allâh ﷻ. She converted to Islâm, spent all her wealth and worldly goods to help

me spread this faith, and this too at a time when the entire world seemed to have turned against me and persecuted me. And it is through her that Allâh ﷻ blessed me with children."

Khadîjah رضي الله عنها was born in Makkah in the year 556 CE. Her mother's name was Fâtimah bint Zâ'id, and her father's name was Khuwaylid bin Asad. He was a very popular leader among the tribe of Quraish, and a very prosperous businessman who died while fighting in the famous battle of Fujjâr. Khadîjah رضي الله عنها thus grew up in the lap of luxury. She married Abu Hâlah Malak bin Nabash bin Zarrarah bin At-Tamimi. She bore him two children, Hâlah and Hind. She wanted to see her husband prosper and financed him in setting up a big business. But unfortunately he passed away. Sometime later, the young widow married 'Ateeq bin 'Aith bin 'Abdullâh Al-Makhzûmi, and she had a daughter by him as well named Hindah. But the marriage soon broke up on grounds of incompatibility. After this all her attention was devoted to the upbringing of her children, and building up the business she inherited from her father.

Her astuteness and business acumen made hers one of the most widespread businesses among the Quraish. Her policy was to employ hardworking, honest and discriminating managers to deal on her behalf. There was no network of travel and communication as there is today and a lot depended on the integrity of the employees who traveled far and wide on her behalf. She exported her goods to far away markets like Syria, and her managers bought goods from those markets to be sold at home. Makkah being strategically located on the trading caravan routes and the center of international trade fairs, was a very profitable market for the goods brought back. The managers would get fifty percent of the profit, and this was enough incentive for them.

Khadîjah رضي الله عنها had heard of the integrity, honesty and principled behavior of the Prophet ﷺ, and sent a job offer to him to head her trading caravans. He gladly accepted the offer and started working for her. Khadîjah sent him on a business trip; her old and trusted slave Maisarah being delegated to accompany and serve him.

This trip proved to be an extremely profitable venture and Maisarah was astounded by some very remarkable scenes he witnessed on this trip. He was impressed and completely won over by the Prophet's integrity, strength of character, adherence to principles, his amicable dealings and his business abilities. On the way back from Syria, the Prophet ﷺ lay down under a tree to rest for a while. Nestor, a Christian monk, noted for his knowledge of religion and for his insight saw him and asked Maisarah who he was. Maisarah told him all about Muhammad ﷺ and his reputation for honesty and intelligence. Nestor then told him that this man would be elevated to Prophethood in the future, as no man had ever rested under that particular tree but Prophets.

Tradition has it that Maisarah saw two angels bearing a cloud over the Prophet's head to protect him from the glare and heat of the sun. He was stunned and overcome by a sense of gratitude that he had been given the opportunity of benefiting from the close companionship of this man soon to be chosen by Allâh ﷻ as His Messenger.

When he returned home, Maisarah reported to Khadîjah رضي الله عنها all that had taken place on the trip to Syria. She was deeply moved and impressed, and started thinking of proposing marriage to Muhammad ﷺ. But how could she express her thoughts to him? She already rejected several proposals of marriage from men belonging to some of the noblest families of the Quraish. How would her tribe react? What would her family say? And what was more, would her proposal be acceptable to this young, yet unmarried man of the tribe of Quraish?

As she pondered over these questions and debated within herself, one night she dreamt that the shining sun had descended from the heavens into her courtyard, radiating her home. When she woke up she went for the interpretation of this wonderful dream to her cousin, Waraqah bin Nawfal, a blind man noted for his skill in interpreting dreams, and for depth of his knowledge, particularly of the Torah and the Injîl. When he heard her dream, he gave a serene smile, and told her not to worry, as this was a very promising dream. The glorious sun she saw descending into her courtyard indicated that the Prophet ﷺ whose advent had been predicted in the Torah and the Injîl was to grace her home and she would gain from his presence in her life.

After this meeting with Waraqah she became stronger in her desire to marry Muhammad ﷺ. But she was still not sure how to go about it. One of her very close friends, Nafeesah bint Manbah knew of her inclination. One day she told Khadîjah that what was bothering her so much was not a major problem, and she herself would help her to solve it. She went immediately to Muhammad ﷺ, and without much ado she requested his permission to ask him a very personal question. When he said he had no objection, she asked why he had not yet got married. He said he did not have the financial resources to do so. Then she asked him if he would be willing to marry a beautiful lady from a noble and wealthy family, who was inclined towards marriage with him. He asked whom she was referring to; when he learnt her identity he said that he was willing, provided she was willing to marry him. Of course Khadîjah رضي الله عنها was overjoyed. The Prophet ﷺ was then twenty-five years of age and Khadîjah رضي الله عنها was forty years old. (According to one tradition, she was twenty-eight).

The two uncles of the Prophet ﷺ, Hamzah ؓ and Abu Tâlib approached her uncle 'Umar bin Asad with the formal proposal. It was accepted and the date was fixed. The two families began preparing for the wedding. On the date that had been fixed, the families and friends gathered and the marriage was solemnized. Halimah Sa'adiyah who nursed the Prophet ﷺ in his infancy was specially invited for the wedding and traveled to Makkah from her village. When she left after the festivities, Khadîjah presented her with household goods, a camel and forty goats as an expression of gratitude to the lady who had taken such good care of Muhammad ﷺ in his infancy.

Khadîjah was very blessed in the marriage, and had six children: first two sons, Qâsim and 'Abdullâh; followed by daughters, Zainab, Ruqayyah, Umm Kulthum and Fâtimah رضي الله عنهم. They were wonderful, intelligent children and it was a very happy, peaceful and content household. But all this did not seem enough. Muhammad ﷺ felt something was missing, and he was extremely restless. He would retire for a month once a year to the Cave of Hirâ' to dedicate himself entirely to prayer and meditation.

One day he felt the presence of another being who held him in his arms in a tight embrace. Then he loosened his hold and asked him to '*Read*';

Muhammad ﷺ answered that he was illiterate. But the person repeated the same act and the same command again and again. Then finally he read these *Âyât* which are the first revelation of the Qur'ân. They are from *Surah Iqrâ* or *Al-'Alaq* of the Noble Qur'ân:

> "Read! In the Name of your Lord Who has created (all that exists). He has created man from a clot. Read! And your Lord is the Most Generous. Who has taught (the writing) by the pen. He has taught man that which he knew not." (96:1-5)

Then the being disappeared. This was such an overwhelming experience that the Prophet ﷺ returned home sweating and shaking. He called out to Khadîjah asking her to cover him with a sheet or a blanket. After lying down for some time he became a little more relaxed. When he had calmed down to some extent, he told his wife that he feared for his life, and narrated the whole incident to her.

Khadîjah, a picture of loyalty and serenity consoled him saying that Allâh ﷻ would surely protect him from any danger, and would never allow anyone to revile him as he was a of man of peace and reconciliation and always extended the hand of friendship to all. He never lied, was always hospitable, carried the burdens of others and helped those who were in trouble. These soothing and encouraging words of sympathy and understanding from Khadîjah gave him immeasurable strength and confidence.

She then took him to meet her cousin, Waraqah bin Nawfal, who immediately guessed the identity of the being in the Cave of Hirâ' as the Angel Jibrîl ﷺ, the Messenger of Allâh who had visited Mûsa (Moses) ﷺ as well. Waraqah, who was very old, wished that he could live to see the time when the Prophet Muhammad ﷺ would be forced into exile by his people. The Prophet ﷺ was very surprised and asked if his people would really do this to him. Waraqah assured him that it was typical of human beings that they would never appreciate or follow a Prophet who rose among them. As the proverb has it, *"A Prophet is never honored in his own land."* Waraqah added that he wished he were alive at that time and be able to help him. He added that if what he had been told were true then surely it meant that her husband was the Prophet of Allâh whose advent had been mentioned in the scriptures.

As mentioned earlier, the Prophet ﷺ had six children by Khadîjah رضي الله عنها: four daughters and two sons. The four daughters grew up to be faithful and courageous daughters of Islâm. They were named Zainab, Ruqayyah, Umm Kulthûm and Fâtimah رضي الله عنهن. They all migrated to Madinah, with the Prophet ﷺ. Zainab رضي الله عنها was married to Abul 'Aas bin Rabee'ah and Ruqayyah رضي الله عنها was married to 'Uthmân ﷺ. When she passed away he married Umm Kulthûm رضي الله عنها; Fâtimah رضي الله عنها was married to 'Ali bin Abi Tâlib ﷺ. The first three daughters died during the lifetime of Muhammad ﷺ, and his beloved daughter Fâtimah رضي الله عنها lived just six months after he passed away.

The Prophet ﷺ had three sons, two by Khadîjah رضي الله عنها and Ibrâhîm, a third son by Maria Qibtiyyah رضي الله عنها. The first son was named Qâsim and the Prophet ﷺ came to be known as Abu'l Qâsim.[1] The second son, 'Abdullâh was also known as Tâhir (the pure) or Tayyib (the good). Both died in their childhood and the disbelievers were overjoyed that the Prophet ﷺ had no heirs to carry on his noble mission. The third son, Ibrâhîm was born by his wife, Maria Qibtiyyah رضي الله عنها. He also died in infancy. When he saw Ibrâhîm dying, he gently picked him up and said that he was helpless and could do nothing before the Will of Allâh ﷻ:

> 'We know that death is inevitable and is a fact of life. We also know that those who are left behind will catch up with those who have gone ahead; if this were not so we would grieve even more for Ibrâhîm. The heart mourns and the eye weeps, but it is not fitting that we utter words which might displease our Rabb, our Creator and Sustainer.'

On the day Ibrâhîm passed away there was a solar eclipse. The Arabs of ancient times were superstitious and associated these phenomena of nature - lunar and solar eclipses — with a great man's death. Many Muslims even started associating the solar eclipse with Ibrâhîm's death. But the Prophet ﷺ immediately went up to the pulpit and in his sermon said:

> 'Solar and lunar eclipses are signs of Allâh. They never occur because of the death of any human being. When you see any of these offer Salât.'

His enemies now started calling him *Abtar*, the one who had no descendants, whose lineage was cut off. But, Allâh ﷻ had more lasting

---

[1] Father of Qâsim

bounties in store for him. He then revealed to him the beautiful Verses of *Surat Al-Kawthar*, the 108th *Surah* of the Noble Qur'ân:

"Verily, We have granted you Al-Kawthar. Therefore turn in prayer to your Lord and sacrifice. For he who hates you, he will be cut off." (108:1-3)

When the disbelievers saw that Islâm was attracting more and more followers in spite of all their tactics, they had a meeting to decide what steps should be taken to stop the spread of this new religion. They decided to declare an open and total political and economic boycott of the tribe of Banu Hâshim. This took place in the seventh year after the Prophet ﷺ declared himself the Messenger of Allâh ﷻ.

The boycott was so severe that innocent children faced starvation and hunger, and adults survived eating the leaves of trees. Yet the firm followers of Muhammad ﷺ did not turn away from their true religion and they came out of the ordeal stronger and purer than before.

Khadîjah رضي الله عنها who had been brought up in luxury in her wealthy father's home now faced the economic hardships with patience and courage, which are a necessary part of any siege.

Khadîjah's nobility of character and conduct pleased Allâh ﷻ so much that He sent special greetings for her. This incident was narrated by Muhammad ﷺ to Abu Hurairah ﷜ and quoted in a *Hadîth* of *Sahih Al-Bukhâri*.

Khadîjah رضي الله عنها was an ideal wife and mother. The Prophet ﷺ lived in her house which became a blessed place due to his presence and the fact that Jibrîl عليه السلام came often to visit him there with Qur'ânic revelations. It became the center of Islâm, where the Companions and women Companions visited often to partake of the hospitality of Muhammad ﷺ and his wife.

After the *Hijrah* (migration) of the Prophet ﷺ to Madinah, the house was occupied by the brother of 'Ali. Later Mu'âwiyah bin Abu Sufyân ﷜ who transcribed some of the Divine Revelations purchased this house and built a mosque. Thus the site of the house of Khadîjah رضي الله عنها became a place of prayer and worship for all time. She had been used to praying two *Rak'aât* (units) of *Salât* (prayer), in the mornings and evenings with the Prophet ﷺ, even before prayers were made compulsory by Allâh ﷻ.

There is one incident recorded in history regarding this. After accepting Islâm she became more contemplative and inclined towards worship; she found a blessed feeling of peace in prayer. 'Afif Kindi relates that 'Abbâs bin 'Abdul Muttalib ؓ was a great friend of his and he used to visit him often in Yemen in connection with his business in perfumes. On one occasion when they were standing and chatting in Minâ, they saw a handsome young man approach. He carefully washed his hands and feet and then stood respectfully with his arms crossed on his breast. Soon a dignified lady of noble bearing and a young handsome young lad joined him.

'Afif asked 'Abbâs ؓ what they were doing and whether this was a new form of exercise. 'Abbâs ؓ replied that the youth was his brother 'Abdullâh's son, and the lady was his wife. She was a woman of great wealth and virtue, and an ideal wife and mother. The lad was his brother Abu Tâlib's son. He added that Muhammad ﷺ had announced that he was a Messenger of Allâh and had started preaching a new religion called Islâm. In due course 'Afif accepted Islâm, but he always regretted the fact that he had not joined the Prophet ﷺ and his Companions in their prayers and supplication on that memorable day in Minâ, when he had first heard of Islâm.

Khadîjah رضي الله عنها passed away just three years before the *Hijrah*, or the Prophet's migration to Madinah. She died at the age of sixty-five, having given almost twenty-five years to Muhammad ﷺ and the cause of Islâm. When Muhammad ﷺ saw her in the throes of death he consoled her saying Allâh ﷻ had so ordained it, and that the thing she was dreading, would prove favorable for her. Her eyes lit up and as she gazed at her beloved husband, and her soul left its earthly body. Her grave was prepared at a place called Hujjoon, near Makkah. Muhammad ﷺ stepped into it to see that everything was as it should be, and with his own hands lowered her gently into it. Thus passed away the 'Mother' of all Muslims, the one who had sacrificed her all for Islâm.

The same year the Prophet's greatest supporter and protector from among his family, his uncle Abu Tâlib passed away. Thus within the space of a few months two of his closest companions, supporters and benefactors had passed away. Besides his personal sense of loss and bereavement, Muhammad ﷺ was deeply disturbed by the fact that his work of spreading the word of Allâh ﷻ was faced with problems and obstacles. His uncle had protected him at critical moments with his influence and authority; his wealthy wife gave her all generously to the cause, and also provided great moral and emotional support. Her house was a haven of peace for him as she took upon herself all of the responsibilities of running the household and bringing up four young daughters. Whenever he was abused by the disbelievers she provided moral support and unflagging faith.

One of the ladies of the Quraish, Khawlah bint Hâkim, visited the Prophet ﷺ to console him, and saw his state of depression and grief and remarked on it. He replied it was only natural that he should be touched by her absence, as she had been a loving mother to his now neglected children; she had been a loyal and sympathetic wife who shared his secrets. It was only human and natural that he should feel her loss as she was there for him during his most difficult times.

A Companion of the Prophet ﷺ narrates that whenever any gift was brought to him he would immediately send it to some lady who had been a friend of Khadîjah رضي الله عنها. 'A'ishah رضي الله عنها, a favorite wife of Muhammad ﷺ says that whenever a goat was slaughtered the Prophet ﷺ would send some meat to Khadîjah's friends; when she remarked about this on one occasion he told her:

> '*I have great regard for her friends, as she has a special place in my heart.*'

'A'ishah رضي الله عنها said she never experienced such a feeling of natural feminine jealousy for any other wife of the Prophet ﷺ as she did for Khadîjah رضي الله عنها.

She also narrates that whenever Muhammad ﷺ spoke of her he would talk at great length and praise her qualities, and pray for her forgiveness.

As Allâh ﷻ says in *Surah Al-Fajr* in the Noble Qur'ân that it will be said to the pious believers:

> "*O the one in complete rest and satisfaction! Come back to your Lord – well-pleased (yourself) and well-pleasing (unto Him)! Enter you then among My (honored) servants, and enter you My Paradise.*" (89:27-30)

Saudah bint Zam'ah رضي الله عنها

The Prophet ﷺ said:

"*Allâh has commanded me to marry only the women of Paradise.*"

'A'ishah رضي الله عنها said:

"*I did not wish seeing any woman except Saudah bint Zam'ah رضي الله عنها, if I could be in her skeleton.*"

Saudah bint Zam'ah رضي الله عنها

The first lady to enter the household of the Prophet ﷺ after the passing away of Khadîjah رضي الله عنها was Saudah رضي الله عنها who was obedient, generous and loyal with a sense of sacrifice. 'A'ishah رضي الله عنها was very impressed by her simple and selfless nature. She was among the first to accept Islâm, and also had the distinction of emigrating twice, first to Abyssinia and then to Madinah. Her life is a beacon for all Muslim women.

Her mother Shammoos was from the tribe of Banu Najjâr, a branch of the Quraish; her father was also from a branch of the Quraish, Banu 'Âmir bin Lua'i. She was married to her cousin, Sakran bin 'Amr, and then married to the Prophet ﷺ on his death. All her husband's brothers, Suhail, Sahl, Hâtib and Saleet had the honor of being Companions of the Prophet ﷺ. Both she and her husband accepted Islâm in its earliest days and they both had the distinction of migrating to Abyssinia for the cause of Allâh, joining the second band of migrants. They were blessed with a lovely boy whom they named 'Abdur-Rahmân. They stayed in Abyssinia for a considerable period of time before returning to Makkah.

One day Saudah رضي الله عنها dreamt that the Prophet ﷺ entered her house and caught hold of her by the nape of her neck. When she told her husband about her dream, he interpreted it to mean that after his death she would marry Muhammad ﷺ. Sometime later she had another dream; she saw the moon descending into her lap. She told Sakran about this dream as well; again he interpreted it for her. His death was imminent he said, and she would marry the Prophet ﷺ. A few days later he fell ill, and passed away. She was left lonely and it seemed as if there was no purpose to life.

One of her friends was Khawlah bint Hâkim رضي الله عنها, the wife of Uthmân bin Madh'oon. One day she visited the Prophet ﷺ and remarked that he was leading a very lonely and sad life with the responsibility of bringing up his four daughters, and was missing his wife Khadîjah رضي الله عنها. He replied that she was right and that Khadîjah رضي الله عنها had been a remarkable and great lady. She suggested to him that he should get married. He asked who he could possibly marry, who would be willing to take on the responsibility of his household and daughters.

She replied that she had in mind a certain lady and if he agreed she would approach that person. On learning the identity of the lady the Prophet ﷺ agreed. Khawlah رضي الله عنها was very happy that her suggestion was accepted and immediately went to see Saudah رضي الله عنها. She told her that she had great news for her. When she heard of the proposal, she was over-come by the honor being bestowed on her. But she said Khawlah رضي الله عنها should also discuss this matter with her elderly father who was going blind. Of course her father was too happy that his widowed daughter had been chosen to be the companion and wife of the Prophet ﷺ.

Khawlah رضي الله عنها then visited Muhammad ﷺ with the good news. Soon the marriage took place and Zam'ah performed the ceremony. The Prophet ﷺ gave a *Mahr*[1] of 400 Dirhams to his wife Saudah رضي الله عنها on the occasion. Her brother 'Abdullâh had not yet converted to Islâm and was very upset and saddened by the news; he expressed his grief in a barbaric and uncivilized manner by throwing dust on his head. Later when he converted to Islâm, he realized his mistake and how disgracefully he had received the greatest honor possible to himself and his family.

---

[1] Dowry either payable at the time of marriage or at a mutually agreed time.

Saudah bint Zam'ah رضي الله عنها

Saudah رضي الله عنها was of course very happy, having moved into the house of Khadîjah رضي الله عنها where Prophet Muhammad ﷺ lived with his daughters, Umm Kulthûm and Fâtimah رضي الله عنهما. She felt she was very fortunate that now her future was assured. She would often relate her memorable experiences in Abyssinia, and talk especially about his daughter Ruqayyah رضي الله عنها and her husband, Uthmân bin Affân ؓ and the Prophet ﷺ would listen with great interest.

On one occasion Ruqayyah رضي الله عنها visited Makkah. The sisters received her with mixed emotions of joy and sorrow, joy on seeing her after so many years and sorrow because they were meeting each other for the first time after the death of their mother. Saudah رضي الله عنها stepped forward and embraced Ruqayyah. Ruqayyah and Saudah رضي الله عنهما never expected that they would be meeting again after their days in Abyssinia, now as mother and stepdaughter. But it was a very cordial relationship and the Prophet ﷺ was extremely happy to meet his daughter and son-in-law.

He got news of the latest developments, of how the refugee *Sahâbah* were faring, and of the hospitality of the ruler Najâshi. The social conditions in Makkah continued to be bad, the Muslims were cruelly treated and oppressed; and the disbelievers were not prepared to change their policy. Every day brought fresh stories of torture and harsh treatment of the Muslims, and the only alternative appeared to be migration. The Prophet ﷺ, keeping all these circumstances in view, now decided his followers should migrate to Madinah. A few days later Allâh ﷻ ordered him to migrate as well. So the Prophet ﷺ set out on his sacred journey in the company of his most trusted Companion, Abu Bakr Siddeeq ؓ.

On reaching Madinah they stayed over at the house of Abu Ayyub Ansâri ؓ. Once he was settled he sent Zaid bin Harithah ؓ and Abu Rafi' ؓ to Makkah with some camels and 500 Dirhams to bring all the members of his family. These two trusted Companions reached there and immediately left for Madinah with Saudah, Ruqayyah, Umm Kulthûm, Fâtimah رضي الله عنهن. Umm Aiman رضي الله عنها the wife of Zaid bin Harithah ؓ and his son Usamah ؓ were also part of the caravan, which was put up at the house of Hârithah bin Nu'mân Ansâri ؓ on reaching Madinah. During his stay in Makkah, the Prophet ﷺ had married 'A'ishah رضي الله عنها, who now came to live with him in his household.

Later at different stages in his life the Prophet ﷺ married Hafsah bint 'Umar, Zainab bint Jahsh, Umm Salamah رضي الله عنهن and others who had the good fortune to be associated with him. It was an age when the desert of Madinah bloomed into a garden whose heady perfumes seemed to have enchanted the world. The pebbled streets of Madinah became the focal point for all believing Muslims, and the axis on which the whole Islâmic world revolved. The bustling activity and the liveliness as a new city-state evolved were magnified by the charismatic presence of Muhammad ﷺ. Even the angels seemed envious of these early Muslims and the role they were playing in spreading Islâm across the world, and the Angel Jibrîl ﷺ visited this glorious city many times.

When Saudah bint Zam'ah رضي الله عنها became old she feared that Muhammad ﷺ would divorce her, so she decided that a settlement be made. Her desire was to be raised on the Day of Judgment with the other members of the Prophet's wives, so she said she would voluntarily allocate 'A'ishah رضي الله عنها the time allotted to her. It was at this point of time that *Âyah* of *Surat An-Nisâ'* was revealed to the Prophet ﷺ:

> "And if a woman fears cruelty or desertion on her husband's part, there is no sin on them both if they make terms of peace between themselves; and making peace is better." (4:128)

'A'ishah رضي الله عنها was very touched by her gesture and they became even closer than before. Her heart was so pure that it was totally free of jealousy or malice.

Saudah رضي الله عنها was a tall, healthy woman with a sense of humor. Ibn Sa'ad mentions how once she was offering voluntary night prayers, standing behind the Prophet ﷺ. The next morning she told him how his very long prayer made her fear that her nasal vein would burst and her nose would bleed! So she said that while in the bowing position, she held on to her nose! This comical image that she presented of herself made the Prophet ﷺ burst into laughter. She was a very warm and simple person.

She had a slow lumbering walk because of her build and when she went with the Prophet ﷺ on *Hajj* she took special permission to leave for Muzdalifah earlier as to avoid the crowds. 'A'ishah رضي الله عنها who was also part of the group, later wished she had also left with her since she really enjoyed her company and missed her liveliness.

When Saudah رضي الله عنها first heard about the Dajjâl[1] from the Prophet ﷺ she was terrified. Being the simple person that she was, it became a pastime for the others to talk about it and frighten her and then laugh at her. On one occasion 'A'ishah رضي الله عنها and the Mother of the Believers Hafsah رضي الله عنها started talking about it in front of her. She was so scared that she immediately ran into a dark room full of cobwebs to hide from the monster. When Muhammad ﷺ walked in he found the two enjoying the joke. He asked them what was so amusing. On being told what had happened he called out to Saudah رضي الله عنها to come out as there was no monster around. She came out sheepishly laughing at herself.

On one occasion, the Prophet ﷺ, 'A'ishah and Saudah رضي الله عنهما were sitting together and chatting. The former had cooked a special dish and offered it to the latter. But she declined. 'A'ishah رضي الله عنها was a lively young person, and threatened to forcibly feed Saudah رضي الله عنها. And when she continued to remain serious, she actually splashed it all over her face! So this lighthearted gaiety and spirit of camaraderie was very much part of the Prophet's household. There was no malice and jealousy in this pure atmosphere. It was reflective of the pleasant ambience in the household of the Prophet ﷺ where there was always loving concern and affection for all. But when the call to prayer, or *Adhân* was given by the *Mu'adhdhin*, Muhammad ﷺ would immediately rise and leave for the mosque as if he did not even know the family members gathered around him.

---

[1] A one-eyed man, the anti-Christ who will appear just before the Day of Judgment.

The History of At-Tabari, *Kâmil* of Ibn Atheer, and the *Seerah* of Ibn Hishâm have recorded an incident that occurred after the victory in the Battle of Badr. The triumphant Muslim army was on its way back to Madinah with many prisoners; among them was Suhail bin 'Amr, the brother of Sakrân bin 'Amr, the first husband of Saudah رضي الله عنها. He was under the care of Mâlik bin Dakhtham.

On the way he told his captor that he wished to relieve himself, and managed to escape. When the Prophet ﷺ was informed, he asked the army to stop and ordered that the escaped prisoner should be captured or killed where ever found. The *Mujahideen* [1] fanned out to search and soon found him, hiding behind a tree. His hands were bound together and tied to his neck; in this state he entered the city.

When Saudah رضي الله عنها saw him, she involuntarily exclaimed that he should have died a noble death, rather than live to see such a shameful day. She did not realize that the Prophet ﷺ had heard her. He told her that she was stirring up the prisoner against Allâh ﷻ and his Prophet ﷺ; how could the death of one fighting against the forces of Allâh ﷻ be noble? She was very ashamed at this and immediately apologised, saying that she just could not take what she had seen and blurted out what first came to her mind. She said she was really loyal and obedient to the Will of Allâh ﷻ and His Prophet ﷺ, and was sorry if she was offensive in any way. The Prophet ﷺ relented with a smile, and announced that the captors should treat all prisoners with consideration. The result was that the *Mujahideen* first fed the prisoners in their charge and then ate themselves. And ultimately, because of this kind treatment many disbelievers, among them Suhail bin 'Amr and his brothers, converted to Islâm.

After the Prophet's Farewell *Hajj*, he told his wives that they should remain in their homes as it was the Will of Allâh ﷻ:

---

[1] Those fighting the *Jihâd*.

"And stay in your homes." (33:33)

Thus, Saudah and Zainab bint Jahsh رضي الله عنهما did not travel after the death of Prophet Muhammad ﷺ, and they stayed in their homes in Madinah, saying that they had performed *Hajj* and *'Umrah* in the company of the Prophet ﷺ and would follow the command of Allâh ﷻ.

Saudah رضي الله عنها was extremely generous. During his rule 'Umar bin al-Khattâb ؓ, sent her a bag full of Dirhams. She asked what it was, and on learning that it was money she was very surprised and said this was like dates being packed in a bag! She then distributed the money among the poor and needy.

There are five authentic *Ahâdîth* attributed to her, according to Imâm Dhahabi. She narrated how when one of their goats died they used the skin until it got worn out. Thus it is proved that it is permissible to use the skin of a dead animal. Similarly in the *Musnad* of Imâm Ahmad the following *Hadîth* is attributed to Saudah رضي الله عنها:

> *A man came to the Prophet ﷺ and asked if it was possible to perform Hajj for his aged father, who could no longer undergo its rigors. The Prophet ﷺ asked if he would pay his father's debts if he had any, and if this would be acceptable. The man replied that it would. Then Muhammad ﷺ told him that Allâh ﷻ was Oft-Forgiving and Most Merciful and he should perform the Hajj on behalf of his father.*

The Caliphs who succeeded after the Prophet's death thought it a great honor to look after the welfare of the Mothers of the Believers, and diligently did their duty by them.[1] Saudah رضي الله عنها lived to the ripe old age of eighty. She passed away during the caliphate of 'Umar bin al-Khattâb ؓ and was buried in *Jannatul-Baqi'*.

As Allâh ﷻ says in *Surah Al-Fajr* in the Noble Qur'ân that it will be said to the pious believers:

---

[1] Thus, *Ummul Mu'mineen* Saudah رضي الله عنها with her maturity, simplicity and amiable nature came at an opportune moment into the Prophet's household providing support for her husband, motherly love for the girls and a carefree and pleasant atmosphere in the home. (*Translator's note*)

"O the one in complete rest and satisfaction! Come back to your Lord – well-pleased (yourself) and well-pleasing (unto Him)! Enter you then among My (honored) servants, and enter you My Paradise." (89:27-30)

'A'ishah bint Abu Bakr رضي الله عنها

'A'ishah رضي الله عنها said:

"Angel Jibrîl ﷺ brought my picture wrapped in the cover of green silk in a dream and said:

'She is your wife in this world and in the Hereafter.'"

(*Tirmidhi* in the chapter of *Fadhâ'il*)

'A'ishah bint Abu Bakr رضي الله عنها

A'ishah رضي الله عنها was the favorite daughter of one of the closest friends, Companion and associates of the Prophet ﷺ, Abu Bakr Siddeeq. Several *Âyât* of the Noble Qur'ân which were revealed were associated with her, and she was justifiably proud of this honor. She was in an enviable position among the Mothers of the Believers in that she was considered the foremost among them. Allâh had chosen her Himself in the heavens as a bride for Muhammad ﷺ; a portrait of hers, wrapped in silk, was brought to him in his dream by the Angel Jibrîl عليه السلام. He told him that he was to marry her, and she would be his consort in the life hereafter as well.

She had a brilliant mind and a remarkable memory; and the distinction of being the source of the most *Ahâdîth* (narrations) because of her long association with Muhammad ﷺ. Her knowledge of the many branches of religion like *Fiqh* (jurisprudence) and *Sharî'ah* (Islâmic legislation), her wisdom in interpretation, her mastery of the teachings of the Prophet ﷺ, her trustworthiness and integrity -- all these qualities made her one of the most remarkable personalities of the time. She was very tender-hearted and no needy person left her house empty-handed. The Angel Jibrîl عليه السلام personally greeted her. During her lifetime the Prophet ﷺ gave her the wonderful news that she earned a place for herself in Paradise. It was while resting in her lap that the Prophet ﷺ passed away, and it was her apartment that became his final resting-place. Angels surrounded her apartment even during her lifetime and for all time the blessings of Allâh ﷻ will be showered on it, since it is in the center of the sanctuary at Madinah.

She said that there were nine blessings of Allâh ﷻ which distinguished her from all other women in the world except Maryam bint 'Imrân, the mother of 'Isa ﷺ.

- The Angel Jibrîl ﷺ had presented her portrait wrapped in green silk to Muhammad ﷺ and told him that this was the picture of the lady chosen by Allâh ﷻ to be his consort both in this world and the next.
- She was the only virgin to have become the wife of the Prophet ﷺ.
- When the Prophet ﷺ passed away, he was resting in her lap and was buried in her apartment.
- Many times angels encircled her apartment with love and respect.
- Very often divine revelation would come to Muhammad ﷺ when they were lying together resting in peace and tranquillity.
- She was the daughter of the loyal and true friend of the Prophet ﷺ, Abu Bakr Siddeeq ﷺ.
- *Âyât* acquitting her of any wrongdoing had descended from the heavens from Allâh ﷻ, proving her innocence.
- She was born a Muslim and had been brought up in a pure environment, and spent her formative years with the purest and best of creatures, the Prophet ﷺ.
- Allâh, the Lord, the Sustainer of the Universe promised her Divine Forgiveness and abundant bounties.

'A'ishah رضي الله عنها had claims to noble birth from both sides of the family. Her mother was Umm Rummân رضي الله عنها and her father was Abu Bakr Siddeeq ﷺ. Umm Rummân earlier married 'Abdullâh Azdi and had a son by him named 'Abdur-Rahmân. 'A'ishah رضي الله عنها was born in 614 CE. Her father Abu Bakr Siddeeq ﷺ is mentioned in the Noble Qur'ân in glowing terms. He was a pure Allâh-fearing man, the foremost and staunchest supporter of the Prophet ﷺ, whom he loved dearly, even more than his life, and thus 'A'ishah's cradle was the cradle of Islâm. Abu Bakr Siddeeq ﷺ had the honor of being buried next to his beloved leader and Prophet ﷺ, in the sanctuary of Madinah. He will, Allâh Willing, enter Paradise in the company of the Prophet ﷺ.

'A'ishah bint Abu Bakr رضي الله عنها

'A'ishah's favorite pastimes as a girl were swinging and playing with dolls. Once on a visit to her father, Muhammad ﷺ saw her playing with a winged horse; she was barely five years old at the time. He asked her what it was; she replied it was a horse. He smiled and answered that horses do not have wings! She promptly retorted that the Prophet Sulaimân عليه السلام had winged horses! This incident reveals several things about her — she was intelligent, quick-witted, well-informed on religious and historical matters — and at such a tender age! She had a formidable memory, which never seemed to fail her. She hardly ever forgot something once she heard it. At the time of the *Hijrah*, (migration) of the Prophet ﷺ to Madinah, she was barely eight years old, yet she remembered years later even minor details about that historic and momentous move, when the first Islâmic state was on the rise.

She was barely nine years of age when she joined the household of the Prophet ﷺ. This was the time when he was grief stricken by the loss of his loving and supportive wife Khadîjah رضي الله عنها. Both she and his uncle Abu Tâlib, had protected him against the most powerful chieftains of the two foremost tribes of Arabia. With their deaths he felt lonely and isolated. Then, he and his faithful followers faced the cruelest religious prosecution seen in history.

When 'A'ishah رضي الله عنها joined his household in Madinah, she did not find herself in a royal mansion. A number of small rooms were constructed in the locality of Bani Najjâr, around the Prophet's Mosque, and she occupied one of these, located on the eastern side of the Mosque. It was about six feet wide, had earthen walls and the roof was made of leaves and twigs. To prevent the rain water from seeping in the roof was covered with a blanket. The roof was so low that a person standing upright could touch the roof. There was a single shuttered door, which was never closed; a blanket served as a curtain. Close to the room, on a slightly higher level was another small room, which Muhammad ﷺ occupied on the one occasion when he had boycotted the Mothers of the Believers. A mat, a thin mattress, a pillow filled with the bark of trees, a leather water bag, a small plate for dates and a glass for drinking water were all the things in the room. There were none of the signs of worldly wealth and pomp, but this little room was filled with spiritual treasures. The Prophet ﷺ liked the lack of riches and material comforts; he often prayed that he should live and die in poverty, and be reborn on the Day of Judgment in the company of the poor and the needy.

Bilâl ؓ was in charge of the arrangements and provided for the needs of the families of the Prophet ﷺ. It was he who used to distribute the annual supply of grain. At times it became necessary to even borrow money in order to fulfill their needs. When the whole of Arabia was under the authority of Islâm, huge quantities of grain and cash flowed into the central treasury. But on the day that Muhammad ﷺ passed away, there was not even food for a single day in his household. 'A'ishah رضي الله عنها maintained this tradition of generosity and liberality right up to her last days. During the days of prosperity, abundant riches arrived daily, but she always distributed them among the needy by the time evening fell. The most outstanding trait of her character was her innate magnanimity and benevolence. Her generosity was well-known, and no beggar left her door empty-handed.

'Abdullâh bin Zubair ؓ mentioned that 'A'ishah رضي الله عنها and her sister, Asmâ' رضي الله عنها were both very large-hearted and benevolent. They spent all that they would receive in the Name of Allâh ﷻ. The only difference between them was that 'A'ishah رضي الله عنها would collect a sizable amount gradually and then give it away in charity; Asmâ' رضي الله عنها on the other hand, would give whatever she had in hand. In fact she would even fall into debt to help someone in need. When asked why she took on debts unhesitatingly, she replied that if a person had every intention of repaying the debt, Allâh ﷻ would help him or her. She added she was looking for His Mercy and Help.

On one occasion, at one sitting, 'A'ishah رضي الله عنها gave away 70,000 Dirhams in charity for Allâh ﷻ and got up showing her empty handkerchief to the people seated there. One evening she received 100,000 Dirhams from Amir Mu'âwiyah ؓ who was in Syria and by nightfall the entire sum had gone to charity. Her maid reminded her that she was fasting and she should have kept something for herself. She asked her why she had not reminded her earlier. On another occasion, 'Abdullâh bin Zubair ؓ sent her 100,000 Dirhams, and similarly they were also given away as early as possible.

One day she was fasting and a beggar came to her apartment and asked for some food. She told her maid to give the lady the piece of bread they had. The maid answered that there was nothing else with which she could break her fast. 'A'ishah رضي الله عنها answered curtly that she should help the hungry woman and the evening would take care of itself. By the evening someone sent her a dish of cooked meat; she said to the maid that Allâh ﷻ had provided her with something even better than what she had given away. She owned a house which she sold to Mu'âwiyah ؓ and gave away all the money in charity.

She loved her sister's son, 'Abdullâh bin Zubair ؓ, very deeply. He in turn loved her very much and always looked after her needs. On one occasion he remarked that her generosity needed to be restrained. 'A'ishah رضي الله عنها was very upset and angry when she heard this; she swore she would never talk to him. She demanded who on earth thought that he could stop her from spending in the way of Allâh ﷻ. She asked how he could even dare to say such a thing. And finally, when she calmed down and made up with him, she freed several slaves as penance for breaking her oath.

'A'ishah رضي الله عنها was very tender-hearted, and broke into tears easily. On one occasion when a beggar woman carrying two small children came to her door; she had only three dates in the house. These she gave her; the woman gave one each to the children and started eating one herself. One of the children ate his share quickly and started looking longingly at his mother eating her date. The woman could not bear her child's hunger and took the date from her mouth, broke it into two halves, and gave a piece to each of the children. When 'A'ishah رضي الله عنها saw this heartrending scene she could not control her tears.

'A'ishah رضي الله عنها was a modest, pure, and pious lady, yet even she could not escape the slanderous and malicious plotting of the Hypocrites. In the month of *Sha'bân*[1] in the fifth year of the *Hijrah*, Muhammad ﷺ, led the Muslim army towards Qadeed, and a minor battle ensued between them and the tribe of Banu Mustaliq. Several Hypocrites were also part of the army during this particular battle. A few

---

[1] The 8th month of the Hjirah calendar.

people were killed, but most were captured. The army was camped on the banks of a stream named Al-Muraisa'.

'A'ishah رضي الله عنها, a very slim and petite fourteen-year old had also accompanied the Prophet ﷺ on this expedition. She had borrowed a delicate necklace from her sister Asmâ' رضي الله عنها. On the way back when the army had camped in the desert, she went far into the desert to relieve herself. Suddenly she realized that the necklace had fallen somewhere along the way. She retraced her footsteps looking for it and luckily found it, but after a very long search. By the time she reached the camping site, the caravan left. Now the normal procedure was that the ladies, who were segregated from the men folk, would get into their litter[1] and draw the curtains. Then the camel drivers would place the litter on the camel's back. Since 'A'ishah رضي الله عنها was very light no one realized her absence. When she came back after her search to the camping site, she found that the caravan had left. Fearless as she was she just lay down, waiting for her companions to return for her when they found her missing.

Safwân bin Mu'attal had the responsibility of checking the camp site for things which might have been left behind inadvertently after the departure of the caravan; at daybreak he arrived to find a figure lying down wrapped in a *Jilbâb*.[2] When he saw it was a lady, he moved away after alighting from the camel, so she could get on to it. When 'A'ishah رضي الله عنها heard him, she woke up and got on to the camel. He then walked leading the camel by the bridle.

In the afternoon when the caravan had just reached the next camp site to rest, they saw 'A'ishah رضي الله عنها arriving with Safwân bin Mu'attal. She got off the camel in front of all the people assembled there. This incident became the material for a scandal for the Hypocrites, led by 'Abdullâh bin Ubayy bin Salool. His intrinsic nature, his natural propensity for foul and wicked suspicions, made him indulge in slanderous gossip. The whole of Madinah was flooded by this

---

[1] A litter was like a palanquin or howdah, but with curtains, and placed on camels for the ladies.

[2] A cloak that covers the entire body.

scandalous talk that cast aspersions on the character of 'A'ishah رضي الله عنها. Regrettably, Hassân bin Thâbit, Hamnah bint Jahsh, and Mistah bin Athâthah also joined the Hypocrites in this mud-slinging. The Prophet ﷺ was naturally extremely disturbed when he heard this talk about a member of his household, and his favorite wife; but 'A'ishah رضي الله عنها was blissfully ignorant of all this gossip going around about her and Safwân bin Mu'attal.

One night she went out with the aged mother of Mistah bin Athâthah. The old lady tripped and started cursing her son. 'A'ishah رضي الله عنها was surprised; remonstrating with her and said that he was a Companion of the Prophet ﷺ who fought courageously in the Battle of Badr and deserved respect. The old lady retorted that 'A'ishah رضي الله عنها was ignorant of the fact that he was involved in an awful and frightening plot; then she revealed what had been taking place behind her back. 'A'ishah رضي الله عنها was appalled at the depths to which sheer willful malice can make a person fall.

After returning home, she took the permission of Muhammad ﷺ, and went to visit her parents. They also corroborated the story she had heard. She was heartbroken and started weeping. Her sympathetic and loving mother tried to console her, but she failed to stem the flood of tears. She told her that since she was the favorite of Muhammad ﷺ, people jealous of her position had deliberately hatched this plot. She advised her to be patient and everything would be cleared up. Her father also tried to soothe her and calm her down.

But 'A'ishah, the living image of purity and integrity, could not accept the fact that people could descend to such cruel depths, and life could be such a mental torture. After two days and nights of continuous weeping she fell ill. On the third morning her parents were sitting with her and trying to comfort her, when the Prophet ﷺ came to see her. He told her very gently that if she erred she should ask Allâh for His forgiveness. At this her tears dried up and she asked her mother to answer him. But her mother remained silent, sorrowful and tearful. When she saw that her mother was speechless she appealed to her father, Abu Bakr Siddeeq ؓ to speak to Muhammad ﷺ, but he too did not say anything. Finally she spoke to her husband and said that if she denied she was guilty, nobody would believe her; but she was innocent and only Allâh ﷻ knew it. The best answer to these accusations was to quote the answer of the father of Yûsuf:

"So (for me) patience is most fitting. And it is Allâh Whose help can be sought against that (lie) which you describe." (12:18)

She later recalled that she was so disturbed, that even though she tried very hard, she just could not remember the name of Ya'qoob ﷺ, the father of Yûsuf ﷺ. At precisely this moment, the *Âyât* of announcing her innocence were revealed to the Prophet ﷺ.

When the revelation was over his brow was full of beads of perspiration from the exertion; he then turned to 'A'ishah with a smile and started reciting the: *Âyât*

"Verily, those who brought forth the slander are a group among you. Consider it not a bad thing for you. Nay, it is good for you. Unto every man among them will be paid that which he earned of the sin, and as for him among them who had the greater share therein, his will be a great torment. Why then, did not the believers, men and women, when you heard it (the slander), think good of their own people and say: This (charge) is an obvious lie? Why did they not produce four witnesses? Since they (the slanderers) have not produced witnesses! Then with Allâh they are the liars. Had it not been for the Grace of Allâh and His Mercy unto you in this world and in the Hereafter, a great torment would have touched you for that whereof you had spoken. When you were propagating it with your tongues, and uttering with your mouths that whereof you had no knowledge, you counted it a little thing, while with Allâh it was very great. And why did you not, when you heard it, say: It is not right for us to speak of this. Glory be to You (O Allâh)! This is a great lie. Allâh forbids you from it and warns you not to repeat the like of it forever, if you are believers. And Allâh makes the Âyât (proofs) plain to you, and Allâh is All-Knowing, All-Wise. Verily, those who like that (the crime of) illegal sexual intercourse should be propagated among those who believe, they will have a painful torment in this world and in the hereafter. And Allâh knows and you know not. And had it not been for the Grace of Allâh and His Mercy on you, (Allâh would have hastened the punishment upon you). And that Allâh is full of Kindness, Most Merciful. O you who believe! Follow not the footsteps of Shaitân. And whosoever follows the footsteps of Shaitân, then, verily, he commands

'A'ishah bint Abu Bakr رضي الله عنها

Al-Fahshâ' (illegal sexual intercourse), and Al-Munkar (evil and wicked deeds). And had it not been for the Grace of Allâh and His Mercy on you, not one of you would ever have been pure from sins. But Allâh purifies (guides to Islâm) whom He wills, and Allâh is All-Hearer, All-Knower." (24:11-21)

Her parents were overpowered by a proud sense of relief; pride that their daughter had been honored with a Qur'ânic revelation, and relief that she was acquitted of any wrongdoing. They asked their daughter to rise and thank her husband, but 'A'ishah رضي الله عنها promptly replied that she was grateful to her Allâh ﷻ for He had revealed Qur'ânic *Âyât* Verses that exonerated her honor. And these would be recited until the Day of Judgment. This episode is known in Islâmic History as the Event of *Ifk*.

After this incident the Prophet's respect for 'A'ishah رضي الله عنها increased even more. 'Amr bin al-'Aas once asked Muhammad ﷺ who he loved most in this world, and he replied that he loved 'A'ishah رضي الله عنها more than anyone else. Then he asked him about the men folk. And the Prophet ﷺ answered that he loved Abu Bakr Siddeeq ؓ the most. On one occasion 'Umar ؓ told his daughter Hafsah رضي الله عنها not to try and compete with 'A'ishah as Muhammad ﷺ respected her and valued her very highly. One of the reasons for this was her mastery and knowledge of the decrees and articles of faith as well as her brilliant interpretation of Islâmic law.

The Prophet ﷺ loved to listen to 'A'ishah رضي الله عنها talking and always smiled when she spoke. He always tried to please her. On one *'Eid* day there were some Africans displaying their skill with spears; 'A'ishah رضي الله عنها wanted to watch this sport, so the Prophet ﷺ stood in front of her so she could enjoy herself and not be seen. And he did not move until she got tired of it. Often just to entertain themselves they would narrate stories to each other. The Prophet ﷺ told her the story of a man called Kharâfah whom the *Jinn* had taken away. 'A'ishah رضي الله عنها narrated a detailed story about eleven ladies who were friends and how each of them described her husband. The Prophet ﷺ listened intently as she spoke.

The eleven women agreed that they would be frank and not conceal anything about their husbands. The first one said that her husband was like a piece of camel meat placed on top of a mountain -- there was no means by which one could reach it; and in any case it was not anyone's to take.

The second one said there was so much to say about her husband that if she started she didn't know what she would leave out; it was really better not to start.

The third friend said that her husband had such a foul temper that if she spoke against him he would immediately divorce her, and if she didn't that would be another problem. It was as if she was married, yet not married.

Now it was the turn of the fourth friend. She said her husband was like the nights of Hijâz, neither too cold nor too warm, he had a very balanced temperament.

The fifth lady said her husband was like a cheetah in the house and a lion outside; if he gave his word he never broke it, and did not even need to be reminded about it.

The sixth lady said her husband never followed the middle path in anything. When he started eating he ate up everything that was set before him; the same with any drink that was there. Even when he slept, he would pull the whole sheet to cover himself. He would not even ask how his wife was managing.

The seventh one said her husband was a useless man who had a vile temper. In his rage he could break a person's head or crush his bones.

The eighth lady said her husband was as soft and delicate as a rabbit to the touch, and he smelt like the sweet-smelling jasmine.

The ninth wife was very happy describing her husband; she said that he was tall, lived in a huge mansion, and was a very open-hearted and generous man.

The tenth friend said her husband was better than all those described, he was a very wealthy man who owned many camels. He was so hospitable that he entertained frequently, and took pleasure in slaughtering his camels for his guests.

The eleventh lady was very proud of her husband, Abu Zara'a, because he was rich and had loaded her with gifts of jewelry. His

'A'ishah bint Abu Bakr رضي الله عنها

smiling and pleasant face kept her happy. He first saw her when she was just a shepherd's daughter, but he brought her into a home, which was rich in grains, and had plenty of livestock, camels and horses. There was plenty on all sides, and a pleasant atmosphere; even if she slept late in the morning he would never disturb her. His mother was a very great lady and also very well to do. She had lots of clothes and a large house. His son took up very little space and ate only the best of delicacies, which was goat's meat. His favorite daughter was well mannered and obedient to her parents. Abu Zara'a's maidservant was a loyal woman who did not carry tales about the happenings in the house; she was very faithful and honest and kept the house clean and tidy. And so the story went on and on.

The Prophet ﷺ listened to 'A'ishah رضي الله عنها, totally engrossed and then told her that he was as good a husband for her as Abu Zara'a was for Umm Zara'a. But all this pleasant entertainment could not distract Muhammad ﷺ from his duty to Allâh ﷻ. Just at the moment when he was enjoying himself, the *Mu'adhdhin's* call to prayer would be heard, and immediately he would rise and prepare to go the mosque. 'A'ishah رضي الله عنها said that it seemed as if he did not even know his family or friends; the love for Allâh ﷻ had priority over all other affections and interests.

> *"How perfect Allâh is and I praise Him. How perfect Allâh is, the Supreme."*

Another incident which brought the blessings of revelation occurred on a journey when 'A'ishah رضي الله عنها was travelling with the Prophet ﷺ. Her father and many Companions had accompanied them. They camped at a place in the desert and once again 'A'ishah's necklace fell off. Some of the Companions were sent to search for it, but it could not be found. The Prophet ﷺ was resting in his tent, when the call for morning prayers was given. But there was no water for their ablutions. The Companions were worried about the morning prayers, and they said that 'A'ishah رضي الله عنها was responsible for this predicament. Abu Bakr Siddeeq ﷺ curtly rebuked his daughter for creating a situation, which might lead to the *Fajr* prayers being missed. Exactly at this moment this: *Âyâh* was revealed to the Prophet ﷺ,

> *"And if you are ill, or on a journey, or one of you comes after answering the call of nature, or you have been in contact with women*

(by sexual relations) and you find no water, perform Tayammum[1] with clean earth and rub therewith your face and hands. Truly, Allâh is Ever Oft-Pardoning, Oft-Forgiving." (4:43)

Immediately the very same people who had been criticizing and complaining about 'A'ishah started praising her and expressed their appreciation and thanks for such a great favor that Allâh ﷻ had granted because of her. The noted Companion, Usaid bin Hudhair ؓ, said that the family of Abu Bakr Siddeeq ؓ had often been responsible for the many favors and blessings bestowed by Allâh ﷻ. Abu Bakr Siddeeq ؓ himself who just a few minutes earlier had been rebuking his daughter, now was full of smiles. He said he had not realized until that moment how pleased Allâh ﷻ was with her, that He had revealed such verse which would be a source of blessings for the Muslim *Ummah* until the Day of Judgment. He prayed for a long and happy life for her, as she had been a source of great ease and comfort for all followers of Islâm. After the prayer when the camels were ready for departure, the necklace was found under one of them.

❖తఠ❖తఠ❖తఠ❖

By the ninth year after *Hijrah*, the might of Islâm had spread over most of the Arabian Peninsula. The newly founded center of Islâm, Madinah, had become a flourishing city-state. Some of the wives of the Prophet ﷺ had been used to a luxurious life style before marriage, and when they saw that there were riches and comforts to be had, they presented a request for their allowances to be suitably reviewed and increased. This desire of his wives for worldly comforts disturbed the Prophet ﷺ. He declared that for one month he would separate himself from his wives, and he went into seclusion in the little room above the apartment of 'A'ishah. During this period he was suffering from an injury after having fallen from his horse.

Naturally this caused a furor among the households. After 29 days he came down to 'A'ishah's apartment, and told her that she could make

---

[1] Striking your hand on earth and passing the palm of each on the back of the other and then blowing off dust from them and then wiping your face with them; this is called *Tayammum*. (*Editor's note*)

her choice after consulting her parents: either she could choose him and a life of hardship and near starvation, or she could leave him and lead a life of comfort and ease. 'A'ishah رضي الله عنها had no doubt whatsoever in her mind; she immediately answered that both she and her parents would willingly sacrifice their lives for him if the need arose. She said there was no need to consult her parents and she would prefer life with him to the world and its attractions and temptations. A beautiful smile lit up his face. And then Allâh ﷻ revealed the following: Âyât,

> "O Prophet (ﷺ)! Say to your wives: 'If you desire the life of this world, and its glitter, then come! I will make a provision for you and set you free in a handsome manner (divorce). But if you desire Allâh and His Messenger, and the Home of the hereafter, then verily, Allâh has prepared for the good-doers among you an enormous reward.'" (33:28-29)

After telling him what she felt about the matter, 'A'ishah رضي الله عنها very naively asked him to keep it a secret as she wanted to see what the others would say, uninfluenced by her decision. He told her, smiling very gently, that he had been sent as a teacher and not as a dictator or oppressor by Allâh ﷻ. Finally, all the wives took the same decision as 'A'ishah رضي الله عنها, and the wave of tension which had Madinah in its grip changed; and the same era of joy, peace and tranquillity returned.

There are two recorded incidents when 'A'ishah رضي الله عنها herself saw the Angel Jibrîl ﷺ personally.

❖ca❖ca❖ca❖

On one occasion, 'A'ishah رضي الله عنها saw the Prophet ﷺ with his hands on the mane of a horse talking to the rider. She asked him who he was; the Prophet ﷺ sounded rather surprised and asked if she had seen him. Then he told her that it was the Angel Jibrîl ﷺ in the form of a human and he requested that his greetings be conveyed to her. She prayed spontaneously that Allâh ﷻ should give a good reward to the honored guest and to his noble host.

❖ca❖ca❖ca❖

Anas ؓ narrates how once the Prophet ﷺ was praying in 'A'ishah's apartment, when she saw a stranger standing outside the door. She informed him, and he finished his prayers and stepped out. Who should he see but the Angel Jibrîl ﷺ. Muhammad ﷺ requested him to enter, but the Angel replied that they did not enter places where there were dogs or pictures. When the Prophet ﷺ looked around he saw a puppy in a corner of the room; when he was chased out, the Angel Jibrîl علیه السلام entered.

'A'ishah رضي الله عنها attained a lofty status because of the knowledge and wisdom with which she had been blessed. She was consulted by the other Companions and women Companions on the finer points of religion. Many of the traditions and authentic *Ahâdîth* originate from her. From among the many Companions associated with the Prophet ﷺ, there are only seven noble ones to whom thousands of *Ahâdîth* are attributed. Among these are:

- Abu Hurairah 'Abdur-Rahmân bin Sakhr Dawsi ؓ. (5374 *Ahâdîth*)
- 'Abdullâh bin 'Umar bin al-Khattâb ؓ. (2630 *Ahâdîth*)
- 'A'ishah رضي الله عنها. (2210 *Ahâdîth*)
- 'Abdullâh bin 'Abbâs ؓ. (1660 *Ahâdîth*)
- Jâbir bin 'Abdullâh Ansâri ؓ. (1540 *Ahâdîth*)
- Sa'ad bin Mâlik Abu Sa'eed al-Khudri ؓ. (1540 *Ahâdîth*)
- Anas bin Mâlik ؓ - (2286 *Ahâdîth*)

Imâm Dhahabi wrote that 'A'ishah رضي الله عنها was superior to all other women in her knowledge and wisdom. She was a theologian of the highest order. And he was just in his evaluation; after all she was born and nurtured under the tutelage of a father liked Abu Bakr Siddeeq ؓ, spent her married life with the Prophet ﷺ from a very tender age. She imbibed divinely inspired knowledge and wisdom from the very fountainhead of Prophethood; she was an eyewitness to the problems and questions that the divine revelations answered. Her apartment was the center where *Âyât* were revealed by the divine Mercy of Allâh ﷻ. Thus she was given the title of 'Horizon of the Ladies of Islâm'.

During the caliphate of the *Khulafâ-ar-Râshideen*, [1] her *Fatwâ*[2] was accepted. Once someone asked Masrooq if 'A'ishah رضي الله عنها had

---

[1] The first four caliphs after the Prophet; Abu Bakr Siddeeq, 'Umar bin al-Khattâb, 'Uthmân bin Affân, Ali bin Abi Tâlib رضي الله عنهم.
[2] A judicial decree or verdict.

mastery over the *Sharî'ah* laws regarding inheritance. He swore that he had personally seen revered Companions asking her questions about the finer points of the laws of inheritance. 'Urwah bin Zubair رضي الله عنها, her sister's son often visited her to discuss religious issues with her. Other Companions envied him as he could freely approach her at any time to clear his doubts as he was the son of her sister Asmâ' رضي الله عنها, and thus her *Mahram*.¹

The Prophet ﷺ deeply loved and respected her because of her command over religious matters and other praiseworthy qualities. On one occasion when the Prophet ﷺ was ill, 'A'ishah رضي الله عنها also was not feeling well. The Prophet ﷺ said that if she died before him he would personally bathe her and shroud her and lower her into her grave and pray for her. She lightheartedly replied that it seemed as if he would celebrate her death; and she told him that in case she died before him, he should bring a new wife into her apartment. The Prophet ﷺ smiled at this; but it was during this illness that he left this world to join his Lord.

'A'ishah رضي الله عنها narrated that she was proud that when it was her turn, in her apartment, in her lap, the Prophet ﷺ passed away. Her brother, 'Abdur-Rahmân came in during his last moments with a *Miswak*² in his hand; the Prophet ﷺ looked longingly at it. 'A'ishah رضي الله عنها understood what he wanted, and asked him if she could offer one to him. When he nodded, she took it from her brother; since it was hard she softened it with her teeth and offered it to him. He cleaned his teeth; and dipping his hand frequently into a bowl of water kept near him, he kept wiping his face again and again, repeating the words:

"*There is none worthy of worship but Allâh. Verily, death has pains.*"

Then he pointed upward with his hand and said:

"*Toward the best friend.*"

---

¹ Certain relatives with whom marriage is forbidden
² Twig of a tree used to clean the teeth and mouth.

Thus the soul soared up from the prison of the body.

Previously 'A'ishah رضي الله عنها had a dream that three moons descended into her apartment. When the Prophet ﷺ passed away he was buried in her apartment. Then her father told her that part of her dream had come true that day — the first moon irradiated her apartment. Later, her father was buried next to the Prophet ﷺ, and still later 'Umar Farooq ﷺ. Thus, the prophecy of her dream was fulfilled.

Imâm Dhahabi quoted a saying of the Prophet ﷺ that a Prophet's soul leaves its body in the place that he likes the best. Thus it is proven he died in his favorite place, the apartment of 'A'ishah رضي الله عنها.

She left this earthly existence for Paradise in the year 58 *Hijrah* on the 17th of Ramadhân at the age of 66,

"To Allâh we belong and to Allâh we return."

She was buried in the graveyard at Madinah, *Jannatul Baqi'*. Abu Hurairah ﷺ led the funeral prayers. 'Abdullâh bin Muhammad bin 'Abdur-Rahmân bin Abu Bakr Siddeeq and 'Abdullâh bin 'Abdur-Rahmân bin Abu Bakr Siddeeq رضي الله عنهم placed her gently into her grave.

"O the one in complete rest and satisfaction! Come back to your Lord – well-pleased (yourself) and well-pleasing (unto Him)! Enter you then among My (honored) servants, and enter you My Paradise." (89:27-30)

Hafsah bint 'Umar رضي الله عنها

One day the Angel Jibrîl عليه السلام visited the Prophet ﷺ and narrated about Hafsah رضي الله عنها:
"*She is a lady who often fasts and worships, and she will be your wife in Paradise too.*"
(*Mustadrak Hâkim 4/15*)

Hafsah bint 'Umar رضي الله عنها

❁❁❁❁❁❁❁❁

Hafsah رضي الله عنها was the daughter of 'Umar Farooq ﷺ, and the niece of another famous *Sahâbi* (Companion), 'Uthmân bin Madh'oon ﷺ who was fortunate to have the Prophet ﷺ led the funeral prayer and buried him himself in *Jannatul Baqi '*— the first *Sahâbi* to be buried there. Her uncle from the paternal side, a martyr and a General of the Muslim army was Zaid bin al-Khattâb. 'Umar Farooq ﷺ acknowledged the superiority of his brother when he said that Zaid ﷺ accepted Islâm before him and attained martyrdom before him. 'Abdullâh bin 'Umar رضي الله عنهما, who was declared by the Prophet ﷺ to be an excellent man, was her brother.

Hafsah رضي الله عنها was an extremely religious lady who used to spend her time in prayer and fasting. An excellent writer and orator, an ardent follower of Islâm, she could number seven of her family members among the warriors at Badr: her father 'Umar bin al-Khattâb, her paternal uncle Zaid bin al-Khattâb, her husband Khunais bin Hudhayfah, three of her mother's brothers, 'Uthmân bin Madh'oon, Qudâmah bin Madh'oon, and 'Abdullâh bin Madh'oon, and Sâ'ib bin 'Abdullâh bin Madh'oon رضي الله عنهم. All of them had taken part in the Battle of Badr and fought so courageously in the cause of Islâm that the Prophet ﷺ said that they would surely enter Paradise.

Hafsah رضي الله عنها had such noble qualities and such an amiable nature that 'A'ishah رضي الله عنها remarked that among wives of the Prophet ﷺ

only she could compare with her. Her life is exemplary, brought up as she was by a Companion of the calibre of 'Umar bin al-Khattâb ﷺ.

❖❖❖❖❖❖❖❖

Five years before the Prophet ﷺ was chosen to be the Messenger of Allâh the renovation of the Ka'bah took place. When it came to the point when the Black Stone had to be re-installed in the walls of the Ka'bah, an argument erupted. This argument could very well have turned into a lengthy series of battles among the tribes, each of whom wanted to have the honor of installing it into the wall of the Ka'bah. Finally it was decided that the matter would be left to chance. Whoever entered the House of Allâh first in the morning would install the Black Stone.

Though Muhammad ﷺ had not yet attained the status of a Prophet, from his early years, he was well known for his honesty, integrity and wisdom. So when he entered first, the tribal chiefs were happy, and agreed that he would have the honor. But he was too wise to accept a spur of the moment decision that might have set off serious complications and rivalries in the future. He stunned the people by asking for a large sheet; picking up the Black Stone, he placed it in the center of the sheet. Then he asked each of the chiefs to hold the edges of the sheet and raise it. Picking up the Black Stone, he placed it in the niche in the wall. Thus, a thorny issue was very simply yet wisely resolved.

Word of the wise yet simple decision taken by Muhammad ﷺ became the subject of conversation everywhere. It was during this period that a daughter, Hafsah رضي الله عنها, was born in the family of a great warrior and wrestler, 'Umar bin al-Khattâb ﷺ who was well known for his martial skills. In her growing years she was brought up in a completely Islâmic environment, both her parents and her aunts and uncles having already converted to the new religion. When she was old enough, she was married to Khunais bin Huthayfah as-Sahmi. He was influenced by the teaching of Abu Bakr Siddeeq ﷺ and had accepted Islâm.

When the leaders of the Quraish first heard about Khunais bin Hudhayfah as-Sahmi ﷺ becoming a Muslim they were enraged, and he was also subjected to the worst cruelty and oppression possible. He therefore joined the caravan of the persecuted migrants leaving for

Hafsah bint 'Umar رضي الله عنها

Abyssina. It is said this was around the time when the Prophet ﷺ had not yet started educating the new converts. But Khunais ؓ was very homesick there and just could not settle down. He sorely missed Makkah where he had spent his childhood and youth and decided to return. Again he faced the sufferings that were inflicted on the followers of the new religion. After some time the call was given by the Prophet ﷺ to migrate to Madinah. Khunais ؓ answered the call, thus becoming one of the few faithful followers who went through the rigors of migrating twice in obedience to the Prophet's call. This time around he was with his wife Hafsah رضي الله عنها. Here he was welcomed by Rafâ'h bin 'Abdul Manzar ؓ and stayed in his house as his guest. After practically all the Muslims had reached Madinah, the Prophet ﷺ also undertook the journey. He entrusted all the things that the people left with him to 'Ali ؓ for safekeeping. Escaping the watchful eyes of the enemy who had surrounded his house, he reached the house of Abu Bakr Siddeeq ؓ; accompanied by him he set out on his historic journey. The first stop they made was for three days in the Cave of Thawr; then they continued on the second lap of the journey. The disbelievers tried their very best to track him, but they failed. Abu Jahl, one of his greatest enemies set a very large reward on his head — a hundred camels — but met with no success. If Allâh Almighty wills to protect someone, no earthly enemy can cause him any harm.

On reaching Madinah, the Prophet ﷺ strengthened the bonds of brotherhood between the migrants and their hosts, the *Ansâr*. For instance, Abu 'Abbâs bin Jâbir Ansâri and Khunais bin Hudhayfah as-Sahmi رضي الله عنهما were declared brothers in Islâm. Both were students in the best school of all — the school of the Prophet ﷺ — and both were accomplished horse riders in the battlefield.

Both Khunais and Hafsah رضي الله عنهما loved the new life in Madinah. Hafsah رضي الله عنها made special arrangements to memorize the *Âyât* of the Qur'ân as and when they were revealed. Then she would give deep thought and attention to the meaning and interpretation of the *Âyât*. Her husband meanwhile was enthusiastically preparing himself for *Jihâd* and improving his martial skills. He was constantly alert to the movements of the enemy and was ever ready to meet them head on.

News came that the Quraish of Makkah – after making elaborate preparations for a war to wipe out the Muslims – were marching towards Madinah. Abu Jahl had sworn to reach the plains of Badr, camp there for three days, slaughter camels and have an orgy of dance and music before attacking the small band of Muslim soldiers. He believed that once people heard of his huge forces, no Arab tribe would have the courage to face them. Even if the puny Muslim army dared to confront him, he would teach them a lesson they would never forget.

The heavily armed forces of Abu Jahl set out; the Muslims under the leadership of the Prophet, practically unarmed, reached Badr and set up camp taking control of the only source of water. All they had with them was their strong faith in Allâh. When the army of Abu Jahl was sighted, the Prophet ﷺ prayed to the Almighty that if this small band of the faithful were destroyed there would be no one left on the face of the earth to pray to Him.

Khunais bin Hudhayfah, 'Umar Farooq رضي الله عنهما, and the maternal and paternal uncles of Hafsah رضي الله عنها and her cousin were all part of this courageous band. Her husband was determined to win the battle for Allâh and bring to dust the pomp and grandeur of Abu Jahl's forces. Finally the forces met and Khunais bin Hudhayfah went tearing through the ranks of the enemy. He was seriously wounded, but most of the leaders of the disbelievers were killed, and Islâm triumphed. It is one of the greatest battles fought in history where a handful of unarmed and outnumbered men routed a powerful and well-equipped army.

The Prophet ﷺ stayed at Badr for three days, while the injured were attended to; then he led the victorious and jubilant Muslim forces back to Madinah. When Hafsah رضي الله عنها heard of her husband's heroic deeds she was very happy, and praised his valor in battle; but she also realized that in his condition he would need the best care possible. She immediately recited the Âyâh of Surat Al-Anfâl which were revealed in connection with the Battle of Badr:

> "Allâh made it only as glad tidings, as that your hearts be at rest therewith. And there is no victory except from Allâh. Verily, Allâh is All-Mighty, All-Wise." (8:10)

Hafsah bint 'Umar رضي الله عنها

These Words of the Almighty Allâh promising victory inspired her and she happily turned to the task of nursing her husband back to health. But it was not to be, for he was to be blessed with an exalted position. A few days later he succumbed to his injuries and joined the ranks of those who are blessed with eternal life. When the Prophet ﷺ heard of his passing away he arranged for him to be buried in *Jannatul Baqi'*, next to the uncle of Hafsah رضي الله عنها; he personally led the funeral prayers. Hafsah رضي الله عنها was, naturally, grief stricken, but being a true believer she respectfully submitted to the Will of Allâh. She turned towards her Maker and courageously gave herself even more than before to prayer and meditation. She was at this time barely twenty-one years old.

◈ↄ◈ↄ◈ↄ◈ↄ◈

For her father it was very painful to see his daughter in this state. Her silent courage under these circumstances, her patient prayers and her study of the Qur'ân irradiated her countenance with a spiritual beauty and innocence, but there was also a sadness because of the harsh loneliness that had become part of her life. After deep thought 'Umar Farooq ؓ decided to approach 'Uthmân bin Affân ؓ, whose wife Ruqayyah رضي الله عنها the Prophet's daughter, had passed away. He thought that sharing a common bond would help to alleviate their sorrow in losing worthy spouses. So, having taken this decision he went direct to 'Uthmân ؓ. After the formal greeting and expression of condolences on his wife's death he broached the topic closest to his heart. 'Uthmân ؓ lowered his eyes and then after a few moments' pause, he said he needed time to think it over.

'Umar Farooq ؓ met him again after a few days and asked him if he had thought over the proposal. 'Uthmân ؓ answered that he was not presently planning on marriage. From there he went to Abu Bakr Siddeeq ؓ and offered him his daughter in marriage. He too lowered his gaze and did not answer him. Imâm Al-Bukhâri in his book of *Hadîth, As-Sahih Al-Bukhâri*, has given a whole chapter to the topic of an honorable man offering his sister or daughter in marriage.

'Umar Farooq ؓ was very upset because both the men he approached had either avoided or refused marriage to his daughter. He was confident of a willing and joyful acceptance but things turned out otherwise. He was very upset and worried at the turn of events; in a sense it was an affront to him and his position as a sincere defender of the faith. People, he thought, would consider it an honor to have an alliance by marriage with him. With this grievance he went to the Prophet ﷺ and explained to him the position he found himself in. The Prophet ﷺ smilingly answered that he should neither grieve nor worry, and Allâh willing he would find a husband better than 'Uthmân ؓ for Hafsah رضي الله عنها, and 'Uthmân ؓ in turn, would find for himself a better wife than Hafsah رضي الله عنها.

'Umar Farooq ؓ was pleased on hearing this from the Prophet ﷺ himself, but also a little perplexed over who such a man could be? A few days later the Prophet ﷺ married his daughter, Umm Kulthûm رضي الله عنها to 'Uthmân ؓ. 'Umar Farooq ؓ realized that one part of the prediction had come true, but he continued to puzzle over the second half of the statement. Who could possibly be a better man than 'Uthmân ؓ?

One day the Prophet ﷺ proposed marriage to Hafsah رضي الله عنها. 'Umar Farooq ؓ could not believe his ears; his daughter would have the honor of joining the select band of women who were known as the Mothers of the Believers! 'A'ishah and Saudah رضي الله عنهما were already part of the Prophet's household. It seemed too good to be true. Thus Hafsah رضي الله عنها was joined in marriage to the Prophet ﷺ in the third year after *Hijrah*, before the Battle of Uhud. She was about twenty-two years old at the time. On seeing off his daughter to her husband's house, 'Umar Farooq ؓ told her that she should never try to compete with 'A'ishah رضي الله عنها, who was the Prophet's favorite and better than her in many respects. He said she should respect her sincerely and live happily as a member of the first and foremost family.

Sa'eed bin Musayyab, a learned scholar, states that the Prophet's prediction that he was a better husband for Hafsah رضي الله عنها than 'Uthmân ؓ was proved right, as was his statement that Umm Kulthûm رضي الله عنها was a better wife for 'Uthmân ؓ than Hafsah رضي الله عنها. After the marriage Abu Bakr Siddeeq ؓ met with 'Umar Farooq ؓ and told him the truth was that the Prophet ﷺ had mentioned to him that he planned to marry Hafsah رضي الله عنها. That was the reason he had remained silent, as it would not have been proper to betray his confidence. If matters were different he would have been only too

Hafsah bint 'Umar رضي الله عنها

happy to accept her hand in marriage. 'Umar Farooq ؓ expressed his happiness by quoting the following: *Âyâh*,

> *"This is by the Grace of my Lord – to test me whether I am grateful or ungrateful! And whoever is grateful, truly, his gratitude is for himself; and whoever is ungrateful, (it is for the loss of only himself). Certainly my Lord is Rich, Bountiful."* (27:40)

After attaining the position of the Mother of the Believers, Hafsah رضي الله عنها became even more absorbed in studying the finer points of religion. She memorized the different *Âyât* as and when they were revealed. She would store in her mind conversations of Muhammad ﷺ for a better understanding of Islâm. Often she would discuss the points that arose in her mind about the *Sharî'ah*. Jâbir bin 'Abdullâh Ansâri ؓ narrates an incident which was related to him by Umm Mubashir. She and Hafsah رضي الله عنها and the Prophet ﷺ were sitting and chatting together. He said that all the people who had given the Pledge of Allegiance at Hudaibiyah under the tree would go to Paradise, and not to Hell. She asked how that was possible. The Prophet ﷺ got annoyed, but Hafsah رضي الله عنها did not give up and quoted an *Âyâh* from *Surah Maryam*.

> *"There is not one of you but will pass over it (Hell)."* (19:71)

In reply he quoted the very next *Âyâh*, also from *Surah Maryam*.

> *"Then We shall save those who use to fear Allâh and were dutiful to Him. And We shall leave the wrongdoers therein to their knees (in Hell)."* (19:72)

This news of Hafsah رضي الله عنها disputing with the Prophet ﷺ spread in Madinah. On that day the Prophet ﷺ was very disturbed; and when 'Umar Farooq ؓ heard about it he chided his daughter. She replied that 'A'ishah رضي الله عنها too spoke in the same manner to him. Her father again cautioned her not to compete with 'A'ishah رضي الله عنها and maintain a certain decorum, or else she would bring trouble on herself.

Among the Mothers of the Believers, 'A'ishah, Umm Habîbah, Saudah and Hafsah رضي الله عنهن all belonged to the tribe of Quraish. The others came from various other tribes. Every day after the *'Asr* prayer, the Prophet ﷺ would visit them all for a little while to see if they needed anything; the time of the visits was routine and each would wait eagerly for his arrival. On several occasions, it so happened that he spent more time with Zainab رضي الله عنها. This upset 'A'ishah رضي الله عنها and she spoke about it to Hafsah and Saudah رضي الله عنهما. They got together and found out that a certain relative had sent Zainab رضي الله عنها a special kind of honey and she used to offer it to the Prophet ﷺ every day. This was his favorite and he used to be delayed in her apartment, enjoying it. 'A'ishah رضي الله عنها was so fond of the Prophet ﷺ that she could not bear for him to be late coming to her apartment. Because of her regard for him she could not object directly. So she consulted with the other two – Hafsah and Saudah رضي الله عنهما – and they decided that when he came to each of them by turn, they would all say that there was a strange smell emanating from his mouth. When he heard the same thing from all three of them he thought it was due to the honey he had, and decided to give it up for good. If this had been an incident in the life of an ordinary person it would have been of no consequence. But this was with the last Prophet of Allâh ﷺ, and his every word and every action would become the law or *Sharî'ah* for all Muslims for all time to come. Thus it had a special significance.

So Allâh ﷺ rebuked him in *Âyâh* of *Surat At-Tahreem*.

> "O Prophet! Why do you forbid (for yourself) that which Allâh has allowed to you, seeking to please your wives? And Allâh is Oft-Forgiving, Most Merciful." (66:1)

It was around the same time that the Prophet ﷺ confided a secret matter to Hafsah رضي الله عنها, and warned her not to speak to anyone about it. But she told 'A'ishah رضي الله عنها. Allâh then revealed to the Prophet ﷺ what happened. Allâh revealed this in the following *Âyâh* of *Surat At-Tahreem*,

> "And when the Prophet disclosed a matter in confidence to one of his wives, then she told it. And Allâh made it known to him; he informed part thereof and left a part. Then when he told her thereof, she said: "Who told you this?" He said: "The All-Knower, the All-Aware has told me." (66:3)

Hafsah bint 'Umar رضي الله عنها

By the ninth year after *Hijrah*, most of the Arabian Peninsula was under the Islâmic government at Madinah; the granaries were full and all the riches were reaching the center from the different regions of Arabia. Many of the ladies in the household of the Prophet ﷺ had been brought up in the lap of luxury; so when they saw this reign of prosperity, they too put forward demands for an increase in their household allowances. When 'Umar Farooq ؓ heard of this he was very upset; he told his daughter Hafsah رضي الله عنها that she should ask her father if she needed anything and not make any demands on the Prophet ﷺ. He also advised all the Mothers of the Believers not to make any demands. Umm Salamah رضي الله عنها did not quite like this and felt that he had the habit of interfering in every matter. She told him frankly that he should refrain from meddling in the affairs of the Prophet's wives.

It was at this time that the Prophet ﷺ had fallen from his horse and been injured; keeping all these things in view he decided to go into seclusion and moved to an upper room adjacent to the apartment of 'A'ishah رضي الله عنها. The whole city was buzzing with the gossip the Hypocrites spread saying that he divorced his wives. But actually no such thing happened. All the Companions were disturbed by this situation, but no one had the courage to approach the Prophet ﷺ and talk to him directly.

Finally 'Umar Farooq ؓ known for his forthrightness went to him and asked him if the rumor was true. When he denied it he was delighted. Then he asked if he could announce this good news to the rest of the Muslims. When he received permission, he joyfully informed the community that everything was fine with the Prophet's household. The whole city was relieved that the Messenger of Allâh ﷺ had not been offended in any way. On the twenty-ninth day he came down into the apartment of 'A'ishah رضي الله عنها. She asked him smilingly why had he come down before the month was over. He replied that often the lunar month did consist of only twenty-nine days. Hafsah رضي الله عنها promised her father that she would never ever ask for a raise in her allowance and she stood by her word to the end of her life.

◈ෲ◈ෲ◈ෲ◈ෲ◈

Hafsah رضي الله عنها, died in the year 41 after *Hijrah*, aged fifty-nine. At the time of death she was fasting. The funeral prayers were led by the governor of Madinah, Marwan bin Hakam. Abu Hurairah, and Abu Sa'eed Khudri رضي الله عنهما, the eminent Companions of the Prophet were among those who carried the bier to *Jannatul Baqi'*. Her two brothers, 'Abdullâh bin 'Umar and 'Asim bin 'Umar رضي الله عنهما placed her gently into her final resting place. Sâlim bin 'Abdullâh, 'Abdur-Rahmân bin 'Abdullâh and Hamzah bin 'Abdullâh, all the sons of 'Abdullâh bin 'Umar رضي الله عنهم also attended funeral.

So a righteous and learned writer and reciter of the Noble Qur'ân who devoted herself from her youth to prayer, fasting and meditation passed into history.

These *Âyât* from *Surat Al-Qamar* express an apt tribute to this great Mother of the Believers:

"*Verily, the pious will be in the midst of Gardens and Rivers (Paradise). In a seat of truth, near the Omnipotent King.*" (54:54-55)

Zainab bint Khuzaymah رضي الله عنها

The Prophet ﷺ said:

"Allâh has commanded me to marry the women of Paradise only."

She is the lady who was known as *'Umm-ul-Masâkeen'* (The Mother of the Distressed)' because she would give charity to deserving people.

Zainab bint Khuzaymah رضي الله عنها

The Prophet ﷺ said that Allâh had ordained that he would marry only those women deserving of Paradise. And Zainab رضي الله عنها was a lady who was known as 'The Mother of the Distressed' because she was the most generous among the ladies of the household.

She was born thirteen years before Muhammad ﷺ was chosen as the Messenger of Allâh. When he declared himself as the chosen Prophet of Allâh he caused a furor in Makkah. Even those who loved and respected him, those who called him 'Truthful' and 'Trustworthy', turned into enemies who wanted to kill him. But there were some who were fortunate enough to be guided to answer his call immediately, and pledge allegiance to Allâh and His Messenger. Among the righteous band of people who first proclaimed his truthfulness was Zainab bint Khuzaymah رضي الله عنها. She had been married to 'Abdullâh bin Jahsh ﷺ. This highly respected Companion attained martyrdom during the Battle of Uhud. The widows and orphaned children of the martyred Companions found security with other Companions who married the widows and took the children under their protection. Thus Zainab bint Khuzaymah رضي الله عنها after the death of her husband attained the enviable position of becoming a wife of the Prophet ﷺ.

The husband of Hamnah bint Jahsh رضي الله عنها was also martyred during the Battle of Uhud and she was also grief stricken. Seeing this the Prophet ﷺ said:

"The place a husband holds in his wife's heart could not be taken by any other."

Hamnah told him sighing deeply that it was the thought of the orphaned children that troubled her most and she asked him to pray that Allâh ﷻ should give her patience and strength. The Prophet's prayers for her were accepted and she married the noble Companion Talhah bin 'Abdullâh ﷺ. He was an ideal husband and a loving father for the orphaned children of her first husband.

Zainab رضي الله عنها was in the same plight as Hamnah رضي الله عنها, but she did not appeal to any human being. She entrusted her affairs entirely to Allâh and devoted herself to prayer and meditation. So when she received a proposal from the best man possible, the Prophet ﷺ, she was overjoyed with the good fortune that Allâh had bestowed on her.

The Prophet ﷺ married her with a dowry of four hundred Dirhams, and an apartment was constructed for her near those of Hafsah and 'A'ishah رضي الله عنهما. Thus she joined the selected band of pure and virtuous ladies of the Prophet's household. Allâh in the Noble Qur'ân speaks of these ladies of his Prophet's household:

> *"Allâh wishes only to remove evil deeds from you, O members of the family (of the Prophet), and to purify you with a thorough purification."* (33:33)

And also:

> *"O wives of the Prophet, You are not like any other women."* (33:32)

Zainab bint Khuzaymah رضي الله عنها, even before the advent of Islâm was known as 'Mother of the Distressed'. This was because she could not bear to see a person hungry or in dire need. She was eulogized in verse by some of the famous poets of the time.

Ibn Katheer wrote that she earned the title because of her deeds of charity and generosity.

Qastalâni writes that she was known by this name even during pre-Islâmic times.

This great quality of generosity became even more pronounced and intense when she converted to Islâm, which has always strongly advocated giving in charity.

Zainab bint Khuzaymah رضي الله عنها

The two ladies who were already part of the household – 'A'ishah and Hafsah رضي الله عنهما – welcomed this new friend and tried their best to give her their sincere sympathetic companionship. They knew that the Prophet ﷺ married Zainab رضي الله عنها because she was deeply affected by the death of her first husband. Because of the kind behavior of these two noble ladies, her grief was lightened and she felt more at peace. Yet she lived barely eight months after her marriage to the Prophet ﷺ. She was just thirty years old when she passed away. The Prophet led the funeral prayers and she was buried in *Jannatul Baqi'*. Khadîjah رضي الله عنها was the first wife to have passed away in the lifetime of Muhammad ﷺ, and Zainab رضي الله عنها was the second.

May Allâh be pleased with them and they with Him.

Umm Salamah bint Abu Umayyah رضي الله عنها

The Prophet ﷺ said:

"Allâh has commanded me to marry only the women of Paradise."

Umm Salamah رضي الله عنها participated in the Pledge of Ridhwân, therefore, she deserved Paradise.

Umm Salamah bint Abu Umayyah رضي الله عنها

Her real name was Hind bint Abu Umayyah who became famous by the name Umm Salamah. She was noble by birth, intelligent, learned, wise and skillful. She was first married to 'Abdullâh bin 'Abdul Asad Makhzoomi known as Abu Salamah. He was the son of the Prophet's paternal aunt Barrah bint Abdul Muttalib. He too belonged to the select band of people who were the first to accept Islâm. He was known for his integrity, valor, generosity, tolerance and patience. He was the eleventh person to come into the fold of Islâm. He was also the foster brother of the Prophet ﷺ by suckling.

Umm Salamah رضي الله عنها was also one of the earliest converts to Islâm. Her mother was 'Atikah bint 'Âmir bin Rabee'ah bin Mâlik bin Khuzaymah. Her father Abu Umayyah bin 'Abdullâh bin 'Amr bin Makhzoom was a very wealthy man and famous throughout the Arab world for his public service and charity. People who traveled with him did not have to carry food and necessities for the journey because they were always treated as his guests, and he bore all the expenses. Umm Salamah رضي الله عنها seemed to have inherited this trait from her father. She was always amiable and kind to her neighbors. When she married the handsome and brave son of the equally wealthy family of Makhzoom, she carried a friendly demeanor of pleasant serenity into her new household. There was an atmosphere of gaiety and love in the home of the newly married couple.

But things changed radically when the couple embraced Islâm. The whole family turned against them; mischievous and wicked elements like Waleed bin Mughairah Makhzoomi started creating problems for them. Finally, when matters were at their worst, the Prophet ﷺ advised his staunch followers to migrate to Abyssinia where the Christian King was more tolerant of the new religion. Sixteen people set out on that historic first migration of the followers of Islâm — twelve men and four women.

These were the people who had that honor.

- 'Uthmân bin 'Affân ؓ
- Abu Hudhaifah bin 'Utbah ؓ
- Abu Salamah 'Abdullâh bin 'Abdul-Asad Makhzoomi ؓ
- 'Âmir bin Rabee'ah ؓ
- Zubair bin 'Awwâm ؓ
- Mus'ab bin 'Umair ؓ
- 'Abdur-Rahmân bin 'Awf ؓ
- 'Uthmân bin 'Awf ؓ
- Abu Sibrah bin Abi Raham ؓ
- Hâtib bin 'Amr ؓ
- Suhail bin Wahb ؓ
- 'Abdullâh bin Mas'ood ؓ

The following four noble ladies were also part of this migrant group:

- Ruqaiyyah رضي الله عنها bint Muhammad ﷺ, wife of 'Uthmân bin 'Affân ؓ
- Sahlah bint Suhail رضي الله عنها, wife of Abu Hudhaifah bin 'Utbah ؓ
- Umm Salamah رضي الله عنها, wife of Abu Salamah ؓ
- Laila bint Abi Hashmah رضي الله عنها, wife of 'Âmir bin Rabee'ah ؓ

When this caravan reached the shores of the ocean, two trading vessels were waiting for departure. They got on board and set sail for

Abyssinia. The next group of immigrants that left for Abyssinia consisted of eighty-three men and nineteen ladies. Ja'far bin Abi Tâlib ﷺ was among them.

Umm Salamah رضي الله عنها narrated that life was very peaceful in Abyssinia, free of all religious persecution. She first gave birth to a daughter, whom they named Zainab. Then she had a son Salamah, hence her name and her husband's name.

The next child was also a son, 'Umar. Finally they had another daughter who they named Durrah. So life was very smooth and time passed uneventfully, in peace and happiness. The ruler of Abyssinia, Najâshi, was very kind to the migrants. When the leaders of the disbelievers heard this news they were enraged and thought that the Muslims were becoming a real source of danger for them. They decided to take strong measures to stem the rising tide of Islâm.

After a great deal of thought they evolved a plan of action. They sent the leading politician of the Arab world, 'Amr bin al-'Aas and 'Abdullâh bin Abi Rabee'ah with expensive gifts for Najâshi, in order to persuade him to hand over the Muslim migrants to their custody. Before meeting the ruler personally, they met the important advisers and ministers laden with gifts for them as well. This was to lay the ground for the final talks with Najâshi, himself. They presented their viewpoint and arguments for demanding custody of the migrants very strongly, and appealed to them for help in persuading the ruler. The ministers assured them of full cooperation and help.

Finally, they presented themselves before Najâshi, and after offering their gifts and respectful salutations, they proceeded to present their case. The refugee Muslims who were persecuted for their religious beliefs they called "crazy rebels", who were sowing discord within families and tribes because of their 'heretic' views. Fathers were opposed to sons and brother was fighting brother. They were breaking away from the traditions and beliefs of their forefathers, and were following some strange new faith. They had been allowed to live peacefully because of the generosity and liberal views of Najâshi, but they were not to be trusted. They could cause trouble in his country as well, since they did not believe in the Christian faith either. The best solution would be to hand them over to the Quraish, who knew best how to deal with them.

Najâshi looked towards his courtiers for their opinion. They agreed with the viewpoint of the Quraish that this was an internal dispute and the political refugees should be handed over to the representatives of the Quraish. Najâshi was a fair minded, far-sighted and frank man. So he called for the leader of the refugees to present their case. The delegation chose Ja'far bin Abi Tâlib ؉ as their leader.

When the delegation reached the court of Najâshi, they wished him and took their seats. 'Amr bin al-'Aas immediately found fault with them, saying they were too arrogant; they should have followed the formal protocol of the court and prostrated themselves before the ruler. Najâshi asked them why they had not observed the decorum of the royal court. Ja'far ؉ replied that they believed that they should prostrate only before the Creator and not before any of the creation of the Almighty. This would amount to worship of a being other than Allâh.

Najâshi replied that he had heard that they adopted a strange new religion. Ja'far ؉ explained to him eloquently the tenets of Islâm.

He said,

> "Your Royal Highness, we were an uncivilized people who used to worship idols, eat dead carcasses, and have drinking orgies. Internal and tribal feuds were common with us and these could go on for a hundred years. We did not maintain good relations with our own kith and kin; we forgot that our neighbors had rights upon us. The law of the jungle prevailed, and might was right. In short we lived like animals.
>
> Then Allâh sent a Messenger to guide us to the right path. He was one of our own from a tribe and a family known to us. We all acknowledged that he was an exceptional man of integrity, honesty and modesty. He invited us to worship Allâh, to always speak the truth and be honest in our dealings and keep our promises. He taught us what is lawful and to abstain from what is not lawful. He said the orphans, the poor, the distressed and women – all had rights in society, and it was wrong to

usurp these rights. He taught us the values of chastity and virtue, and asked us to abstain from slander and backbiting. He said we should remember Allâh in prayer and fasting; we should pay our poor dues so that there could be equitable distribution of money. And soon it was as if we became a new people. Lawlessness, crime, debauchery and constant feuding – all were forgotten. The same people now became a caring community; each wanted for his brother what he wanted for himself.

The nation turned against us because of our virtuous behavior and started torturing us. But we were not ready to sink into that morass of evil again, and when persecution reached its peak, we decided to flee and come to you, as we had heard that your rule was just, and you were tolerant, sympathetic and hospitable to refugees."

Najâshi then answered that he had heard their Prophet received revelations from his Allâh, and that he would like to hear to some of these.

Ja'far took advantage of the opportunity to recite *Surah Maryam* in such a heartrending manner that Najâshi started shaking, tears started coursing down his cheeks and his beard. The courtiers were speechless. Finally, gaining control, Najâshi said that it seemed these *Âyât* and those in the Bible had the same Divine origin. The people in his court were stunned and they thought to themselves that the same magic that Muhammad had used to bewitch and entrance people in Makkah was now working on their ruler as well. Najâshi then told the emissaries of the Quraish that these were people of good character and could continue to live in Abyssinia as long as they wished. Further, he would continue to give every kind of protection necessary, and the delegation from Makkah could leave carrying back their gifts. If someone gave him even a mountain of gold in exchange for these righteous people he would not surrender them. 'Amr bin al-'Aas and 'Abdullâh bin Abi Rabee'ah felt really small after this open snub, and started looking at each other. How would they face their leaders after the failure of their mission?

All their plotting came to nothing. They then left, but not for home; they could not give up so easily and started discussing alternative strategies to gain their ends.

Finally, 'Amr came up with an idea. He said he would tell Najâshi something that would really enrage him. He felt confident that this scheme could not fail. 'Abdullâh asked him what he would tell the king.

'Amr said that the Muslims looked upon 'Isa ﷺ as a human being and the servant of Allâh, but the Christians called him the son of God. This new revelation, they thought, would certainly change the attitude of Najâshi. He said the whole court would be mesmerized by this new revelation.

After reaching Najâshi's court the next morning, they greeted him and plunged in with the information, they said they had forgotten to bring to his attention. These Muslims were so insolent that they refused to acknowledge 'Isa ﷺ as the son of God and claimed that he was an ordinary mortal and servant of Allâh. They requested the king to call the Muslims and ask them what their opinion about 'Isa ﷺ was.

The Muslims were summoned to the court and questioned about the status of 'Isa ﷺ. Ja'far ؓ replied that their Prophet ﷺ told them that he was the servant and Messenger of Allâh; and he was also the spirit and Word of Allâh. Najâshi was so happy to hear this complete answer that he beat his palm on the floor, and exclaimed that what he had heard was exactly right and there was absolutely no difference between this statement and what 'Isa ﷺ had stated about himself. Then he told the migrant Muslims that they could live with peace and goodwill in his country; no one could dare to harm them in even the smallest degree. Then he turned to the representatives of the Quraish and said they could return to their country with their gifts; by the grace of Allâh he and his people had enough and more.

The embarrassed delegates returned empty-handed, mission unfulfilled! Umm Salamah رضي الله عنها has written about this memorable first migration of the Muslims, and described the greatness of Najâshi in such a moving manner that it has become an integral and important part of Islâmic history.

Umm Salamah bint Abu Umayyah رضي الله عنها

Umm Salamah رضي الله عنها narrates that their life in Abyssinia was very peaceful and Najâshi was very kind, but all the same they were homesick for Makkah. They continued longing for the time when peace would finally prevail so they could return to their beloved country. One day news reached that 'Umar bin al-Khattâb ؓ accepted Islâm and that the conditions in Makkah had changed completely. It was said that because of the authority and influence of 'Umar the persecution of Muslims came to an end. They were all so excited at this good news, writes Umm Salamah رضي الله عنها that they decided to set out for their homes. 'Uthmân bin 'Affân ؓ also set out with them with his family. On reaching Makkah they realized it had been just a rumor and things were much worse than before. Muslims were the targets of worse crimes and persecution. But it was too late.

An accepted tradition states what had actually happened. The disbelievers heard the Prophet ﷺ reciting Âyât from the Noble Qur'ân, and prostrated involuntarily at one Âyâh with him. Like all rumors this too ballooned into news that the Quraish had converted to Islâm. In reality this was not so.

Weary of the constant problems they faced, they decided to leave for Abyssinia again. It was at this time that the Prophet ﷺ ordered Muslims to migrate to Madinah. The delegation from there had brought the news that those who swore allegiance to Allâh and His Prophet ﷺ at 'Aqabah had invited Muslims to settle there, and he accepted. The Ansâr of Madinah, (as they came to be called), had said they would look after their migrant brethren.

Abu Salamah ؓ with his family left on camels for Madinah. When members of her family saw this they caught the bridle of the camel and told him that he could go where he wanted but he would have to leave behind their daughter. They said it seemed like a joke — he was always off somewhere or the other, Abyssinia, then Madinah! He never seemed to give her a peaceful, settled life.

When Abu Salamah's family heard this they were enraged. They came and took her sons away, saying she could not take them with her; they were their flesh and blood and they would bring them up. So, in a moment the whole family was split up in three different places. Abu Salamah ؓ left for Madinah, his wife was left with her parents and the sons were with the grandparents. It was such a shock – this being torn apart from husband and sons – that she just could not stop weeping. Every day she used to visit the spot from where her husband and children had been torn away from her and weep for her loved ones. One day one of the members of her tribe passed that way and saw her grieving and asked her what happened. She told him about her plight. He then went and gave a piece of his mind to the elders of both families, rebuking them for their cruel behavior towards a noble and helpless lady. His emotional and blunt outburst made them realize how unjust they were and they relented. They gave back her sons to her, and her family too gave her permission to proceed to Madinah.

But how could she travel alone? No one was willing to accompany her. Finally, gaining courage and solace from the fact that she now had her sons with her, she set out for Madinah. When she reached Tan'eem she met 'Uthmân bin Talhah 'Abdari, who had not up to that time converted to Islâm. He asked her where she was travelling all alone. She replied that she was going to join her husband. He was surprised that not a single member of the family accompanied her. She said no one agreed to go with her and she was totally dependent on Allâh Almighty who was her Defender and Protector; only He would protect her. 'Uthmân bin Talhah 'Abdari took the bridle of the camel and said he would help her in reaching her destination.

Umm Salamah رضي الله عنها said that such a decent, pure-hearted man, with not a trace of evil in him would be difficult to find. Whenever they reached a camping site he would tie the camel to a tree and move far away to lie down and rest. So she also had some privacy and could rest at ease, relaxed with her children. When it was time to resume the journey he would bring the camel and make it sit down. Once she got on the camel's back with her children, he would take the bridle in his hand and start walking. After several days they reached Qubâ which is in the outskirts of Madinah. Banu 'Amr bin 'Awf were settled there; he said that since Abu Salamah ﷺ was also there he could leave her and return. Umm Salamah رضي الله عنها says in her book that his chivalrous behavior and his goodness affected her deeply. When she finally saw her family after so long her joy knew no bounds. In this

Umm Salamah bint Abu Umayyah رضي الله عنها

way, this divided family once again was at peace and the children had the benefit of a good upbringing that only united and happy parents can provide.

Abu Salamah ؓ took part in the Battle of Badr and once again had the honor of fighting for Islâm in the Battle of Uhud. But in this last mentioned battle Abu Usâmah Jashmi wounded him seriously in the side with his spear. He underwent treatment for a month but to no avail. The wound apparently healed, but that was only on the surface, and it continued to fester inside.

Barely two months after the battle of Uhud the Prophet ﷺ received news that Banu Asad was planning to attack the Muslims. He ordered his men to prepare for battle, and made Abu Salamah ؓ the Commander of the Islâmic forces. This, in spite of the fact that worthy and experienced heroes like Abu 'Ubaidah bin Al-Jarrah and Sa'd bin Abi Waqqas رضي الله عنهما were present. When the Prophet ﷺ gave the army flag to Abu Salamah ؓ he outlined the strategy to be adopted. He told him to reach the territory of Banu Asad and camp there, then attack them before they had a chance to do so. Abu Salamah ؓ obeyed the Prophet's orders and with his band of a hundred and fifty men he suddenly swooped down on the Banu Asad immediately after crossing their border.

The clang of swords and the battle cries of the warring *Mujâhideen*, who had sworn to win or die in the attempt, challenged Banu Asad who had been taken unawares. This was a very crucial battle for Islâm, as it would be a compensation for the defeat at Uhud. A decisive victory was essential to impress the tribes in the surrounding territories. So every *Mujâhid* played on his life to fight and win. Abu Salamah ؓ forgot his grievously wounded side and fought valiantly; he moved like lightning and the enemies fell under his sword. But his wound which had only healed on the surface it started bleeding. The battle was won, and Banu Asad was crushed. The Muslims got the rich spoils of a war well fought. After twenty-nine days on the 8th of *Safar* in the fourth year after *Hijrah*, the army re-entered Madinah. But Abu Salamah ؓ was totally spent. When Umm Salamah رضي الله عنها saw his grievous injuries she became extremely worried.

Abu Salamah ؓ was lying in a very serious condition when the Prophet ﷺ came to visit him. He realized that he was approaching death, and patting his hand consoled him. The Prophet ﷺ prayed for him and Abu Salamah ؓ also prayed and asked Allâh to give his family a protector and provider like him. And he also asked Him to give Umm Salamah رضي الله عنها a husband who would give her neither sorrow nor hardship.

After this prayer he passed away. The Prophet ﷺ closed his eyes with his hands. Umm Salamah رضي الله عنها often thought of her husband's last prayer for her and wondered who could possibly be better than Abu Salamah ؓ. She asked the Prophet ﷺ what she should ask Allâh for herself. He taught her to pray for forgiveness both for herself and for Abu Salamah ؓ and ask Allâh to give her a better future.

Umm Salamah رضي الله عنها says that she prayed thus and Allâh ﷻ granted her prayer. When she finished the prescribed period of waiting, Abu Bakr Siddeeq ؓ sent a proposal of marriage to her, but she refused. Then 'Umar bin al-Khattâb ؓ proposed and she refused him as well. Then the Prophet ﷺ proposed. She told him that she had three reservations regarding his proposal. She was hot-headed and had a temper; she felt she might be rude to the Prophet of Allâh ﷺ, and thus lose the reward for all her good deeds. Secondly, she was an elderly lady; thirdly, she had many children. The Prophet answered that he would pray to Allâh, and Allâh willing, her temper would subside. As far as age was concerned, he was also an elderly man. Thirdly, as far as her children were concerned — that was the precise reason for proposing to her — he wished to be their guardian and share the responsibility. She writes that this answer gave her great happiness and thus she attained the honor of becoming part of the Prophet's household. Thus Allâh granted both hers and Abu Salamah's prayer, and she married the Prophet ﷺ in the month of *Shawwâl*, in the fourth year after *Hijrah*.

'A'ishah رضي الله عنها narrated that it was the habit of the Prophet ﷺ to visit each of his wives in turn after the *'Asr* prayers. He would inquire about their welfare and if they needed anything. He would start from the

Umm Salamah bint Abu Umayyah رضي الله عنها

apartment of Umm Salamah رضي الله عنها because she was the eldest among them, and finish his rounds at the apartment of 'A'ishah رضي الله عنها.

Umm Salamah رضي الله عنها, because of her beauty, knowledge and wisdom held an eminent position. After the truce of Hudaibiyah, the Prophet ﷺ ordered his Companions to sacrifice the animals they brought along for the purpose, and shave their heads. But they all seemed reluctant and did not rise to obey his command. When Umm Salamah رضي الله عنها saw the situation she suggested that he should not speak about the subject to anyone, but just go out from the tent and offer the sacrifice and shave his head. Then he could see the effect of his action. And what she expected happened — all the Companions followed suit.

Umm Salamah رضي الله عنها was a very astute and wise lady. She was educated and devoted to the welfare of the destitute and needy.

Several of the *Âyât* of the Noble Qur'ân were revealed to the Prophet ﷺ when he was in her apartment. For instance: *Âyât* in *Surat Al-Ahzâb*,

> "And Allâh only wishes to remove evil deeds from you, O members of the family (of the Prophet), and to purify you with a through purification." (33:33)

Also some of the *Âyât* of *Surat At-Taubah* were revealed while he was with her.

> "And (there are) others who have acknowledged their sins, they have mixed a deed that was righteous with another that was evil. Perhaps Allâh will turn unto them in forgiveness. Surely, Allâh is Oft-Forgiving, Most Merciful." (9:102)

He also said:

> "And (He forgave) the three who did not join till for them the earth, vast as it is, was straitened and their own selves were straitened to them, and they perceived that there is no fleeing from Allâh, and no refuge but with Him. Then, He forgave them that they might beg for His pardon. Verily, Allâh is the One Who forgives and accepts repentance, Most Merciful." (9:118)

This *Âyâh* refers to the turning towards Allâh ﷻ of Ka'b bin Mâlik, Hilâl bin Umayyah and Murarah bin Ar-Rabi' رضي الله عنهم in sincere repentance. These three Companions, without any valid reason, avoided joining the Muslim army in the Battle of Tabuk. They were therefore ostracized by the Prophet ﷺ and the rest of the Companions. They were so stricken by guilt that they kept praying for Divine Forgiveness, until finally Allâh ﷻ granted it to them. The Prophet ﷺ was sleeping in the apartment of Umm Salamah رضي الله عنها when this last *Âyâh* was revealed to him. He woke up in the late hours of the night and told her that the supplications for forgiveness of these three Companions had been accepted. She asked him if this good news should be conveyed to them immediately. He said they should not be disturbed so late at night; after the *Fajr* prayers he sent for them and congratulated them. They were overjoyed and so were all the other Companions.

Umm Salamah رضي الله عنها also had the distinction of taking part in many battles of significance in the history of Islâm. She was with the Prophet ﷺ during the Battles of Bani Mustaliq, Tâ'if, Khaybar, Hunain and the conquest of Makkah. She was present at the signing of the historic Treaty of Hudaibiyah where the *Bai'at ar-Ridhwân* (Oath of Allegiance) had taken place.

Salmân Fârsi ؓ narrates that someone mentioned to him that the Angel Jibrîl had come down from the Heavens and was in conversation with the Prophet ﷺ. When he went there he saw that the person with the Prophet was Dihyah al-Kalbi, and that Umm Salamah رضي الله عنها was also present. When the conversation ended, the Prophet ﷺ asked if they knew who that person was. She said he was one of his most faithful followers, Dihyah al-Kalbi. Thereupon the Prophet told her, smiling, that it was actually the Angel Jibrîl in human guise.

Umm Salamah رضي الله عنها was very learned in religious matters. She knew three hundred and eighty-seven *Ahâdîth* of the Prophet ﷺ by heart. She knew very well the finer points of Islâmic law about foster-relations through suckling and divorce. 'Abdullâh bin 'Abbâs رضي الله عنهما used to consult with her for many points of *Sharî'ah*, (Islâmic

Umm Salamah bint Abu Umayyah رضي الله عنها

legislation). On the top of the list of names of Companions whose judgments on points of law were regarded as valid is the name of Umm Salamah رضي الله عنها.

The following is the list of Companions who were known for their ability to give legal verdicts:

- Umm Salamah رضي الله عنها
- Anas bin Mâlik ؓ
- Abu Sa'eed al-Khudri ؓ
- Abu Hurairah ؓ
- 'Uthmân bin 'Affân ؓ
- 'Abdullâh bin 'Amr bin al-'Aas
- 'Abdullâh bin Zubair ؓ
- Abu Musâ Ash'ari
- Sa'd bin Abi Waqqâs ؓ
- Salmân Fârsi ؓ
- Jâbir bin 'Abdullâh ؓ
- Mu'âdh bin Jabal ؓ
- Abu Bakr Siddeeq ؓ
- Talhah bin 'Ubaidullâh ؓ
- Zubair bin 'Awwâm ؓ
- 'Abdur-Rahmân bin 'Awf ؓ
- 'Imrân bin Husain ؓ
- 'Ubâdah bin Sâmit ؓ
- Mu'âwiyah bin Abi Sufyân ؓ

Umm Salamah رضي الله عنها had hardly any equal in mastery over language. When she spoke her words and phrases were well chosen and exactly appropriate for the expression of ideas. Her written language was suited for literary expression. Many Companions and followers have noted down traditions attributed to her.

❖✽❖✽❖✽❖

She lived to the ripe old age of eighty-four and died in the year 62 after *Hijrah*. She lived to see the rule of *Khulafâ' Ar-Râshideen*. Zainab bint Jahsh رضي الله عنها was the first among the Mothers of the Believers to pass away and Umm Salamah رضي الله عنها the last. This was during the rule of Yazîd bin Mu'âwiyah and she was laid to rest beside the other wives of the Prophet ﷺ in *Jannatul Baqi'*.

> *"O the one in (complete) rest and satisfaction! Come back to your Lord – well pleased and well pleasing. Enter you then among My (honored) servants, and enter you My Paradise."* (87:27-30)

Zainab bint Jahsh رضي الله عنها

One day Allâh's Messenger ﷺ said to the Mothers of the Believers:

"*Among you she would meet me first in the hereafter whose hands are the longest.*"

Amongst the Mothers of the Believers, Zainab رضي الله عنها was the lady who died first, and she became the guest of Paradise. Zainab رضي الله عنها would often give charity. Generosity is referred to 'having long hands'.

Zainab bint Jahsh رضي الله عنها

۞۞۞۞۞۞۞۞

She was the daughter of Umaimah bint 'Abdul Muttalib bin Hâshim, who was the paternal aunt of the Messenger of Allâh ﷺ. Her brother was the distinguished general, 'Abdullâh bin Jahsh ؓ. Another brother was a noted author of religious poetry, Abu Ahmad bin Jahsh ؓ. Her sister was another famous woman Companion, Hamnah bint Jahsh رضي الله عنها. Among her paternal uncles were the 'Leader of the Martyrs' Hamzah bin 'Abdul Muttalib ؓ, and 'Abbâs bin 'Abdul Muttalib ؓ, who was renowned for his works of charity. Her paternal aunt was Safiyyah bint 'Abdul Muttalib bin Hâshim رضي الله عنها.

Known for her generosity and sympathy for the needy, sobriety, abstinence and devotion in prayer, she was first married to Zaid bin Hârithah, the adopted son of the Prophet ﷺ. After her divorce she was married to the Prophet ﷺ at the express command of Allâh ﷻ, in order to destroy the pre-Islâmic custom of giving the same status to adopted children as to their own flesh and blood. At the banquet given at her wedding the *Âyah* of *Hijâb* was revealed.

She was an innately good woman who used to devote a great deal of her time to prayer and fasting. On her death she left a house which was bought by Waleed bin 'Abdul Malik for fifty thousand Dirhams and included by him in the precincts of the Prophet's Mosque at Madinah. The Prophet ﷺ told 'Umar bin al-Khattâb ؓ that she was a God-fearing woman, hospitable and modest. She was so generous and soft-hearted that the poor and distressed of the city broke into tears when they heard they lost their benefactress and patron. She was also one of the fortunate whom the Prophet ﷺ said would go to Paradise.

◈⋘◈⋘◈⋘◈⋘◈

She was born about thirty years before the *Hijrah* of the Prophet ﷺ. She was influenced by the teachings of her brother, 'Abdullâh bin Jahsh ؓ, to convert to Islâm. Beautiful, intelligent, wise and of noble birth she was the envy of many.

The increasing popularity and influence of Islâm roused a towering rage among the Quraish; the new converts faced indescribable tortures. Some were made to lie on beds of coal, while some others were dragged naked across the burning desert sands. Still others were wrapped up in straw mats and strung over smoke, to suffocate them and stop them from breathing. Every day saw new methods of the art of torturing these people who had sworn allegiance to Allâh. The sole purpose was that they should give up the belief and practices of Islâm. It seemed as if Makkah had become too small to hold both the Muslims and the Quraish. The Prophet ﷺ exhorted his followers and friends to be patient and brave, but finally he gave them orders to migrate; first to Abyssinia and then to Madinah.

Under the leadership of 'Abdullâh bin Jahsh ؓ his entire family set out. The caravan included the blind poet Abu Ahmad bin Jahsh ؓ, who was admired for his linguistic mastery. He wrote an epic poem depicting in detail the tortures inflicted by the Quraish, the reasons for migration and the heroic deeds of the Muslims. This poem is considered to be a masterpiece of Arabic literature.

Muhammad bin 'Abdullâh bin Jahsh, Zainab bint Jahsh, Hamnah bint Jahsh who was the wife of Mus'ab bin 'Umair and Umm Habîbah bint Jahsh, wife of 'Abdur-Rahmân bin 'Awf رضي الله عنهم were all companions on this journey. Since all the members of the family had left, their house was lying vacant. Taking advantage of this opportunity, Abu Sufyân, the leader of the Quraish, occupied it. The very house in which people used to pray to Allâh and read the Noble Qur'ân, was now in the possession of idolaters.

'Abdullâh bin Jahsh ﷺ, was upset to hear this and on the occasion of the conquest of Makkah, he spoke to the Prophet ﷺ. When he saw this ardent follower in such distress, he asked him if he would not prefer to have a far better house in Paradise. Of course, 'Abdullâh ﷺ replied, he would much prefer to have a house in Paradise. Upon which the Prophet ﷺ consoled him saying he did, indeed, have a better home there.

Time passed peacefully in Madinah, and the ties between the immigrants and the *Ansâr*, the original inhabitants created an atmosphere of brotherly love and affection. It seemed as if they were members of one united family. The best individual in the society was neither master nor slave, neither man nor woman, neither rich nor poor, but a God-fearing person of good character and morals.

In the context of such an ideal society the Prophet ﷺ suggested to his cousin Zainab رضي الله عنها that he had decided to get her engaged to Zaid bin Hârithah ﷺ, his adopted son and a freed slave. When Zainab رضي الله عنها heard this she was stunned; she told him that she was from a noble family and she was neither keen nor willing to marry a freed slave. She was doubtful if they could get along with each other. He answered that he had chosen Zaid ﷺ for her and she should accept him. Before Zainab رضي الله عنها could answer him, an *Âyâh* was revealed to the Prophet ﷺ. This was the *Âyâh* of *Surat Al-Ahzâb*,

> "It is not for a believer, man or woman, when Allâh and His Messenger have decreed a matter that they should have any option in their decision. And whoever disbelieves Allâh and His Messenger, he has indeed strayed into a plain error." (33:36)

Thus Zainab رضي الله عنها and Zaid ﷺ were married, but separated soon after, as they were from totally different social backgrounds, they were never happy, and their marital life was far from peaceful.

Zainab رضي الله عنها was biased and from the very beginning the relations were always strained. Zaid ﷺ felt that the respect that a husband should get from his wife was never given to him. Disappointed in his marriage, he went to the Prophet ﷺ and told him that he was very upset as he and Zainab رضي الله عنها seemed totally incompatible. The advice that he received from his mentor, has been incorporated in the Noble Qur'ân:

> "Keep your wife to yourself, and fear Allâh." (33:37)

But in spite of all the best efforts the marriage did not work out, and finally he divorced Zainab رضي الله عنها.

The Arabs thought it was wrong for a man to marry the widow or divorcee of his adopted son. Allâh wanted to abolish this uncivilized custom, so He sent Jibrîl to tell the Prophet ﷺ in secret that Zainab رضي الله عنها would one day be his wife. He was very distressed as it was against the accepted norm of behavior. He feared social censure and was very ashamed and embarrassed at the implications. But the decision had been made in the heavens by Allâh ﷻ, and soon he received the revelation:

> "And (remember) when you said to him (Zaid bin Hârithah ؓ) on whom Allâh has bestowed grace (by guiding him to Islâm) and you have done favor (by manumitting him): "Keep your wife to yourself, and fear Allâh." But you hid in yourself that which Allâh will make manifest, you did fear the people (i.e., their saying that Muhammad married the divorced wife of his manumitted slave) whereas Allâh had a better right that you should fear Him. So when Zaid had accomplished his desire from her (i.e. divorced her), We gave her to you in marriage, so that there may be no difficulty to the believers in respect of (the marriage of) the wives of their adopted sons when the latter have no desire to keep them. And Allâh's Command must be fulfilled." (33:37)

When Zainab رضي الله عنها completed her period of waiting, the Prophet ﷺ sent her a proposal through Zaid bin Hârithah ؓ. When he went to her, she was kneading dough; keeping his back turned to her, he gave her the Prophet's message, that he wanted her to join the select group of the Mothers of the Believers. She said she could not answer immediately, but would have to consult her Maker. She began praying to Allâh for guidance. She was still in the middle of her prayer, when the Prophet ﷺ received a revelation that the marriage had already been performed in the Heavens by Allâh ﷻ Himself. After this Heavenly order, the Prophet ﷺ immediately went to Zainab رضي الله عنها, without observing any of the formalities that were observed with acquaintances and friends. He did not inform her in advance nor did ask for permission. There are some exceptional points to be noted regarding this marriage.

- Only the order of the Qur'ân was based as a guardian or a witness.

- It abolished a pre-Islâmic custom that equated a blood relationship with an adoptive one; in which the father could not marry an adopted son's ex-wife or widow.

- Zainab رضي الله عنها used to say very proudly to the other Mothers of the Believers that her marriage had been performed not by her family but by Allâh above the Heavens with His beloved Prophet.

- When the Hypocrites criticized the Prophet ﷺ for this marriage, Allâh ﷻ replied:

"There is no blame on the Prophet in that which Allâh has made legal for him. That has been Allâh's way with those who have passed away of (the Prophets of) old. And the Command of Allâh is a decree determined. Those who convey the Message of Allâh and fear Him, and fear none save Allâh. And Sufficient is Allâh as a Reckoner." (33:38-39)

And to clarify the finer points still further He revealed the *Âyah* which again is part of *Surat Al-Ahzâb*:

"Muhammad is not the father of any of your men, but he is the Messenger of Allâh and the last of the Prophets. And Allâh is Ever All-Aware of everything." (33:40)

On this occasion Allâh revealed the order clarifying the position of adopted sons as:

"Nor has He made your adopted sons your real sons. That is but your saying with your mouths. But Allâh says the truth, and He guides to

the (Right) Way. Call them (the adopted sons) by (the names of) their fathers, that is more just with Allâh." (33:4-5)

On the occasion of this wedding Allâh revealed revelation regarding *Hijâb* and also made it clear that no man could marry any of the Mothers of the Believers after the Prophet ﷺ. These two commands were revealed in : *Âyah* of the same *Sûrat*,

> *"O you who believe! Enter not the Prophet's houses, unless permission is given to you for a meal, (and then) not (so early as) to wait for its preparation. But when you are invited, enter, and when you have taken your meal, disperse without sitting for a talk. Verily, such (behavior) annoys the Prophet, and he is shy of (asking) you (to go); but Allâh is not shy of (telling you) the truth. And when you ask (his wives) for anything you want, ask them from behind a screen that is purer for your hearts and for their hearts. And it is not (right) for you that you should annoy Allâh's Messenger, nor that you should ever marry his wives after him (his death). Verily, with Allâh that shall be an enormity."* (33:53)

'A'ishah رضي الله عنها says that in terms of values and position, Zainab رضي الله عنها was her equal. She said she had never seen any other person who was so eager to get closer to Allâh ﷻ. To gain nearness to Him she was more charitable than most, and her generous behavior with relatives was impeccable. When 'A'ishah رضي الله عنها was wrongfully accused, the whole of Madinah was polluted with gossip and slanderous talk; in fact even the Prophet ﷺ was disturbed. The Prophet ﷺ asked Zainab رضي الله عنها what her opinion was of 'A'ishah رضي الله عنها. The noble character of this lady is revealed in her answer; she promptly said she did not wish to be involved, and did not want to defile and taint her ears, her eyes and her tongue with such terrible accusations. Swearing by Allâh ﷻ she said, she found 'A'ishah رضي الله عنها to be a truly Allâh-fearing lady of exemplary character. She found in her the most wonderful traits of integrity, sincerity and honesty. She said she had not seen in her anything but goodness and virtue. 'A'ishah رضي الله عنها narrated that Zainab رضي الله عنها very easily have taken advantage of the situation and passed derogatory remarks about her, for after all, in a sense they were rivals. 'A'ishah رضي الله عنها says she never forgot the fact that she stood by her at the worst time in her life when almost the whole world had turned against her.

On one occasion Zainab رضي الله عنها called Safiyyah رضي الله عنها a Jewess and this deeply distressed the Prophet ﷺ. In fact he was so upset that he stopped talking to her. Zainab رضي الله عنها felt guilty and realized that she committed a grave mistake and offended the Prophet ﷺ. Finally she requested 'A'ishah رضي الله عنها to advocate her case with him and tell him that she was sincerely repentant; she was the only one who could talk to him in such a direct manner. When the Prophet ﷺ visited 'A'ishah رضي الله عنها she looked for an opportune moment and brought up the subject, pleading the case for Zainab رضي الله عنها. The Prophet ﷺ forgave her and life returned to normal in the household.

When Zainab رضي الله عنها passed away 'A'ishah رضي الله عنها recalled an occasion when the Prophet ﷺ said that among the Mothers of the Believers, she would meet him first who had the longest arms. Zainab رضي الله عنها was short compared to the others and naturally her arms were also shorter. All the ladies took this statement literally and started measuring their arms. It was only upon the death of Zainab رضي الله عنها that they realized what the statement meant. It really meant that the person with the longest arms was the most generous or liberal person, who only thought of how she could benefit others. There was an implicit prophesy in this statement, which became clear when Zainab رضي الله عنها passed away. It meant she would meet him in Paradise before the others. And she passed away before any of the other wives of the Prophet ﷺ.

'A'ishah رضي الله عنها says Zainab رضي الله عنها worked with her own hands, and what she thus earned she spent on works of charity. She says she was an Allâh-fearing, straightforward lady who practiced abstinence. All her actions were aimed at pleasing Allâh ﷻ. Sometimes she could lose her temper, but then she was quick to repent and ask for forgiveness. She was very pure at heart and never carried resentments and grudges.

The Prophet ﷺ had a very organized routine. After the 'Asr prayers he would visit the different apartments to inquire about the well being of the ladies of his household. He was always very just in the attention he paid to them and the amount of time he spent with each one of them. Once Zainab رضي الله عنها received some special honey from a relative, and it so happened that this was the Prophet's favorite. Whenever she offered it to him he would spend some time longer in her apartment, as it took time to flavor and enjoy it. The other wives felt impatient and restless waiting for their turn with him. So 'A'ishah, Saudah, and Hafsah رضي الله عنهن worked out a plan. Each of them would tell him that there was a peculiar smell in his mouth. And if all of them said the same thing he would certainly believe them and realize that the only thing which could have given him bad breath would have been the honey he just had. Since he was very concerned about personal hygiene, he would definitely stop eating the honey. Of course the three Mothers of the Believers did what they did, not out of spite, but because they loved him and wanted him to come to them sooner. In fact Allâh ﷻ has Himself spoken of them in the highest terms of respect in the Qur'ân:

> "O wives of the Prophet (ﷺ)! you are not like any other women." (33:32)

And it happened as they planned; the Prophet ﷺ developed a distaste for honey and decided he would never eat it again. In the case of an ordinary human being this may not have been a problem. But the Prophet ﷺ was swearing not to have something that actually was not forbidden by Allâh ﷻ; this could lead to any of his followers to similarly forswear something not forbidden by Allâh ﷻ.

So Allâh ﷻ rebuked him:

> "O Prophet! Why do you forbid (for yourself) that which Allâh has allowed to you, seeking to please your wives? And Allâh is Oft-Forgiving, Most Merciful." (66:1)

As a result the Prophet ﷺ broke the oath he had taken and performed the penance for this in accordance with the injunctions of Allâh ﷻ.

❖ca❖ca❖ca❖ca❖

Zainab رضي الله عنها made a little mosque in a corner of her house and used to spend a lot of time there in prayer and meditation. The Prophet ﷺ would also pray there sometimes. She believed strongly in

Zainab bint Jahsh رضي الله عنها

asking Allâh ﷻ for counsel through prayer and supplication, before taking any action. All her life's major decisions were made in this way. In fact even when the Prophet ﷺ proposed she turned to prayer for guidance.

This righteous lady died during the caliphate of 'Umar Farooq ؓ at the age of fifty-three. When she realized she was about to meet her Maker, she told the people around her that she already prepared a shroud for herself. If 'Umar Farooq ؓ sent one for her, one should be used and the other given away in charity. She was such a modest lady that a curtain was drawn in front of her dead body, even though it was wrapped in a shroud.

'Umar Farooq ؓ led the funeral prayers and all her close relatives – Usamah bin Zaid, Muhammad bin 'Abdullâh bin Jahsh , 'Abdullâh bin Abi Ahmad bin Jahsh and Muhammad bin Talhah bin 'Abdullâh رضي الله عنهم – got down into the grave to lower her gently into her final resting place in *Jannatul Baqi'*.

> "O the one in (complete) rest and satisfaction! Come back to your Lord – well pleased and well pleasing. Enter you then among My (honored) servants, and enter you My Paradise." (87:27-30)

Juwairiyah bint Hârith رضي الله عنها

The Prophet ﷺ said:

"*Allâh has commanded me to marry only the women of Paradise.*"

'A'ishah رضي الله عنها said:

"*I did not see any lady except Juwairiyah رضي الله عنها who became a source of blessing for her tribesmen more than herself (Juwairiyah) رضي الله عنها, because hundreds of her tribesmen were liberated from slavery by her action.*"

Juwairiyah bint Hârith رضي الله عنها

Islâm had begun to spread rapidly and a major portion of the Arabian Peninsula was under the influence of Islâm by the fifth year after *Hijrah*. Madinah had by now become the center of a stable and rapidly expanding Islâmic state. The Islâmic forces were on a triumphal march, inspired by spiritual strength.

The entire tribe of Banu Khuzâ'ah was sympathetic to the cause of Islâm and the Prophet ﷺ, except one of their branches, Banu Mustaliq, who planned to attack Madinah. The chieftain of this tribe was Hârith bin Abi Dhirâr, who was an arrogant man, drunk with his power and wealth. He had a beautiful daughter, Juwairiyah رضي الله عنها, who was born just before the advent of Islâm. She was brought up in the lap of luxury, and had all the refinements and graces of a princess. Intelligent and wise, she mastered language and literary style. This was an accomplishment much prized by contemporary Arabs. She was happily married to one of the rising youths of the tribe of Banu Khuzâ'ah, Musâfa' bin Safwân.

It was at this time that the Prophet ﷺ received news that Hârith bin Abi Dhirâr was making elaborate preparations to attack the Muslim forces at Madinah. So he sent one of his most trusted Companions, Buraidah bin Haseeb ﷺ, to survey the situation and get facts and information about the enemy in order to work out an appropriate strategy. Buraidah ﷺ met with Hârith and many other important people who were close to him. He noted that there was a lot of activity and that the young men were busy making preparations for war. There were many weapons to be seen, and from his discussions with people it was quite obvious that they were planning to go to war. Buraidah ؓ came back and informed the Prophet ﷺ of all that he had seen and heard. The Muslim forces were now alerted by their leader and they too started preparing for battle. Within no time at all, an army of seven hundred was ready to leave, under their General, the Prophet ﷺ himself. 'A'ishah رضي الله عنها accompanied him on this march.

Al-Muraisi' was an important strategic point for the tribe of Banu Mustaliq as it was the source which provided water for drinking as well as for other purposes. The Muslim forces reached this important position and sent a message to the Banu Mustaliq to accept Islâm. If they did so, they could continue to live in their lands in peace and security as before. But, instead of accepting Islâm, they came out on to the plains and declared war. One of the soldiers of Banu Mustaliq, shot an arrow which lodged in the body of a *Mujâhid*. Wild fighting then broke out. The Prophet ﷺ ordered his troops to keep to their ranks and launch a united attack on the enemy, who were cornered and found no way of escape. Ten people were killed and about seven hundred captured. The husband of Juwairiyah رضي الله عنها, Musâfâ' bin Safwân was among those who were killed. Among the captives there were women as well. The *Mujâhideen* also got two thousand camels and five thousand goats.

On reaching Madinah, the spoils of war were distributed among the *Mujâhideen*. According to the custom of those days, men and women were distributed as slaves. Juwairiyah bint Hârith رضي الله عنها was given to the famous companion of the Prophet ﷺ, Thâbit bin Qais al-Ansâri. All who saw Juwairiyah رضي الله عنها were stunned by her exceptional beauty. Brought up as she had been in one of the foremost families of the time, she was not only beautiful but graceful, elegant and eloquent. At the first opportunity she went into the presence of the Prophet ﷺ and pleaded her case with him. She told him that she was the daughter of a chieftain and used to command. Because of unfortunate circumstances she found herself in this helpless position. From a throne made of gold she had fallen into dust. She had been given to Thâbit bin Qais al-Ansâri for a ransom of gold, but from

Juwairiyah bint Hârith رضي الله عنها

where could she get the gold to give in exchange for her freedom? How could she possibly live the life of a slave? She pleaded with the Prophet ﷺ to take notice of the pitiful and desperate condition in which she found herself.

The Prophet ﷺ was moved by her sorrowful plea and asked her if she would like to live as a free woman and be part of his household if he paid her ransom. She had never in her dreams expected this offer. Moved deeply by this unexpected elevation in her status, she exclaimed she would be more than happy to accept. She was freed, and swearing allegiance to Islâm, she married Prophet Muhammad ﷺ.

When the *Mujâhideen* heard of her conversion and marriage to the Prophet ﷺ they too freed all the slaves of the tribe of Banu Mustaliq. So in this way not only did she become free, but she also became one of the Mothers of the Believers. This action of hers had the far-reaching result of liberating all her tribe from slavery. And thus Juwairiyah رضي الله عنها became a source of blessings for her tribe.

When 'A'ishah رضي الله عنها first saw Juwairiyah رضي الله عنها she exclaimed that she was as beautiful as a fairy. On another occasion she said she had yet to see a lady who proved to be such a source of blessings for her people. Through her, Allâh blessed a hundred families of her tribe with freedom.

Before her marriage to the Prophet ﷺ her name was Barrah, but Muhammad ﷺ changed it to Juwairiyah رضي الله عنها. Zainab bint Jahsh, Zainab bint Abu Salamah and Maimoonah bint Hârith were also named Barrah, but the Prophet ﷺ changed their names as well.

In his book, *Dalâi'l An-Nubuwwah*, Imâm Baihaqi has quoted Juwairiyah رضي الله عنها, as saying that three days before the Prophet ﷺ arrived she saw in a dream the moon coming towards her from the direction of Madinah and falling into her lap. She did not like to talk about it to anyone, but when they were conquered and she was made a prisoner she hoped that her dream would be realized. Then the Prophet ﷺ freed her and subsequently married her.

In his book *Siyar A'lâm an-Nubalâ* Imâm Dhahabi quoted her as saying that when the Prophet ﷺ married her she was a girl of twenty. Imâm Dhahabi adds that she was an extremely beautiful lady.

Some time later, her father and all the men who had been freed on the occasion of her marriage presented themselves before the Prophet ﷺ and accepted Islâm as their religion. Thus, Juwairiyah رضي الله عنها was blessed with a twofold honor – first of freeing her tribesmen from slavery, and then of bringing them into the fold of Islâm.

Most of the time she would be found engrossed in prayer. On one occasion when the Prophet ﷺ left home he found her lost in meditation. On returning in the afternoon he still found her in the very same position of prayer and supplication. He asked her if she had been praying continuously since he had left. When she answered in the affirmative, he asked her if she would like to learn four small sentences that could earn her more reward from Allâh ﷻ than the whole morning's prayers. Then he taught her the following sentence:

'How perfect Allâh is and I praise Him by the number of His creation and His pleasure, and by the weight of His Throne, and the extent of His Words.'

Both Muslim and Abu Dawood quote Juwairiyah رضي الله عنها narrating an incident similar to the one above. She said the Prophet ﷺ told her that after leaving her in the morning he recited the above four sentences, three times each, and these earned him more reward from Allâh ﷻ than her whole morning's prayers.

Ibn Sa'd recorded that from the lands taken after the Battle of Khaybar the Prophet ﷺ fixed for Juwairiyah رضي الله عنها 80 *Wasaq*[1] of dates and 20 *Wasaq* of barley.

After the Prophet ﷺ passed away the first Caliph, Abu Bakr Siddeeq ؓ fixed an equal amount to be given to the Mothers of the Believers for their household expenses. 'Umar bin al-Khattâb ؓ, however, fixed the

---

[1] One *Wasaq* is approximately equal to 124 kg.

Juwairiyah bint Hârith رضي الله عنها

sum of twelve thousand Dirhams for the rest, but for Juwairiyah and Safiyyah رضي الله عنهما he fixed only six thousand Dirhams each. They naturally refused to accept this amount. He explained that the others got double the amount because of their migration. But they argued that he had given preference to the others. Then 'A'ishah رضي الله عنها pointed out to him that the Prophet ﷺ used to make no distinction and divide everything equally between his wives. So 'Umar bin al-Khattâb ؓ decided to revoke his decision and gave them all an equal stipend of twelve thousand Dirhams.

Juwairiyah رضي الله عنها died at the age of sixty-five in *Rabi'ul-Awwal* in the year 50 AH during the caliphate of Mu'âwiyah bin Abi Sufyân. The governor of Madinah, Marwân bin Hakam led the funeral prayer and she was buried in *Jannatul Baqi'*.

"O the one in (complete) rest and satisfaction! Come back to your Lord – well pleased and well pleasing. Enter you then among My (honored) servants, and enter you My Paradise." (87:27-30)

Safiyyah bint Huyayy رضي الله عنها

> The Prophet ﷺ said:
> "*No doubt, you are the daughter of a Prophet, your uncle is a Prophet and you are the wife of a Prophet.*"

Safiyyah bint Huyayy رضي الله عنها

Safiyyah bint Huyayy was the favorite daughter of Huyayy bin Akhtab, the chieftain of the tribe of Banu Nadheer. Her mother was Barrah bint Shamwâl who was the sister of Rafâ'ah bin Shamwâl. She was married to Salâm bin Mashkam first, but they separated soon on grounds of incompatibility. Her second husband was Kinânah bin Rabi' bin Haqeeq who was killed in the Battle of Khaybar, and she was taken as a prisoner of war. One of the Companions, Dihyah al-Kalbi ؓ, asked the Prophet ﷺ for a slave girl, and he gave him the freedom to choose for himself. He chose Safiyyah رضي الله عنها. The others suggested that since she was the chieftain's daughter he should keep her for himself and give some other slave to Dihyah al-Kalbi ؓ. The Prophet ﷺ did as they suggested; then he decided to free her and married her.

There is another tradition too. Wahshi bin Harb ؓ narrates how the Prophet ﷺ asked for their opinion about Safiyyah رضي الله عنها. They told him that she would be more suitable for him and better than any of the others. So he freed her and took her hand in marriage.

Seerat Ibn Hishâm, Dalâil An-Nubuwwah by al-Baihaqi and *Dalâil An-Nubuwwah* by Asbahâni all recorded what Safiyyah رضي الله عنها had to say about her life before her marriage to the Prophet ﷺ. Her father and her paternal uncle, Abu Yâsir, loved her deeply and they used to live in Madinah. When the Prophet ﷺ migrated and came there he first stayed in the valley of Banu 'Amr bin 'Awf, and both her father and her uncle went to see him. On their return both looked tired, fed up and disappointed. They did not pay any attention to her, which was very unusual for her. She became anxious over what could possibly have happened. Her uncle asked her father if this was the same man. He swore by Allâh that it was certainly the same man. Her uncle wanted to confirm again if it really was the same man, and if he had recognized him. Again her father replied in the affirmative. Then her uncle asked him for his sincere opinion about the stranger. Her father answered that he would always treat this man as a foe. Safiyyah رضي الله عنها heard this cryptic conversation filled with malice and vindictiveness and was shocked.

Time passed and the Treaty of Hudaibiyah was signed. When the Prophet ﷺ returned after the Quraish prevented them from entering Makkah, the news spread like wildfire through the entire Arabian Peninsula that the Muslims had bowed down and accepted an unfair treaty. People thought they had weakened, were desperate and fast losing hope. When the Jews in Khaybar heard this news, they thought this was the appropriate moment to strike and started preparing to attack Madinah. They invited all the Jews in the surrounding areas to join forces with them.

When the Prophet ﷺ heard about the warlike preparations of the Jews of Khaybar, he took with him the very same fourteen hundred people who had set out with him to perform *'Umrah* but had not been allowed within the precincts of Makkah after the Treaty of Hudaibiyah. Women also were part of this group of pilgrims. He had returned from Hudaibiyah in the month of *Dhul-Hajjah*, and left for Khaybar with his army in the early days of the month of *Muharram*. When he first sighted Khaybar he ordered his army to stop right there, and lifted his hands in supplication to Allâh ﷻ. Whenever he traveled, it was his usual practice to recite this prayer when his eyes first fell on a city:

> *'O Allâh, Lord of the seven heavens and all that they envelop, Lord of the seven earths and all that they carry, Lord of the devils and all whom they misguide, Lord of the winds and all whom they whisk away. I ask You for the goodness of this village, the goodness of its inhabitants and for all the goodness found within it and I take refuge with You from the evil of this village, the evil of its inhabitants and from all the evil found within it.'*

Safiyyah bint Huyayy رضي الله عنها

It was nightfall when they reached Khaybar. He camped with his forces on the plains just on the outskirts of the city. This again was a typical strategy of his: whenever he led his men to engage in battle, he planned to reach there by nightfall. But he was so principled that he would never attack the enemy at night in order to take them unawares.

The Muslim army was encamped just outside Khaybar, but the people of the city were quite unaware of this. When they woke up in the morning and started going about their usual chores, they were shocked to see a whole army encamped on their doorstep, as it were!

Soon after *Fajr* (early dawn) prayers, the Prophet ﷺ ordered the *Mujâhideen* to advance and attack. The Jews of Khaybar started scattering towards their homes. When the Prophet ﷺ saw them running he called out:

> 'Allâh is Great, Khaybar is deserted, Khaybar is broken, Khaybar is destroyed and ruined!'

By the Grace of Allâh Almighty the Muslims triumphed and all the forts of Khaybar were taken. The father of Safiyyah رضي الله عنها, Huyayy bin Akhthab was killed in the battle of Bani Quraidhah. Her husband Kinânah bin Rabi'ah bin Haqeeq was captured and killed for the crime of misgovernment. And Safiyyah رضي الله عنها was made a prisoner of war.

Dihyah al-Kalbi ؓ was given the option to choose a slave girl for himself, and he chose Safiyyah رضي الله عنها. One of the Companions suggested that it would be better if the Prophet ﷺ kept Safiyyah رضي الله عنها, the daughter of a leader and chieftain, for himself and gave some other slave girl to Dihyah al-Kalbi ؓ. So he chose the sister of Safiyyah's husband Kinânah bin Rabi'ah. The Prophet ﷺ then freed Safiyyah and married her. Her dowry was her liberty, writes Ibn al-Qayyim.

On the return journey to Madinah, the Prophet ﷺ camped with his army twelve miles away from the city. One of the *Sahâbiyât*, Umm Sulaim al-Ansâriyah, dressed up Safiyyah رضي الله عنها in her bridal finery.

In his book, *Siyar A'lâm an-Nubalâ'* Imâm Dhahabi describes the qualities and character of Safiyyah رضي الله عنها. He says she was noble both by birth as well as by nature; she was Allâh-fearing, intelligent, beautiful, patient, tolerant and dignified. When the Prophet ﷺ saw the mark of an injury just above her eye, he asked her how she got hurt. She answered that she had dreamt that the moon had fallen into her lap. When she told her husband about her dream, he slapped her hard and told her that it meant she was in love with the king of Yathrib. When she married the Prophet ﷺ, Safiyyah رضي الله عنها was just seventeen years old.

Safiyyah رضي الله عنها traveled in the company of the Prophet ﷺ from Khaybar to Madinah. She says that she had never come across a person who was more refined and well-mannered than him. He was always pleasant and behaved courteously at all times. When the people of Madinah heard of his approach, they came out to greet him and his victorious army. The faces of the Muslims were glowing with pleasure, and those of the Hypocrites were downcast and gloomy.

All the Mothers of the Believers were waiting impatiently in their apartments, longing to meet the Prophet ﷺ and congratulate him on this great victory. When word came that he had married the young and beautiful daughter of the Jewish leader, 'A'ishah رضي الله عنها was disturbed by a twinge of feminine jealousy, which was but natural. The Prophet ﷺ also did not consider it proper to take his new bride to any of his wives' houses. He went directly to the house of Hârithah bin Nu'mân Ansâri and stayed there. The ladies of Madinah came there to meet Safiyyah رضي الله عنها; and all of them were full of praise for her.

After resting for some time the Prophet ﷺ went to his daughter Fâtimah رضي الله عنها, and met his beloved grandchildren Hasan and Husain رضي الله عنهما. After that he visited each of his wives and inquired about their welfare. He found a certain aloofness and distance in the behavior of 'A'ishah رضي الله عنها, but he thought it better to ignore it for the moment. 'A'ishah رضي الله عنها after some time decided to visit the new bride in the house of Hârithah bin Nu'mân Ansâri. The Prophet ﷺ then asked her for her opinion of Safiyyah رضي الله عنها. 'A'ishah رضي الله عنها, still vexed by her feminine jealousy replied dryly

Safiyyah bint Huyayy رضي الله عنها

that she had seen the Jewess. The Prophet ﷺ gently rebuked her, saying that Safiyyah رضي الله عنها should no longer be referred to as a Jewess as she had accepted Islâm.

'A'ishah and Hafsah رضي الله عنهما were very close friends and the latter was the only person in whom the former could safely confide. Actually it was the intense love that 'A'ishah رضي الله عنها had for the Prophet ﷺ that made her express her emotions in this manner.

Once Safiyyah رضي الله عنها moved into her own place she displayed her noble upbringing by adopting a pleasant and friendly attitude with the other Mothers of the Believers. She brought expensive gold jewelery with her from Khaybar, and she presented this to the other wives. She loved the Prophet's favorite daughter Fâtimah رضي الله عنها and gave her gold earrings as a gift. She tried her best to win a place in the affections of 'A'ishah and Hafsah رضي الله عنهما because she realized the Prophet ﷺ held them in high esteem and loved them dearly. She narrated that on one occasion she mentioned to him that she heard that Hafsah رضي الله عنها taunted her, calling her the daughter of a Jew.

The Prophet ﷺ told her that she should have told Hafsah رضي الله عنها that she could not be better than her: her husband was Muhammad ﷺ, her father was Hâroon عليه السلام and her uncle was Musâ عليه السلام.

On another occasion 'A'ishah رضي الله عنها spoke of Safiyyah رضي الله عنها in very disparaging terms. Prophet ﷺ told her that if the expressions she had used were thrown into an ocean they could make the whole of it bitter.

An incident about Safiyyah رضي الله عنها is mentioned in *Sahîh Al-Bukhâri*. During the last ten days of *Ramadhân* when the Prophet ﷺ was in *I'tikâf* (secluding himself in the mosque) she went to visit him. Afterwards, when she got up to leave, he also rose and accompanied her outside. Two of the *Ansâr* saw him there talking to her, and greeted him.

He asked them to stop and explained to them that the lady was his wife and had come to visit him.

They said in praise of Allâh ﷻ "*Subhânallâh,* O Prophet of Allâh!" And they were upset that he should have felt the need to explain his actions.

He answered that Satan could become part of human beings to such an extent that he could course through the body with their blood. He added that he did not want Satan to sow evil suspicions in their hearts.

❖⋖⋗❖⋖⋗❖⋖⋗❖

Safiyyah رضي الله عنها gave a lot of time to the reading of the Noble Qur'ân, and its effect on her heart was so intense that because of the fear of Allâh ﷻ, tears would course down her cheeks, and she would start sobbing.

In the Qur'ân, Allâh ﷻ says that the true believer is he whose heart starts quaking when the Name of Allâh ﷻ is taken before him. And when he listens to the verses of the Noble Qur'ân being read, his faith grows. If the Name of Allâh Almighty is taken and his heart does not quake with fear if the verses of the Noble Qur'ân are recited, and he does not feel pleasure in listening to them, then it is an indication he should start worrying about the status of his faith and belief in Allâh ﷻ.

Abu Nai'm al-Asfahâni wrote in his book *Hilyatul-Awliyâ'* that once some Companions gathered in the apartment of the Mother of the Believers Safiyyah رضي الله عنها, they mentioned Allâh, recited the Noble Qur'ân and prayed voluntary prayer. Safiyyah رضي الله عنها said to them that their voluntary prayer, recitation and remembrance of Allâh were all good, but they should weep too with the fear of Allâh ﷻ.

In fact if the fear of Allâh ﷻ is strongly rooted in one's heart, then involuntarily the tears will start flowing, and the truth is that it is these tears of penitence which clean and purify the heart; and they are invaluable in the eyes of Allâh Almighty. The eyes which shed these tears will go to Paradise as they are the proof of the intensity and the fervor of the love for Allâh ﷻ.

❖⋖⋗❖⋖⋗❖⋖⋗❖

Safiyyah bint Huyayy رضي الله عنها

Safiyyah رضي الله عنها was an extremely tolerant, patient, loving and kind-hearted woman. Imâm Dhahabi has narrated an incident from her life in his book, *Siyar A'lâm an-Nubalâ'*. He said Safiyyah رضي الله عنها had a slave girl, who went and told the Caliph 'Umar Farooq ؓ that in spite of the fact that her mistress had converted to Islâm, she still observed the Saturday Sabbath of the Jews; and she also kept good terms with the Jews. The Caliph met with Safiyyah رضي الله عنها and questioned her regarding these two accusations. She answered that after Allâh ﷻ had told Muslims about the sanctity and blessings of Friday she stopped giving importance to Saturday. As far as her terms with the Jews were concerned, they were her relatives and she was following the dictates of Allâh ﷻ and His Messenger to maintain good relations with kindred. As human beings, they too deserved sympathetic and kind treatment from her.

She later discovered that it was her slave girl who had carried these tales to Caliph 'Umar Farooq ؓ. She asked her why she had done this. The girl very innocently and nervously answered that it was Satan who had incited her.

She immediately set the girl free. As Allâh ﷻ says:

"Who repress anger, and who pardon men; verily, Allâh loves the good-doers." (3:134)

She was extremely knowledgeable and spent most of her time in reciting the Noble Qur'ân, of which she knew by heart many of the *Surahs*. After leading a full life, she passed away in the year 50 AH, during the caliphate of Mu'âwiyah ؓ, and was buried in *Jannatul Baqi'*. She left a hundred thousand Dirhams that were distributed as per her will.

"O the one in (complete) rest and satisfaction! Come back to your Lord – well pleased and well pleasing. Enter you then among My (honored) servants, and enter you My Paradise." (87:27-30)

Umm Habîbah Ramlah bint Abi Sufyân رضي الله عنها

Pointing towards Amir Mu'âwiyah ﷺ and Umm Habîbah رضي الله عنها, Allâh's Messenger ﷺ said:

"*By Allâh, I wish that she, you and I might partake of the pure drink of Paradise together.*"

Umm Habîbah Ramlah
bint Abi Sufyân رضي الله عنها

W araqah bin Nawfal, 'Uthmân bin Huwarith bin Asad, Zaid bin 'Amr bin Nufail and 'Ubaidullâh bin Jahsh were four friends who were very disheartened by the plague of idol worship which was so widespread in Arabia. They often used to get together and discuss how this terrible evil could be eradicated from their people. They could not talk about it openly, so they used to have their sessions late at night when the entire world was silent and asleep.

They were upset that it was not only the common unenlightened and uneducated man on the street who was involved in this barbaric practice of idol worship, but even the noble tribe of the Quraish had lost their spiritual bearings. How could any rational man believe that the stones they themselves carved with their hands, that were deaf and incapable of moving even a finger, were all powerful and could help them? How could they prostrate themselves before these stones, worship them with all their hearts and souls and believe they could help them solve all life's problems? People used to sacrifice animals before these idols and eat the food and drink the blood of the animals sacrificed!

They came to a decision one night that they should stop worrying about these irrational, uncivilized and shortsighted people and find a way out of this confusion for themselves. The Quraish, the leading tribe had lost their way and these four friends decided they had to find the way to the pure and unsullied religion of Ibrâhîm ﷺ for themselves. They had the strong belief that this was the straight and simple path of virtue and righteousness; the guidance given by their Prophet Ibrâhîm ﷺ. They knew what was the way to salvation, but they had to keep their thoughts and intentions secret as the followers of the barbaric practices could make life difficult for them

They decided they had to set out and search for the truth whatever the cost. With this plan in mind they dispersed from the meeting moving in different directions. Their objective was to find the religion of the Prophet Ibrâhîm ﷺ, in its pure form.

Waraqah bin Nawfal had given up idol worship and had given up eating the flesh of animals sacrificed in the name of idols. He knew the Torah and the Injîl by heart.

He was a cousin of Khadîjah رضي الله عنها, the wife of the Prophet ﷺ, who had taken the Prophet ﷺ to him on the occasion of the first revelation in the cave of Hirâ. When the Angel Jibrîl ﷺ spoke to him, embraced him tightly, and commanded him to '*Read*', the Prophet ﷺ was terrified. His wife consoled him; recognizing the purity and virtuous qualities of her husband, she told him that a person such as he would surely be protected by Allâh Almighty.

Waraqah then told her that the 'being' the Prophet ﷺ had seen in the cave must have been the same Angel who delivered Messages from Allâh to earlier Prophets. He said that Muhammad ﷺ must be the chosen Last Messenger, whose coming was foretold in both the Torah and the Injîl. He would soon be elevated to a great position, the whole nation would turn against him and he would be forced to flee his motherland. Waraqah said that if he remained alive at that time he would certainly help him and stand by him. But he passed away before Muhammad ﷺ openly declared himself the Last Messenger and Prophet of Allâh.

The second friend, 'Uthmân bin Huwarith bin Asad, traveled to Syria, and worked as a missionary to spread Christianity. He became a close friend of the Roman Emperor Caesar and was finally elevated to the papal position.

Zaid bin 'Amr bin Nufail, the third of these companions, accepted neither Christianity nor Judaism. He stopped worshipping idols. He gave up eating dead animals and drinking their blood. He hated eating the flesh of the animals sacrificed to the idols and often talked

Umm Habîbah Ramlah bint Abi Sufyân رضي الله عنها

of the pure religion of the Prophet Ibrâhîm ﷺ. He too died before the proclamation of Muhammad ﷺ as the Messenger of Allâh.

'Ubaidullâh bin Jahsh, the fourth friend, regrettably, fell into such doubts and perplexity that he vacillated between right and wrong, between what to do and what not to do. He married the beautiful, intelligent and well-educated daughter of the Quraishi chieftain, Abu Sufyân Sakhr bin Harb.

It was around this time that Makkah was shaken by the news that Muhammad ﷺ rejected all the idols and declared that they were not deserving of worship, he invited people to worship Allâh ﷻ and proclaimed he was His Last Prophet and Messenger. The leaders of the Quraish were furious and the community was split into two factions. Some people pledged allegiance to Allâh ﷻ and His Prophet and became Muslims. The others challenged the validity of this new religion that went against the practices and beliefs of their forefathers. They became sworn enemies of the Muslims and were determined to persecute and torment them.

But the intelligent and wise daughter of Abu Sufyân, Ramlah رضي الله عنها, accepted Islâm and so did her husband 'Ubaidullâh bin Jahsh. His two brothers 'Abdullâh bin Jahsh and Abu Ahmad bin Jahsh had also become Muslims. The two sisters, Zainab bint Jahsh رضي الله عنها and Hamnah bint Jahsh رضي الله عنها, too had come into the fold of Islâm. The former later joined the select group of the Mothers of the Believers. Abu Ahmad bin Jahsh was a very famous blind poet in those days and wrote about the history and exploits of the Muslim *Ummah* as it was happening. Hamnah رضي الله عنها was the wife of one of the most loyal Companions of the Prophet ﷺ.

The whole family was fortunate to have obeyed the call to Islâm, but while in Abyssinia 'Ubaidullâh had the misfortune to reject Islâm after having accepted it. He became an apostate and heretic and turned to Christianity. He started drinking and died on the same belief. However, his wife Ramlah رضي الله عنها remained faithful to Islâm; in fact her love and support for it grew stronger. And ultimately she joined the ranks of the Mothers of the Believers. Her life is a study in loyalty and steadfastness, in her love for the truth.

Abu Sufyân Sakhr bin Harb was a chieftain of the Quraish, who led the disbelievers in many of their wars. Besides his daughter Ramlah رضي الله عنها, he had two sons, Yazîd and Mu'âwiyah. Both of them were renowned for their services to Islâm. Ramlah accepted Islâm when the Muslims were facing a lot of opposition and were being cruelly persecuted. Abu Sufyân was a very powerful man, but he was helpless in the matter of his daughter Ramlah رضي الله عنها. The human mind is always free though the body can be captured or subdued. She was a helpless, frail girl, but he could not stop her from accepting Islâm. She openly declared herself a Muslim, and the oppression of the Quraish could in no way deter her. What Allâh Wills no one can change, for surely He is All Powerful and can bring the dead to life.

In spite of all his best efforts, Abu Sufyân could not make his daughter recant.

Meanwhile, after surveying the situation the Prophet ﷺ decided that the staunch supporters of Islâm had taken enough of the torture and oppression from the Quraish. They would have to migrate, and he ordered them to leave for Abyssinia, where the ruler was known for his kindness and hospitality to refugees from tyrannical rule.

Ramlah bint Abu Sufyân رضي الله عنها and her husband 'Ubaidullâh bin Jahsh were among the second group of migrants who left for Abyssinia. There Ramlah رضي الله عنها gave birth to a girl who they named Habîbah; hence she was now known as Umm Habîbah رضي الله عنها. So the days passed swiftly for her as she kept busy seeing to the upbringing of her little daughter; all her free time was spent in prayer and meditation.

One night she dreamt that her husband's face was mutilated. She woke up panic stricken, but was too nervous to talk about her dream to her husband. A few days later he told her that he originally had been a Christian and then converted to Islâm. But since coming to Abyssinia he gave a great deal of careful consideration and thought to the matter. He finally had come to the conclusion that Christianity offered the best system of beliefs for leading a successful life. Hence he was recanting and going back to the fold of Christianity. He advised her to do the same and become a Christian.

Immediately it struck Ramlah رضي الله عنها that this was what her dream meant. The metamorphosis of her husband's face from a superior to a

Umm Habîbah Ramlah bint Abi Sufyân رضي الله عنها

lower form and its mutilation meant that he had lost his identity as a Muslim. Then she told him about her dream, hoping that this at least would instill the fear of Allâh in his heart. But he was too far gone on the downward road; not only his face but his heart had been mutilated. 'Ubaidullâh was not bothered; in fact he started drinking. He was so addicted that he was drunk for most of the time. Umm Habîbah رضي الله عنها was now growing desperate, worrying about the future of her daughter and herself. She prayed to Allâh to give her the strength to remain steadfast in her faith.

After some time 'Ubaidullâh died due to heavy drinking. Umm Habîbah رضي الله عنها was relieved, of course, but what was she to do now, how was she to survive? Only two activities kept her occupied – the upbringing of her daughter and her prayers. She would sometimes get together with the other Muslim ladies in Abyssinia to talk of the latest developments. Ruqayyah رضي الله عنها, the daughter of the Prophet ﷺ, Asmâ' bint 'Umais رضي الله عنها and Lailâ bint Abi Hashmah رضي الله عنها were the great ladies with whom she would spend her free time. But these ladies too soon returned home. Still, there were other ladies with whom she was friendly.

Years passed and the map of the Islâmic world changed, as did its history. Madinah was attacked and battles continued to be fought. The Treaty of Hudaibiyah was signed and the obsession of the Quraish for revenge was finally quenched. They, and many others like them, thought that this unequal treaty restrained the growing power and influence of Islâm.

One night while she was fast asleep, Umm Habîbah رضي الله عنها dreamt someone called out to her, *"Mother of the Believers"*. When she woke up she felt a great sense of well-being and not just happiness, but ecstasy. During the time, the Prophet ﷺ had migrated to Madinah, and the first Islâmic state had been established. Someone, while talking to him about the state of affairs in Abyssinia, mentioned the troubles that Umm Habîbah رضي الله عنها was undergoing. The daughter of a wealthy and noble family was living from hand to mouth. After the husband had recanted and died, the daughter of a chieftain of the Quraish was living under tragic circumstances. When the Prophet ﷺ heard this, he sent 'Amr bin Umayyah Adhmri ﷺ to Najâshi with the message that if Umm Habîbah رضي الله عنها liked she could marry him.

When Najâshi got the message he sent his slave girl Abraha to Umm Habîbah رضي الله عنها. Umm Habîbah رضي الله عنها was overjoyed when she heard of the proposal, and could not understand how she could possibly reward the bearer of the message. She was so happy that she rewarded Abraha with all the silver jewelry she was wearing — bangles, anklets and rings. Abraha also told her she should appoint someone as her representative for the ceremony. Umm Habîbah رضي الله عنها nominated her relative from the tribe of Quraish, Khâlid bin Sa'eed bin 'Aas ﷺ.

That very evening Najâshi sent a message to Ja'far bin Abi Tâlib ﷺ asking him to bring all his Muslim friends to his palace. When all the refugee Muslims were assembled in the court, he announced the news of Umm Habîbah's marriage. After praising Almighty Allâh he said he had received a request from His Messenger ﷺ to arrange for his marriage with Umm Habîbah رضي الله عنها, and he was giving her a dowry of four hundred Dinârs.

Then Umm Habîbah's representative, Khâlid bin Sa'id bin 'Aas, read the marriage contract and said,

> 'All Praise is for Allâh, and I praise Him, seek His help and ask His forgiveness. I bear witness that None has the right to be worshipped but Allâh and Muhammad is His Servant and His Messenger, whom He has sent with True Religion and a guidance to the Right Path to overpower His Religion over all the false religions though the polytheists will not like it. I have accepted the proposal of the Prophet ﷺ and married Umm Habîbah bint Abu Sufyân to him. May Allâh bless this marriage and make it fruitful for Muhammad ﷺ.'

Najâshi then gave four hundred Dinârs to Khâlid bin Sa'eed. When all the guests rose to leave, Najâshi asked them to stay on for a dinner he had arranged in celebration of the marriage.

Umm Habîbah رضي الله عنها was so grateful to Allâh for the honor bestowed on her by making her one of the Mothers of the Believers that she sent for Abraha and gave her a sum of fifty Dinârs. She said by the Grace of Allâh she now had plenty, and apologised for not having rewarded her earlier in a suitable manner, as she had that time nothing but the little pieces of jewelry she had given her. She asked Abraha to make clothes and jewelry for herself. Abraha respectfully presented her with a little bag. It

Umm Habîbah Ramlah bint Abi Sufyân رضي الله عنها 131

contained some very expensive perfumes which Najâshi had asked his wives to send for Umm Habîbah رضي الله عنها. And Abraha presented her with the same jewelry she had received earlier from her, apologising for her lack of resources. She also sent a message for the Prophet ﷺ, saying she had embraced Islâm, but had kept it a secret. She said when Umm Habîbah رضي الله عنها met the Prophet ﷺ, beloved of all Muslims, she should convey her greetings without fail and this would be the greatest favor she could do for a poor woman.

When Umm Habîbah رضي الله عنها reached Madinah she told the Prophet ﷺ about the happenings in Abyssinia and about the goodness of Najâshi and how the wedding had been organised. She also told him about the slave girl Abraha and the respectful greetings she had sent him. The Prophet ﷺ was very pleased with her message; returning her greetings, he prayed that Allâh ﷻ should bless her with plenitude. Abu Sufyân heard about his daughter's marriage and he expressed happiness in spite of the fact that he had not yet accepted Islâm. He said the Prophet ﷺ was the youth who would never lose face, and always be honored.

When the Quraish broke the Treaty of Hudaibiyah, he came to Madinah to renew the treaty. He visited his daughter; just as he was about to sit down Umm Habîbah رضي الله عنها quickly stepped forward and rolled up the light mattress which was spread out. He was surprised and asked her if he was not worthy of the mattress, or the mattress was not worthy of him. She replied that actually it was a mattress used by the Prophet ﷺ, and no idol worshipper could sit on it, as he was unclean. She had therefore rolled it up and put it out of his way. Abu Sufyân was very embarrassed and said she had forgotten her manners since moving away from him. She answered that the manners of Islâm had taught her different values and cleanliness had a different meaning for her now. Since he was not familiar with these concepts he was offended. She said that she was thankful that Allâh ﷻ had guided her to the path of Islâm. She expressed surprise that her father — in spite of being an important chieftain of one of the leading tribes of the Quraish — had not yet accepted Islâm. He was in a lofty position by worldly standards, but as far as the norms of a rational religion were concerned, he was really backward. How could he possibly worship a piece of stone that was both blind and deaf, could neither respond to his prayers nor reject them? Abu

Sufyân was not happy with what his daughter told him. He asked her how he could possibly, at this stage, turn his back on a religion his forefathers had followed from generations and left his daughter's house.

❖◌❖◌❖◌❖◌❖

It was the earnest desire of Umm Habîbah رضي الله عنها that her father and brother should come into the fold of Islâm and earn the reward of a blessed Paradise. She did not want them to pass away from this world in a state of disbelief like Abu Jahl, Waleed bin Mughirah, 'Aas bin Wâ'il, 'Utbah bin Rabi'ah and Shaibah bin Rabi'ah. On the occasion of the conquest of Makkah, when Abu Sufyân and Mu'âwiyah pledged allegiance to Allâh and His Prophet, her joy knew no bounds. The following: *Âyah* was revealed,

> "Perhaps Allâh will make friendship between you and those whom you hold as enemies. And Allâh has power (over all things), and Allâh is Oft-Forgiving, Most Merciful." (60:7)

'Abdullâh bin 'Abbâs ؓ says that this particular Verse was revealed on the occasion of Umm Habîbah's marriage to the Prophet ﷺ. This marriage influenced important chieftains and prominent leaders like Abu Sufyân, Mu'âwiyah and Yazîd bin Abu Sufyân to understand Islâm and join the ranks of the Prophet ﷺ.

Abu Al-Qâsim bin Asâkir quoting Hasan ؓ says once Mu'âwiyah was visiting the Prophet ﷺ, while he was seated with Umm Habîbah رضي الله عنها beside him. When he turned to leave, the Prophet ﷺ called out to him and invited him to sit with them.

The Prophet ﷺ then told him that he sincerely wished that they three should sit together and have the pure drink of Paradise there.

These words imply that they will all three, Allâh Willing, be in Paradise. In a similar manner the glad tidings of Paradise for Umm Habîbah رضي الله عنها are implied in a very famous statement of the Prophet ﷺ that he has been commanded by Allâh ﷻ to marry only ladies who were deserving of Paradise.

So this means that in this very earthly existence all the Mothers of the Believers had been given the joyous news that they would go to Paradise in the Hereafter.

❖◌❖◌❖◌❖◌❖

Umm Habîbah Ramlah bint Abi Sufyân رضي الله عنها

The name of Najâshi, the ruler of Abyssinia, was actually Ashamah, meaning 'gift'. Since he was a very generous man who was always giving gifts to the distressed and needy, his name was very appropriate. He was a very kind and sympathetic ruler. He became a Muslim after he saw the Islâmic way of life of the refugees from Makkah. He was very kind to them. He not only promptly solemnized the marriage of Umm Habîbah رضي الله عنها to the Prophet ﷺ, but he also hosted a wedding banquet and provided boats for the journey back. The Angel Jibrîl ﷺ informed the Prophet ﷺ when he passed away due to natural causes. The Prophet ﷺ prayed to Allâh for the forgiveness of his sins. All the refugees – the Companions and women Companions – who had found peace and freedom of religious worship in his kingdom, were very grieved when they received the news of his death. All of them remembered his sympathy, his kindness, his cooperation and the protection he provided them in difficult times. They prayed that his sins be forgiven and he be given a place in Paradise.

Umm Habîbah رضي الله عنها, due to her knowledge, mastery over *Hadîth* and eloquence was ranked third among the Mothers of the Believers. The first in rank was 'A'ishah رضي الله عنها and the second was Umm Salamah رضي الله عنها. There are sixty-five *Ahâdîth* narrated by her. Some of them are quoted by men like Mu'âwiyah, 'Abdullâh bin 'Utbah bin Abu Sufyân, 'Urwah bin Zubair, Sâlem bin Shawâl bin Makki, Abu'l Jarrâh Qurshi. The ladies Zainab bint Umm Salamah al-Makhzoomiyah and Safiyyah bint Shaiba 'Abdariah رضي الله عنهم quoted others.

In *Sahîh Al-Bukhâri* it is mentioned that three days after receiving news of her father's death Umm Habîbah رضي الله عنها applied perfume. She then said there was no need for her to apply perfume that day, but the Prophet ﷺ had said:

> 'It is not permissible for a Muslim woman who believes in Allâh and the Last Day of Judgment to mourn for more than three days for a dead person, except for her husband. Then she should observe mourning for four months and ten days.'

There is another *Hadîth* associated with Umm Habîbah رضي الله عنها quoted by Abu'l Jarrâh Qurshi in *Musnad Abu Ya'lâ* regarding *Miswâk*. She says, the Prophet ﷺ said:

> 'If it had not been so difficult, I would have liked my Ummah (followers) to clean their teeth with Miswâk before every prayer just as they perform the ablution before every prayer.'

Another Hadîth she narrated is quoted in *Musnad Abu Ya'lâ*, *Musnad Abu Ahmad* and by several other authoritative sources of *Ahâdîth* like Abu Dawood, An-Nasâ'i, At-Tirmidhi and Ibn Mâjah. This relates to the noon prayer. The Prophet ﷺ said:

> 'Whoever prays four voluntary Rak'âh (units) of prayer before and after the compulsory noon prayer Allâh will make Hell-fire forbidden for him.'

When someone conveyed the message that 'Uthmân bin 'Affân ؓ was martyred in his house after being besieged, she was so upset that she prayed the killer's hands should be cut off and that he should be disgraced and shamed in public. And Allâh fulfilled her prayer. A man entered the murderer's house and attacked him with a sword; and when the murderer tried to protect himself with his right hand, it got cut off. Then he tried to flee from him and ran into the street, holding his sheet with his teeth. But he could not manage it, the sheet fell, and he was left standing naked in front of all the people on the street.

During her brother Mu'âwiyah's rule she visited Damascus, and it was during his caliphate that she passed away in Madinah in the year 44 AH. Before her death Umm Habîbah رضي الله عنها sent messages to 'A'ishah and Umm Salamah رضي الله عنهما apologising for any offense she might have caused them when disagreements or differences had occurred. Both 'A'ishah and Umm Salamah رضي الله عنهما were very touched by this gesture.

> "O the one in (complete) rest and satisfaction! Come back to your Lord – well pleased and well pleasing. Enter you then among My (honored) servants, and enter you My Paradise." (89:30)

Maimoonah bint Hârith Al-Hilâliyah رضي الله عنها

The Prophet ﷺ said:

"*Allâh has commanded me to marry only the women of Paradise.*"

'A'ishah رضي الله عنها said:

"*By Allâh, Maimoonah was the most Allâh-fearing and nurtured the ties of kinship.*"

Maimoonah bint Hârith Al-Hilâliyah رضي الله عنها

Abu Hurairah and 'Abdullâh bin 'Abbâs رضي الله عنهم narrated that the original name of Maimoonah رضي الله عنها was Barrah, and it was changed by the Prophet ﷺ. Her father was Hârith bin Hazan, and he belonged to the tribe of Banu Hilâl. Her mother's name was Hind bint 'Awf. Umm Al-Fadhl Lubâbah al-Kubrâ and Lubâbah al-Sughrâ, Asmâ' and 'Izzah were her sisters. Umm Al-Fadhl Lubâbah al-Kubrâ was married to 'Abbâs bin 'Abdul Muttalib, and she had the honor of being the second lady to accept Islâm after Khadîjah رضي الله عنها. Lubâbah al-Sughrâ married Waleed bin Mughairah; their son was Khâlid bin Waleed one of the greatest Generals of Islâm. Asmâ' bint Hârith married Ubay bin Khalaf and 'Izzah married Ziyâd bin 'Abdullâh bin Mâlik. Asmâ' bint 'Umais and Salamah bint 'Umais were her sisters from her mother's side.

Asmâ' bint 'Umais was first married to Ja'far bin Abi Tâlib ﷺ. She had three sons by him – 'Abdullâh, 'Awn and Muhammad. When he was martyred she married Abu Bakr Siddeeq ﷺ. She bore him a son, Muhammad bin Abi Bakr. When Abu Bakr Siddeeq ﷺ died, she married for the third time. Her third husband was 'Ali bin Abi Tâlib, and they had a son named Yahyâ. Salamah bint 'Umais married Hamzah bin 'Abdul Muttalib. And her third sister Salâma bint 'Umais married 'Abdullâh bin Ka'b.

Thus Hind bint 'Awf had the unique distinction of being the only woman who was the mother-in-law of the Prophet ﷺ, the first Caliph

Abu Bakr Siddeeq, Hamzah bin 'Abdul Muttalib, 'Abbâs bin 'Abdul Muttalib, Ja'far bin Abi Tâlib and 'Ali bin Abi Tâlib رضي الله عنهم.

One of her grandsons was 'Abdullâh bin 'Abbâs, who was the greatest standard bearer of the Muslim army. He was a learned commentator on the Noble Qur'ân and well versed in *Hadîth* and *Fiqh*. Another grandson was the greatest General mentioned above, Lubâbah al-Sughrâ's son, Khâlid bin Waleed. So, Maimoonah رضي الله عنها came from a very illustrious family of martyrs, warriors and intellectuals.

She was first married to Mas'ood bin 'Amr bin 'Umair Thaqafi, but they soon separated on grounds of incompatibility. Her second husband was Abu Raham bin 'Abdul 'Uzzah 'Amri al-Quraishi. He died shortly after their marriage and Maimoonah رضي الله عنها was widowed at a very early age.

In the seventh year after *Hijrah* the Prophet ﷺ went with his Companions to Makkah to perform *'Umrah*. It is said that Maimoonah رضي الله عنها wished to marry him and become one of the honorable Mothers of the Believers. Soon this wish became an absorbing desire. She even mentioned it to her sisters.

She felt her tribe, Banu Hilâl should also be connected to the Prophet ﷺ in the same way that the other tribes like Banu Tameem, Banu 'Adi, Banu Umayyah, Banu Makhzoom, Banu Asad and Banu Mustaliq were connected – by marriage. Lubâbah al-Kubrâ who was married to 'Abbâs bin 'Abdul Muttalib mentioned her sister's wish to her husband, saying that since he was the uncle and very highly respected by the Prophet ﷺ if he requested him, her sister's wish could be fulfilled.

When 'Abbâs ؓ spoke to the Prophet ﷺ, he requested Ja'far bin Abi Tâlib ؓ to make the arrangements for the marriage. The Prophet ﷺ had finished his *'Umrah* and was free, and Maimoonah رضي الله عنها was on a camel. When she saw him, she involuntarily exclaimed that the camel and its rider were bequeathed to Allâh's Messenger. Thus, she gifted herself to the Prophet ﷺ, and he accepted her very gracefully.

But a more popular tradition says that when he arrived in Makkah for his *'Umrah*, he sent Ja'far bin Abi Tâlib ؓ with his proposal of

Maimoonah bint Hârith Al-Hilâliyah رضي الله عنها

marriage to Maimoonah رضي الله عنها. She asked her brother-in-law, 'Abbâs bin 'Abdul Muttalib ؓ to handle matters. When the Prophet ﷺ finished his *'Umrah*, 'Abbâs ؓ arranged the ceremony.

Allâh said:

> "O Prophet! Verily, We have made lawful to you your wives, to whom you have paid their Mahr, and those (slaves) whom your right hand possesses — whom Allâh has given to you, and the daughters of your paternal uncles and the daughters of your paternal aunts and the daughters of your maternal uncles and the daughters of your maternal aunts who migrated with you, and a believing woman if she offers herself to the Prophet, and the Prophet wishes to marry her, a privilege for you only, not for the (rest of) the believers. Indeed We know what We have enjoined upon them about their wives and those whom their right hands possess, in order that there should be no difficulty on you. And Allâh is Ever Oft-Forgiving, Most Merciful." (33:50)

After his *'Umrah* the Prophet ﷺ stayed in Makkah for three days. Then, on the fourth morning Hawaitab bin 'Abdul 'Uzzâ came with some of the polytheists and told him that since he had finished his *'Umrah*, he ought to leave, according to the terms of the Treaty of Hudaibiyah. The Prophet ﷺ requested that they be allowed to stay for a few more days, and he invited them to attend the dinner he had arranged to celebrate the marriage. Hawaitab answered that they were not interested in any dinner; they just wanted him to go.

The Prophet ﷺ left and pitched camp at a place called Saraf, about nine miles from Makkah, and here he celebrated the marriage. His slave, Abu Râfi' brought Maimoonah رضي الله عنها on a camel to Saraf. It was here that her name was changed from Barrah to Maimoonah رضي الله عنها. Both had completed the rites of *'Umrah*; they changed their garments of *Ihrâm* and the marriage could take place according to *Sharî'ah*.

Maimoonah رضي الله عنها was the last lady that Muhammad ﷺ married. She was twenty-six years old at the time. When they reached Madinah an apartment, which was built next to the Prophet's Mosque, was given to her. The other wives of the Prophet ﷺ warmly welcomed her. She used to pray in the Prophet's Mosque because she heard him saying that one prayer in it was the equivalent to a thousand prayers in all other mosques, except in Masjid al-Harâm at Makkah. One prayer in Masjid al-Harâm was equal to a hundred thousand prayers in any other mosques.

One year several delegations came to Madinah; one of them was from the tribe of Banu Hilâl. One of the members of this delegation was the son of the sister of Maimoonah رضي الله عنها, Ziyâd bin 'Abdullâh bin Mâlik 'Amri. He visited his aunt in her apartment when the Prophet ﷺ happened to be out on some task. When he came back and saw a stranger seated with her he was not pleased. Maimoonah رضي الله عنها, sensitive as she was, sensed his displeasure and immediately introduced him as her sister's son and a member of the visiting delegation. He expressed his pleasure and prayed for Allâh Almighty's blessings for him.

Maimoonah رضي الله عنها was valued highly for her traits like being God-fearing and nurturing good relations with all members of the family. And this tribute was paid to her when she passed away by 'A'ishah رضي الله عنها with the words, 'By Allâh! Maimoonah رضي الله عنها has passed away, she was the most Allâh-fearing and nurtured the ties of kinship.'

Maimoonah رضي الله عنها had an excellent memory, and knew many of the Ahâdîth of the Prophet ﷺ by heart. The most Ahâdîth — two thousand two hundred and ten — are attributed to 'A'ishah رضي الله عنها. Next came Umm Salamah with three hundred and seventy-eight Ahâdîth. Next came Maimoonah رضي الله عنها — seventy-six Ahâdîth were attributed to her. 'Abdullâh bin 'Abbâs, 'Abdullâh bin Shaddâd, 'Ubaid bin Sabâq, Yazîd bin Asam, 'Abdur-Rahmân Sâ'ib Al-Hilâli, 'Ubaidullâh Khaulâni, Sulaiman bin Yasâr and 'Atâ' bin Yasâr رضي الله عنهم have quoted her.

In Sahîh Al-Bukhâri a Hadîth is narrated from 'Abdullâh bin 'Abbâs رضي الله عنهما and attributed to Maimoonah رضي الله عنها. Someone asked the Prophet ﷺ regarding a mouse that had fallen into some clarified butter. He said the mouse and what surrounds it should be thrown out and the rest could be eaten.

Maimoonah bint Hârith Al-Hilâliyah رضي الله عنها

Musnad Abu Ya'lâ, Muslim, Abu Dawood and an-Nasâ'i have quoted another *Hadîth* from Maimoonah رضي الله عنها. This was narrated by the wife of 'Abdullâh bin 'Abbâs ﷺ.

"One morning the Prophet ﷺ looked very worried and he seemed to be in the same mood in the evening. The next day the same mood continued. Maimoonah رضي الله عنها asked him what was troubling him. He said the Angel Jibrîl ﷺ promised to come and visit him, but he had not turned up. Such a thing never happened before. Then the family noticed there was a puppy sitting under a bed. He was chased out and that part of the floor was washed on the directions of the Prophet ﷺ. Soon after that the Angel Jibrîl ﷺ came. Then the Prophet ﷺ asked him why he had not come earlier as promised, and said that this had never happened before. Then the Angel told him that angels do not enter places where there are dogs or pictures."

"Maimoonah رضي الله عنها sometimes used to take loans. Once a member of her family remarked on this and asked her why she did this. She did not quite like this question and replied that the Prophet ﷺ used to say if a Muslim borrowed money and he sincerely believed that Allâh ﷻ would help him to repay the loan, then Allâh ﷻ would surely arrange things in an unexpected manner."

'A'ishah رضي الله عنها relates that the last fatal illness of the Prophet ﷺ started while he was in the apartment of Maimoonah رضي الله عنها. He asked permission of his other wives to spend those days in the apartment of 'A'ishah رضي الله عنها. They all readily agreed. When he passed away he was pleased with all his wives. When his pure soul left his body he was in the apartment of his favorite wife 'A'ishah رضي الله عنها resting his head in her lap. And he was buried in his favorite place, her apartment. Nine of his wives were alive at the time. They were 'A'ishah, Maimoonah, Safiyyah, Juwairiyah, Saudah, Zainab, Ramlah, Hind, and Hafsah رضي الله عنهن.

It was during the caliphate of Mu'âwiyah ﷺ, in the year 51 AH, that Maimoonah رضي الله عنها died. She was in Makkah and she fell ill there. She was very restless and wanted to be taken someplace else. Her relatives took her to Saraf, the same place where she had got married to the Prophet ﷺ. After reaching the exact spot where she spent her wedding night, she passed away. 'Abdullâh bin 'Abbâs conducted the funeral prayers, and she was buried with great honor.

"*O the one in (complete) rest and satisfaction! Come back to your Lord – well pleased and well pleasing. Enter you then among My (honored) servants, and enter you My Paradise.*" (89:30)

Women Companions
Who were Given the
Good News of Paradise

Fâtimah رضي الله عنها bint Prophet Muhammad ﷺ

The Prophet ﷺ told his daughter Fâtimah رضي الله عنها:
"Would you like to be the leader of the women of Paradise?"

Allâh's Messenger ﷺ said:
"One day Jibrîl عليه السلام came and gave me the glad tidings that Fâtimah رضي الله عنها will be the leader of the women of Paradise."

'A'ishah رضي الله عنها narrated,
"She bore a remarkable resemblance to Allâh's Messenger ﷺ. Her way of speaking, sitting, standing and walking — in other words all her manners and gestures were exactly like his."

Fâtimah رضي الله عنها bint Prophet Muhammad ﷺ

She was the youngest daughter of the Prophet ﷺ and his favorite one. She married his cousin 'Ali bin Abi Tâlib ؓ and was the mother of the great martyrs of Islâm, Hasan and Husain رضي الله عنهما. She was born in Makkah a few years before her father was granted Prophethood. Though both Muhammad ﷺ and Khadîjah رضي الله عنها already had three daughters before her, they expressed great happiness at her birth. Going against the accepted custom, her mother did not send her beloved youngest daughter away to be breastfed in any of the surrounding villages, but kept her with her and nursed her herself. She loved her too much to entrust her to anyone else's care. Some years later her father was declared by Allâh ﷻ to be His Prophet ﷺ and last Messenger.

She and her mother and her three elder sisters – Zainab, Ruqayyah, and Umm Kulthoom رضي الله عنهن – accepted Islâm and believed in their father as Allâh's Messenger from the very beginning. She spent her early years under the loving and tender care of her parents. Zeal for the defense of what is sacred and love of the righteous was ingrained in her. She would protect her father and the cause of Allâh ﷻ against all odds and at all times, with courage and conviction. At the very tender age of ten she had gone through the siege of Shi'b Abi Tâlib. And it was by no means a short siege; it lasted for three long years. It was a total social and economic boycott, where children sobbed with the pangs of hunger, and mothers and sisters were tormented by the sight of loved ones suffering. During this period she showed exemplary courage, but this terrible time left an effect on her health which lasted till the end of her life. Just the everyday chores like grinding wheat for bread, fetching water and cooking left her exhausted. When she asked her father for a slave girl from the prisoners of war to help her, he said he would give her something better. And then he taught her some special prayers exalting and glorifying Allâh that would help to dispel her weariness.

'A'ishah رضي الله عنها said that she never saw anyone more devoted to the truth than Fâtimah رضي الله عنها. She stood shoulder to shoulder with the other *Muhâjir* and *Ansâr* women of Makkah and Madinah tending to the injured and the dying in the Battle of Uhud. When she saw her injured and bleeding father, the Prophet ﷺ in the battlefield at Uhud she just could not take it. She helped to stop the bleeding and bandaged his wounds.

Before Muhammad ﷺ proclaimed himself the Last Prophet of Allâh Almighty, he was the most popular, loved and respected man among the Quraish. The most important decisions that had to be made were referred to his wise judgment. If people needed some valuable goods to be left in the care and trust of a reliable person, he was the man they turned to. He was such an eminent and successful trader even in his youth, that experienced businessmen were amazed at his acumen and insight. And when he married Khadîjah رضي الله عنها, the wealthiest businesswoman of her time, people were amazed. And he became even more sought after and popular.

However, once he announced himself to be the Prophet of Allâh and His Messenger, his whole life seemed to turn around. The entire city seemed to be shaken by an earthquake, as it were. He became the most unpopular and reviled man in Makkah and was the center of a storm of objections and accusations. Those who wanted him to recant and give up his claims started using all kind of tactics – from persuasion and torture. The streets he previously frequented were strewn with thorns and filth and garbage was thrown on him from balconies and rooftops. Elaborate plans were made to murder him. Naturally, all these trials and tribulations could not but leave a mark on his home life.

Fâtimah bint Muhammad رضي الله عنها

Fâtimah رضي الله عنها was passing the impressionable years of her childhood in the shadow of these events. Yet, her maturity was such that she faced all this with remarkable patience and determination. She fought like a courageous little tigress to defend her father and protect him. She would stand in front of him to shield him from the attacks of devilish men like Abu Jahl, 'Utbah and Shaibah.

On one occasion, the Prophet ﷺ went into the sanctuary of Makkah with some of his Companions and started to pray, while the disbelievers had just then sacrificed a camel. The filth and bowels of the camel were lying there, when a horrible idea came to Abu Jahl. He asked who among his friends would like to lift all that filth and pile it on the back of Muhammad ﷺ. 'Uqbah bin Abi Mu'eet, the lowest of the low among his friends, got up shrugging his shoulders with satanic glee, and said he would perform the task. And he lifted up the bloody, filthy mess and piled it on the Prophet's back while he was in the act of prostrating before Allâh ﷻ. All of them then broke into peals of uncontrollable devilish laughter.

When news of this dastardly act reached Fâtimah رضي الله عنها in her house, she rushed to the sanctuary. Removing with her pure little hands all the filth she threw it into the distance. She then cleaned her father's back. And furious at the brutal treatment given to her beloved father, she scolded the disbelievers. When the Prophet ﷺ finished his prayers, he lifted his hands in supplication and appealed to Allâh ﷻ to hold these men – Abu Jahl bin Hishâm, Shaibah bin Rabi'ah, 'Uqbah bin Abi Mu'eet and Umayyah bin Khalaf, in His relentless grip. These devils became very nervous because they knew that any supplication made at the sanctuary in Makkah is never rejected by Allâh Almighty. And the Prophet's prayers were answered.

All these men were killed in the Battle of Badr, except 'Uqbah bin Abi Mu'eet. He was taken prisoner and the Prophet ﷺ ordered him to be put to death. Trembling with fear, he asked what would be the lot of his children. Muhammad ﷺ said they would go to Hell. He asked if he would be put to death in spite of the fact that he was a member of the tribe of Quraish. The Prophet ﷺ answered in the affirmative. Then he looked up at his Companions and asked them if they knew what his crime was. Then he told them all this man's doings. Once when the Prophet ﷺ was prostrating before Allâh ﷻ, this vile man placed his foot on his neck and pressed it so hard that his eyes almost popped out of their sockets. The next time again when he was in the same position of prostration, he put offal and filthy blood soaked intestines of a camel sacrificed in the name of one of the idols on his back. Then he narrated how his beloved Fâtimah رضي الله عنها removed it and cleaned his back and his clothes.

Once Abu Jahl was sitting with the disbelievers in front of the Ka'bah planning how to eliminate the Prophet ﷺ for the 'crime' of rejecting the idols installed there as helpless stones which lacked movement. They hated him for propagating the Oneness of Allâh ﷻ and for proclaiming himself as His Last Prophet and Messenger. Fâtimah رضي الله عنها Happened to pass by and heard him. She was so terrified of what these cruel barbarians could do to her beloved father that she went running to tell him of their dastardly plot. As she wept she told him they had sworn in the names of their most famous idols – Lât, Manât, 'Uzzâ and Nâ'ilah – to kill him. All of them would get together and attack him the moment he stepped out of his house. She asked him innocently what would happen, as nothing could stop these men now. The Prophet ﷺ told her to have faith in Allâh ﷻ, as He was her father's Protector. He then got up calmly, made the ablution for his prayers and went to the House of Allâh. When he passed Abu Jahl and his friends who were seated there, he looked up towards the Heavens, then turned his eyes downward. (Saying that Allâh Almighty would cover their faces with dust), he picked up a handful of mud threw it in their direction. These people were so taken aback and overcome that none of them could stir from their places or speak. It was as if the fear of the Almighty had struck them dumb.

Once Fâtimah رضي الله عنها passed by Abu Jahl bin Hishâm on the street and he, for no reason, gave her a tight slap across the face. She went to Abu Sufyân, the leader of the Quraish, and complained to him about Abu Jahl's cruel and uncivilized behavior. Abu Sufyân took her with him to the place where the uncouth barbarian was still sitting and told her to slap him in exactly the same way as he had done. When she went home and narrated this incident to the

Fâtimah bint Muhammad رضي الله عنها

Prophet ﷺ he was very pleased at Abu Sufyân's sense of justice and fair play. He then prayed that his heart should be enlightened, and that he should accept Islâm as the true religion. His supplications for Abu Sufyân were accepted and he finally swore allegiance to Allâh and His Prophet Muhammad ﷺ.

Seven years had passed since Muhammad ﷺ declared himself to be Allâh's chosen Prophet. The whole might of the Quraish had not been able to silence him and his Message; the people who answered the call of Allâh ﷻ were persecuted and tortured in every way possible. They were made to lie on layers of burning coals, and dragged naked across the burning desert sands, but they continued to recite the word of Oneness of Allâh - *'None has the right to be worshipped but Allâh, and Muhammad is His Servant and His Messenger'*. The numbers of the believers kept multiplying, regardless of the consequences they might face in this world.

When Hamzah bin 'Abdul Muttalib and 'Umar bin Khattâb رضي الله عنهما accepted Islâm the whole of Makkah was shaken by an earthquake, as it were. The people started pushing the leaders to take some action otherwise they would lose their hold and all their power and their pomp would fall into the dust and become a story of the past. In the light of these new developments, Abu Jahl called a meeting of the richest and most influential people among the disbelievers. He asked them to suggest the best course of action to be taken against this new movement which was gathering strength against the religion of their forefathers. How could they stem this tide?

One of the devil's right hand men, a libertine and worthless fellow, Nadhr bin Hârith, was present at this meeting. He was an extremely cunning and devious man. His idea was to completely boycott the Muslims - socially and economically. No business, no trade, no intermarriages - nothing should be allowed, he proposed. The tribes of Banu Hâshim and Banu 'Abdul Muttalib and the families who supported them and helped them should be ostracized as well. No food or water should reach them. A very alert and vigilant force should keep an eye on them to see that absolutely nothing reached them; in this way these people would perish and with them their newborn religion. This unusual plan appealed to all those present and was adopted unanimously. There were cries of acclaim from all sides and the Muslims went into a state of siege in Shi'b Abi Tâlib.

This siege lasted for three years. Nothing could melt the hearts of the disbelievers. The screams of hungry children, the sobs of mothers and sisters, the helpless condition of the aged and the infirm – all this could not move their stony hearts. But every student of history was amazed to note that in spite of the worst siege in history being forced on the staunch followers of this new religion, not one man, woman or child recanted and moved out. The truth and righteousness of their cause, the charismatic and magnetic personality of the Prophet ﷺ was their strength. This crucible of suffering burned out all the impure elements and their faith grew firmer and purer. The richest woman of Makkah, Khadîjah رضي الله عنها, her young daughters – the youngest Fâtimah رضي الله عنها, barely ten years of age – stood like rocks by her father. They could give their lives for him. And in a sense little Fâtimah رضي الله عنها did, because this mental and physical ordeal affected her health and physique for the rest of her life.

What is Divine Destiny? Who can fathom the will of Allâh the Almighty? Why did His loved ones who propagated His Faith have to suffer as if they had no one to help or assist them? Man's vision is very limited and he cannot account for the workings of the Divine plan.

Those who live for material benefits cannot understand the workings of the minds of those who do not care for the pleasures of this world. Their trials and tribulations give them a spiritual strength that gives immeasurable and incalculable satisfaction. Their tears seem to purify their souls, wash away the impurities and enlighten their hearts and minds. When the suffering soul of the Allâh-fearing and righteous weeps while prostrating, he is closest to Allâh; perhaps this is why those beloved of Allâh Almighty are made to suffer to achieve nearness to Him. For this is sure: lovers of truth are more deserving of reward in the Hereafter than the lovers of evil.

❖෴❖෴❖෴❖

Fâtimah bint Muhammad رضي الله عنها

Soon after the siege of *Shi'b Abi Talib* lifted, the Prophet ﷺ and Fâtimah رضي الله عنها and her sisters went through the trauma of losing their beloved Khadîjah رضي الله عنها. She had fallen ill during the siege. Ten years passed since Muhammad ﷺ declared himself to be the Messenger of Allâh ﷻ. It was at the same time that the Prophet ﷺ lost his greatest supporter and defender, his uncle Abu Tâlib. The disbelievers became bolder as they thought he was 'helpless.' Fâtimah رضي الله عنها, from a tender age, faced all these troubles, experiencing them first hand side by side with her father. It was also at this time that the Prophet ﷺ went to Tâ'if with the Message of Islâm. The people there were like the Makkans; they welcomed him with stones and he left Tâ'if injured and bleeding. But he did not curse these inhospitable and cruel people; on the other hand he prayed to Allâh ﷻ to guide them to the right path. Umm Kulthoom and Fâtimah رضي الله عنهما were very upset and started weeping when they saw his condition. He affectionately wiped away their tears and consoled them. He said it was inevitable that Allâh ﷻ would help to spread His religion and make it triumph against all odds. Easier times were bound to follow the hard and difficult days.

And sure enough, Mus'ab bin 'Umair ؓ who was the Prophet's ambassador to Madinah gave the good news that the people there were being drawn into the fold of Islâm. They invited Muhammad ﷺ to settle in their city, and promised to help him in any way they could. The Prophet ﷺ accepted their invitation and with the consent of Allâh Almighty decided to migrate to Madinah. He commanded his followers to start the process of migration, and he followed later in the company of his most trusted Companion, Abu Bakr Siddeeq ؓ. He left his two daughters at home in Makkah, with Saudah bint Zam'ah رضي الله عنها, whom he had married after the death of Khadîjah رضي الله عنها.

He sent for them later, and thus these three ladies also had the privilege of becoming migrants for the cause. But the disbelievers could not bear to see them all moving out either. Some mischievous elements caught hold of them on the outskirts of Makkah. One of them was the evil Quraishi youth, Hawairath bin Naqeeth. He started jabbing at the camel on which the Prophet's daughters were riding and the camel reared up in the air, and the two girls fell down. When he saw this he ran away. This little caravan continued on the journey borne by their spiritual faith and strength.

When they reached their destination, the Prophet ﷺ received them. He was very happy to see them alive and well. Those whom Allâh Almighty protects, no one can harm them.

In the second year after *Hijrah*, the Battle of Badr was fought and 'Ali ؓ showed exemplary courage, valor and skill at fighting. The Islâmic forces triumphed and archenemies like Abu Jahl and some other prominent leaders of the Quraish were killed in the battle. Many of the disbelievers were captured as prisoners of war and brought to Madinah. This victory lifted up the spirits of the Muslims as never before.

Fâtimah رضي الله عنها was now eighteen years old and prominent personalities started proposing for her, but the Prophet ﷺ said he was waiting for a sign from Allâh ﷻ. One day 'Ali ؓ came to see the Prophet ﷺ, but he was very shy and diffident and seemed to be holding something back. The Prophet ﷺ realized what was on his mind and asked him if he came to propose marriage to Fâtimah رضي الله عنها. 'Ali ؓ answered that he had. The Prophet ﷺ asked Fâtimah رضي الله عنها what she thought of the proposal. She started to weep silently. He then told her that 'Ali ؓ was a learned, kind-hearted and brave young man. Fâtimah رضي الله عنها accepted her father's decision.

He then asked 'Ali ؓ if he had some money for the dowry. 'Ali ؓ replied that the Prophet ﷺ had seen his life from the cradle and knew his financial position very well. Then the Prophet ﷺ asked him where his shield was, and said that would be the dowry for Fâtimah رضي الله عنها. 'Ali ؓ sent it to the market with his slave to be sold and got four hundred Dirhams for it. This he gave to the Prophet ﷺ, who asked him to keep the money and buy some things for the house and perfume for the wedding. Then he asked Anas bin Mâlik ؓ to bring his Companions – Abu Bakr, 'Uthmân, 'Umar, Talhah, Zubair رضي الله عنهم, and other *Ansâr* and *Muhâjir* friends to attend the ceremony. When all these esteemed people assembled, he asked 'Ali ؓ to read his own marriage speech. Then 'Ali ؓ stood up and recited the words of the ceremony,

Fâtimah bint Muhammad رضي الله عنها

'All Praise is for Allâh. We are grateful to Him for His Bounties and His Blessings. I bear witness that None has the right to be worshipped but Allâh, vouching for Him so it will reach Him and gain His Favor. The Prophet ﷺ has married his daughter, Fâtimah رضي الله عنها, to me and the Mahr has been fixed at four hundred Dirhams. Now all those present please listen to what the Prophet ﷺ has to say and bear witness.'

After that the Prophet ﷺ praised Allâh Almighty and recited the marriage ceremony, after asking Fâtimah رضي الله عنها for her consent. He announced the *Mahr* and told all those present that Allâh ﷻ had commanded him to have Fâtimah رضي الله عنها married to 'Ali ﷺ. After that he prayed for a happy and blessed future for the bride and groom. Then dates were offered to the guests. All those present expressed their happiness and prayed that Allâh ﷻ bless the newly married couple. The next day Hamzah bin 'Abdul Muttalib ﷺ slaughtered a camel to host a banquet to celebrate the wedding of his brother's son, 'Ali ﷺ.

Some basic things were purchased for the house to which 'Ali ﷺ and Fâtimah رضي الله عنها moved. A bed, a pillow filled with the leaves of dried date palm, a plate, a glass, a leather water bag and a grinding stone for grinding flour - these were the few things with which the daughter of the Prophet ﷺ set up her new home. The house that was available was quite a distance from the Prophet's Mosque. The Prophet ﷺ wished his daughter could live closer to him, so that he could see her daily. When one of the Companions Hârithah bin Nu'mân Ansâri ﷺ, came to know of this he approached the Prophet ﷺ very respectfully, saying he had a number of houses close to the Prophet's Mosque and he was welcome to choose any one of them. This would make that particular house dearer to him. The Prophet ﷺ was very moved by this offer and chose one for Fâtimah رضي الله عنها, and prayed for increase and prosperity for his devoted follower. So, 'Ali ﷺ and Fâtimah رضي الله عنها moved in and started the routine of daily life. It was usual for her to grind the wheat, fetch water from the well and cook their meals.

Since she was not very robust and healthy, the siege having left its mark on her, Fâtimah رضي الله عنها used to get very tired with all this hard work. On one occasion after a battle, a lot of money, precious jewelry and prisoners of war, both men and women, were taken by the Muslim army. 'Ali ؓ suggested that she should go to the Prophet ﷺ and ask him for a maid to help, since she used to get very tired with all the housework.

Fâtimah رضي الله عنها went to see her father and requested him for some help. He was not at home and she left a message with 'A'ishah رضي الله عنها. At night, before going to sleep, her father came to visit her. He told her that he would give her something much better than a slave girl. And he taught her some phrases in praise of Almighty Allâh. These, he said, were better than any maid. And he taught her to recite thirty-three times *Subhânallâh* (Glory be to Allâh), thirty-three times *Alhamdulillâh* (All praise is for Allâh), and thirty-four times *Allâhu-Akbar* (Allâh is the greatest).

Fâtimah رضي الله عنها spent her entire life as an Allâh-fearing and pious servant of Allâh ﷻ. Always patient and grateful to her Maker, there was not a word of complaint from her, however difficult the circumstances. The world and its attractions held no charm for her. Her motto in life was always service for Islâm and its *Mujâhideen*. In the battles she was at the front nursing the wounded and the sick. When her father was injured in the Battle of Uhud, it was she who burnt a part of a straw mat and used its ashes to stem the flow of blood. There is a narration in *Sahîh Al-Bukhâri* that when the Prophet ﷺ was asked on one occasion whom he loved best in the world he named his youngest daughter, Fâtimah رضي الله عنها.

'A'ishah رضي الله عنها, talking of her, says she bore a remarkable resemblance to her father. She not only looked like him, but her way of speaking, sitting, standing and walking – in other words all her mannerisms and gestures were exactly like his. Whenever her father visited her she would receive him and kiss his forehead with reverence and respect. They were exceptionally close to each other and whenever she visited her father, he would stand up and receive her. It was as if she left the sweet aura of her personality wherever she went. If he saw her troubled or sad he would also be grieved, and if he saw her happy he would also be pleased.

Fâtimah bint Muhammad رضي الله عنها

One day the Prophet ﷺ heard that there was some misunderstanding between 'Ali and Fâtimah رضي الله عنهما, so he went to meet them. On the way to their house he looked very troubled and sad, and when he left their house he seemed very much at peace. Some of his Companions noted that he was a different man while going to his daughter's house and a different man on the way back. He replied that he just settled some differences between his two children who were very dear to him and his happiness made his face glow.

On one occasion 'Ali made up his mind to marry Abu Jahl's daughter. Somehow Fâtimah رضي الله عنها came to hear about it and told her father that 'Ali was planning to marry into Abu Jahl's family; the Prophet ﷺ was very disturbed when he heard this. He went to the mosque and gave a sermon, saying that Fâtimah رضي الله عنها was a part of his heart and anything that made her unhappy displeased him. He said that the daughter of Allâh's Messenger and the daughter of His enemy could not be married to the same man. 'Ali ؓ changed his mind and apologised to Fâtimah رضي الله عنها for any pain he might have caused her. And things went back to normal.

One day 'Ali ؓ asked the Prophet ﷺ who was dearer to him, himself or Fâtimah رضي الله عنها? The Prophet ﷺ answered that he loved Fâtimah رضي الله عنها more, but 'Ali was dearer to him than her. It was a masterly piece of diplomacy and yet it also was the truth, because he really did love both of them deeply.

Their first son was born to 'Ali and Fâtimah رضي الله عنهما in *Ramadhân* of the third year after *Hijrah*. When the Prophet ﷺ heard the good news he was very happy and immediately went to see the child. He named him Hasan and recited the *Adhân* for him. Then on the seventh day his head was shaved clean, and an amount of silver equivalent to the weight of the hair was distributed among the poor.

In *Sha'bân* of the fourth year after *Hijrah,* a second son was born. The Prophet ﷺ named him Husain, and in his ears too he recited the *Adhân* himself. It is said a third son Muhsin was born but died in his infancy. The Prophet ﷺ loved these two grandchildren dearly. He used to say that they were like scented herbs and would be the leaders of the youths of Paradise. Usâmah bin Zaid ﷺ says that one day he saw the Prophet ﷺ carrying something wrapped in a sheet. He asked him what he was carrying. He opened the sheet and what should Usâmah ﷺ see, but these two little boys all wrapped up in their grandfather's arms. He said that these were his daughter's sons and he would love all those who loved them.

In the fifth year after *Hijrah*, a daughter was born to 'Ali and Fâtimah رضي الله عنهما; the Prophet ﷺ named her Zainab; in the seventh year after *Hijrah* another daughter was born and he named her Umm Kulthoom. When Zainab bint 'Ali رضي الله عنها grew up she married 'Abdullâh bin Ja'far bin Abi Tâlib ﷺ. And Umm Kulthoom married 'Umar bin Khattâb رضي الله عنهما. They had two children Zaid and Ruqayyah. After his wedding 'Umar bin al-Khattâb asked the *Muhâjirs* (immigrants) and the *Ansâr* to congratulate him. They asked him for the reason. He said since he had married Umm Kulthoom, the daughter of 'Ali bin Abi Tâlib ﷺ, and had established links with the family of the Prophet ﷺ, this was a very great honor for him. And everyone wished him happiness and blessed him on this great occasion.

Imâm Ahmad was once asked what he thought of 'Ali and his family members. He said their position in history is unparalleled. According to what the Noble Qur'ân tells us Allâh Almighty had cleaned them of every kind of sin, impurity of faith, disobedience to the Divine Will and social evils.

Ibn 'Abdullâh writes that whenever the Prophet ﷺ came back from any journey or after taking part in a battle, he would first go to his Mosque in Madinah and pray two *Rak'ât* (units), then he would visit Fâtimah رضي الله عنها and then visit the wives in his household.

There is a miraculous incident related in *Al-Bidâyah wa An-Nihâyah*: Once a lady sent Fâtimah رضي الله عنها a couple of pieces of bread and some roasted meat. She put this in a large plate and covered it with cloth. Then she sent a message to her father to come and have his meal at her house. When he arrived she removed the cloth and to her astonishment she found the plate full of bread and plenty of meat. She understood that this abundance and plenty had come from Allâh. She praised Almighty Allâh and asked Allâh to mention and bless His Prophet ﷺ and started to serve the meal to him, beginning with Allâh Almighty's Name. When he saw such a huge amount he smiled and asked who had sent it all. She promptly said Allâh gave it to her and He provides sustenance to whom He pleases without limits. He smiled and thanked Allâh Almighty that He had a daughter who could speak like Maryam. Then the Prophet ﷺ ate of the meal with his daughter, son-in-law and the two grandchildren. Yet there was so much food still left over that it was sent to the Mothers of the Believers. They also ate their fill and then it was distributed among the neighbours.

'Abdullâh bin 'Abbâs رضي الله عنهما says that when Surat An-Nasr was revealed the Prophet ﷺ sent for Fâtimah رضي الله عنها and told her that Allâh had intimated to him that his life on earth was now drawing to a close. Islâm was spreading and hordes of people were now turning to it. When Fâtimah رضي الله عنها heard this she started to weep at the thought of separation from her beloved father. Then he told her that from among his family members she would be the first to meet him. At this she started smiling. When he fell ill and his condition started to deteriorate, she could not bear to see his suffering. He then told her that after that day he would never have to suffer again, as he felt he was about to leave for a better hereafter.

In his book Asad Al-Ghâbah, Ibn Atheer writes that after the Prophet ﷺ passed away no one ever saw Fâtimah رضي الله عنها smile. And her grief remained visible on her face till she passed away, six months later.

"To Allâh we belong and to Him we return." (2:56)

'Ali ؓ and her four children – Hasan, Hussian, Zainab, and Umm Kulthoom رضي الله عنهم were left to mourn her death at a very young age.

She was given her final bath and shrouded by 'Ali, Asmâ' bint 'Umais and Salamah Umm Râf' رضي الله عنهم and buried at night in *Jannatul Baqi'*. 'Ali, 'Abbâs, and Fadhl bin 'Abbâs رضي الله عنهم placed her into her final resting place. Thus the leader of the virtuous women of Paradise set out on her journey to Paradise.

"O the one in (complete) rest and satisfaction! Come back to your Lord – well pleased and well pleasing. Enter you then among My (honored) servants, and enter you My Paradise."

Fâtimah bint Asad رضي الله عنها

The Prophet ﷺ said:

"I gave my shirt to be used as a part of her shroud, so that she would be dressed with the dress of Paradise."

Fâtimah bint Asad رضي الله عنها

Fâtimah bint Asad رضي الله عنها was the mother of 'Ali bin Abi Tâlib ؓ, and the mother-in-law of the Prophet's daughter Fâtimah bint Muhammad ﷺ. Her grandsons, Hasan and Husain رضي الله عنهما are to be the leaders of the youths of Paradise. Besides 'Ali ؓ, she had two other sons. One was Ja'far al-Tayyâr ؓ who was a famous General. He led the forces of Islâm in the Battle of Mu'tah and was martyred in the same battle.

The Prophet ﷺ was an orphan child, his father died before his birth; his mother also died when he was very young. His paternal uncle, Abu Tâlib, had in a sense adopted him. And Fâtimah bint Asad رضي الله عنها, Abu Tâlib's wife, looked after him like her own. She protected him as closely as the heart is protected and enclosed in the human breast.

When he grew up and proclaimed himself to be the Prophet and Last Messenger of Allâh, she still stood by him. All the relentless persecution did not deter her in any way. She was exceptionally fond of her son Ja'far ؓ, but for the sake of Islâm she bore the separation from him and his wife, Asmâ' bint 'Umais رضي الله عنها when they migrated to Abyssinia on the Prophet's orders with the first group of migrant Muslims.

Fâtimah bint Asad رضي الله عنها being one of the first to swear allegiance to Islâm and its concept of the Oneness of Allâh ﷻ, faced the economic and social boycott of Shi'b Abi Tâlib for those three terrible years. She was also a member of the privileged group who migrated to Madinah. Her family and the family of the Prophet ﷺ could be traced back to a common ancestor Hâshim.

Fâtimah bint Asad bin Hâshim bin Abd Munâf bin Qusai bin Kilab رضي الله عنها – that was her lineage. 'Abdul Muttalib, who was a very discriminating man had assessed her nature, her intelligence and her capabilities from the very beginning and sent her a marriage proposal for his son, Abu Tâlib. When the Prophet ﷺ was told by Allâh to spread the Message of Islâm among his kith and kin, it was Fâtimah bint Asad رضي الله عنها who immediately accepted this invitation and swore allegiance and entered the fold of Islâm. When the Prophet's grandfather, 'Abdul Muttalib, passed away, the guardianship of the orphan Muhammad ﷺ passed on to Abu Tâlib. His wife, Fâtimah bint Asad رضي الله عنها, looked after him, loving him as if he were her own son. He remembered in his later life that she would go hungry to feed him. He respected her so highly that whenever she visited him he would stand up and receive her with great love, addressing her as 'Mother'.

His uncle too loved him deeply. Muhammad ﷺ in his childhood was so well mannered and so fastidious about his personal cleanliness that Abu Tâlib would hold him up as an example to his other children. Normally boys would be dirty and tousled from playing rough games with the other boys, but Muhammad ﷺ was always dignified with a neat appearance. People were impressed when they saw him. Abu Tâlib liked all the children to eat together because he felt that whenever Muhammad ﷺ ate with other children, food would be sufficient and when the children ate alone they would remain hungry. Abu Tâlib often told his nephew that he was specially blessed, as there was plenty when he was around.

Fâtimah bint Asad رضي الله عنها did not spare any pains and looked after Muhammad ﷺ in his infancy, boyhood and youth. Once in his childhood he accompanied his uncle on a business trip to Syria. Some very unusual and surprising incidents took place on the journey, and Abu Tâlib described these to his wife Fâtimah bint Asad رضي الله عنها when they came back. She was also very moved and impressed.

Fâtimah bint Asad رضي الله عنها

The same was the case with Maisarah, the slave of Khadîjah رضي الله عنها. He was amazed at some of the strange signs he witnessed on that first business trip to Syria with him. His courtesy, his humane treatment of people, his business acumen, the enormous profit made as well as some of the strange supernatural happenings, the prediction of the monk, Nestor, all these he narrated to Khadîjah رضي الله عنها. Nestor, a Christian monk, noted for his knowledge of religion had predicted that he would be exalted to prophethood by Allâh. Maisarah told Khadîjah about the Prophet ﷺ and his reputation for honesty and intelligence. She was impressed by what she heard and the more she came to know Muhammad ﷺ the more she liked and respected him. And, finally, she proposed marriage, rejecting the offers of marriage from the foremost leaders of the Quraish.

When the Prophet ﷺ placed the invitation to a religion with a new and rational perspective before the Quraish of Makkah, the worshippers of all the false idols in the Ka'bah were infuriated. They could not dream that the Prophet ﷺ would dismiss their gods as useless and helpless creatures, and they became his bitter enemies for propagating a new faith that did away with their traditional and inherited practices. They adopted a very antagonistic attitude and swore to crush him and Islâm. During this period they resorted to the most cruel and sadistic forms of torture to make the converts give up the new faith and return to their old barbaric practices and rituals. It was only the power and influence of Abu Tâlib that prevented them from doing any harm to Muhammad ﷺ. He stood by him with all his love and carried out the responsibilities of a guardian faithfully by giving him his protection. No enemy could dare to do anything to him as long as he was under the mantle of his uncle's protection.

Fâtimah bint Asad رضي الله عنها cooperated with Abu Tâlib wholeheartedly and she reacted as a mother would, as far as the safety and well being of Muhammad ﷺ was concerned. No wonder he loved and respected her so highly. Considering the dangerous conditions which developed for the Muslims in Makkah, he thought it was better that the Muslims migrate to Abyssinia where the ruler Najâshi was known to be tolerant and hospitable. The leader of this first group of migrants was Ja'far bin Abi Tâlib ؓ, the brother of 'Ali ؓ, and the favorite son of Fâtimah bint Asad رضي الله عنها. She loved him more than the others because he resembled Muhammad ﷺ very much, and was extremely intelligent. He seemed to have inherited the family's mastery over language and was also an eloquent speaker who could win people over to his viewpoint. It was with this same skill that he had won over Najâshi when the representatives of the Quraish appealed to him to surrender the Muslims to them.

The Quraish now decided to restrict the Muslims to one small area, besiege them and boycott them. Social and economic sanctions were imposed, and these three years were perhaps the toughest that the followers of Islâm faced. Economically, their condition was certainly the worst ever. Children could be heard on all sides sobbing with hunger, and the elders looked on helplessly with tears in their eyes. To satisfy their hunger they started eating the leaves of trees and grass; they even sucked on wet skins to slake their thirst. Fâtimah bint Asad رضي الله عنها passed this terrible period with fortitude and patience, and did not waver in the smallest degree. Ten years after the first revelation came to Muhammad ﷺ, appointing him the Messenger of Allâh ﷻ, this harsh siege was finally lifted. It was in the same year that the Prophet's wife and most faithful supporter, Khadîjah رضي الله عنها passed away. The pangs of separation from her were very difficult to bear for the Prophet ﷺ. He had not yet recovered from her loss, when he was dealt another terrible blow – his best ally, Abu Tâlib, also passed away. This year is known as 'The Year of Sorrows' in Islâmic history.

The torture and torment, atrocities and cruelties reached such proportions that Allâh ﷻ finally ordered the Prophet to migrate to Madinah. Fâtimah bint Asad رضي الله عنها was among these migrants. When the Prophet's daughter Fâtimah رضي الله عنها married 'Ali ؓ, there were two women named 'Fâtimah' in the family, a mother-in-law and daughter-in-law. 'Ali ؓ narrated how one day the Prophet ﷺ gave him a very large expensive sheet and told him to divide it between the Fâtimahs. At that time there were four Fâtimahs in the family.

Fâtimah bint Asad رضي الله عنها

Fâtimah bint Muhammad رضي الله عنها

Fâtimah bint Hamzah رضي الله عنها

Fâtimah bint Asad رضي الله عنها

Fâtimah bint Shaibah رضي الله عنها, who was the wife of 'Aqeel bin Abi Tâlib ؓ, the brother of 'Ali ؓ.

'Ali ؓ says he did as the Prophet ﷺ told him and divided it among the four Fâtimahs in his family.

Anas bin Mâlik says that when the Prophet ﷺ got news of the death of Fâtimah bint Asad رضي الله عنها he immediately went to her house, sat beside her and prayed for her:

"My dear mother, may Allâh keep you under His Protection. Many times you went hungry in order to feed me well. You fed me and clothed me on delicacies that you denied yourself. Allâh ﷻ will surely be happy with these actions of yours. And your intentions were surely meant to win the goodwill and pleasure of Allâh ﷻ and success in the hereafter."

He gave his shirt to be used as part of her shroud, saying he prayed to Allâh to forgive her and grant her the dress of Paradise.

When the grave was prepared the Prophet ﷺ himself examined it and with his own hands placed her into the grave.

Thus Fâtimah bint Asad رضي الله عنها was one of the few blessed people whose graves were examined and entered by the Prophet ﷺ. The others' names are given below:

Khadîjah رضي الله عنها

'Abdullâh Mazini ؓ – very well known as *Zulbajâdain*.

His son, born by Khadîjah رضي الله عنها, who died in his infancy.

Fâtimah bint Asad رضي الله عنها is that great lady for whom he gave the glad tidings that she would be blessed with a place in Paradise.

May Allâh be pleased with them and they with Him.

Umm Rummân رضي الله عنها

> The Prophet ﷺ said:
> "*If a person wants to see a beautiful Hoor of Paradise, let them look at Umm Rummân.*"

Umm Rummân رضي الله عنها

She was the wife of Abu Bakr Siddeeq ﷺ and the mother of 'A'ishah رضي الله عنها. Thus she was the Prophet's mother-in-law. Her son, 'Abdur-Rahmân bin Abu Bakr Siddeeq رضي الله عنهما was an excellent horseman, and master strategist in war. It was she who taught him the meaning of valor and courage. Her real name was Zainab, but she came to be known by her family name. She was a patient and tolerant lady who did not jump to hasty conclusions, but gave matters deep thought. This was evident in the way she handled the incident when certain people with loose tongues and petty minds accused 'A'ishah رضي الله عنها of adultery. When her husband explained to her the teachings of Islâm she did not linger with doubts about giving up the religion of her forefathers. She immediately saw the greatness of Islâm and accepted it. When the Prophet ﷺ saw her attributes – physical and spiritual – he likened her to a celestial maiden of Paradise.

Umm Rummân رضي الله عنها was brought up in an area of Arabia known as Sarât. When she grew up she married a young man from her tribe named 'Abdullâh bin Hârith bin Sakhbarah Azdi. She had a son by him, who was named Tufail bin 'Abdullâh. They then moved to Makkah, where he became the partner and companion of Abu Bakr Siddeeq ﷺ. However, soon after this 'Abdullâh bin Hârith passed away, and his widow and son were left with no support. Seeing her precarious condition Abu Bakr Siddeeq ﷺ married her. Umm Rummân رضي الله عنها was very happy in her marriage and soon, a son,

'Abdur-Rahmân ؓ and a daughter, 'A'ishah رضي الله عنها were born. Before he came into the fold of Islâm, Abu Bakr Siddeeq ؓ was married to Qateelah bint Abdul-'Uzzâ by whom he already had a daughter Asmâ' رضي الله عنها, and a son, 'Abdullâh. Later in Madinah, Abu Bakr Siddeeq ؓ married Asmâ' bint 'Umais, and by this marriage he had a son, Muhammad bin Abu Bakr ؓ. Then he married Habîbah bint Khârejah and had a daughter whom he named Umm Kulthoom.

It is written in *Tabaqât Ibn Sa'd* that Umm Rummân رضي الله عنها accepted Islâm in the very early days in Makkah. She swore allegiance at the hand of the Prophet ﷺ himself and then migrated with the blessed group of emigrants.

When she witnessed the terrible atrocities committed by the Quraish against the Muslims she would suffer and weep for the innocent victims; but she gained courage when she saw the moral strength and exemplary sacrifice of her husband for the cause of Islâm. She drew inspiration from him and found peace in his presence.

The Prophet ﷺ also used to exhort his faithful followers not to waver, but to be patient and hold steadfast to their faith, for they would surely be rewarded with Paradise in the hereafter . Bilâl ؓ, the first *Mu'adhdhin* of Islâm, was often the worst sufferer. Both he and Khabbâb bin Aratt رضي الله عنهما were encouraged and inspired by the Prophet ﷺ; he told them how in the earlier ages those faithful to Allâh the Almighty also suffered. There were the faithful who did not recant even when their bodies were cut in two with a saw. When he saw the suffering of the family of Yâsir ؓ, he said to them:

> 'O family of Yâsir! Be patient, for your final destination and resting place will be Paradise.'

During this long period Umm Rummân رضي الله عنها remained the epitome of patience, forbearance, courage and bravery. Most of her time was spent in earnest supplications and prayers to Allâh. When she saw her husband's devoted efforts for the propagation of Islâm she expressed her admiration and gave him moral support. She devoted her time to nurturing her children in the traditions of Islâm. The Prophet ﷺ often used to visit the house of his illustrious Companion, Abu Bakr Siddeeq ؓ. He would advise Umm Rummân

Fâtimah bint Asad رضي الله عنها

رضي الله عنها to keep encouraging and instilling the love of goodness in 'A'ishah رضي الله عنها. Khadîjah رضي الله عنها passed away three years before the migration of the Prophet ﷺ to Madinah. The Prophet ﷺ spent a year without marrying . He then married 'A'ishah رضي الله عنها at the command of Allâh as delivered by the Angel Jibrîl عليه السلام.

One day he told 'A'ishah رضي الله عنها that on three consecutive nights he saw her in his dreams. The Angel Jibrîl brought a picture of hers wrapped in a silken cloth, and told him that this was an image of his bride. When he removed the cover he saw that it was her image. 'A'ishah رضي الله عنها was elated to hear that she was chosen to be the Prophet's wife by Allâh ﷻ Himself. Khawlah bint Hâkim told him there were two proposals for him, that of 'A'ishah رضي الله عنها bint Abu Bakr Siddeeq ؓ and Sau'dah bint Zam'ah رضي الله عنها. He accepted both, and thus Umm Rummân رضي الله عنها had the honor of becoming his mother-in-law.

When the Prophet ﷺ was ordered by Allâh ﷻ to migrate to Madinah he went to the house of his closest friend and Companion, Abu Bakr Siddeeq ؓ. Without any questions or hesitation he prepared to accompany the Prophet ﷺ. He packed a few things and took all the cash there was in the house. He left his father, wife and children in the trust and care of Allâh and set off for an unseen destination.

It was a very tough time for Umm Rummân رضي الله عنها: she was separated from her husband and there was a lack of money for household expenses, since he had taken all the available cash with him. But what predominated all other thoughts in her mind were supplications to Allâh ﷻ for the safe arrival of the Prophet ﷺ and her husband in Madinah. On reaching their destination safely, the Prophet ﷺ sent Zaid bin Hârithah and Abu Râfi' رضي الله عنهما to bring his family. Abu Bakr Siddeeq ؓ sent 'Abdullâh bin Uraiqit and wrote to his son 'Abdullâh to bring his family. Umm Rummân and 'A'ishah رضي الله عنهما got on one camel's back. On the way, the camel suddenly seemed out of control and started to jump and almost threw its riders. Umm Rummân رضي الله عنها was worried about her beloved daughter 'A'ishah رضي الله عنها and started calling out, *'O my daughter, O my dear little bride!'* Just then someone called out that they should let go of the reins, and when they did so the camel calmed down and stood still. So the mother and daughter were saved from the impending danger.

When they reached Madinah they stayed at the house of Abu Bakr Siddeeq ؓ arranged for his family. And it was from this house that 'A'ishah رضي الله عنها left as a bride to the Prophet's house. Thus this house became the focal point for the revelations of Allâh ﷻ. Umm Rummân رضي الله عنها expressed great happiness at the thought that her daughter would be one of those who joined the ranks of the blessed Mothers of the Believers. What other greater honor could she want for her family!

❖৻৵❖৻৵❖৻৵❖

When the Hypocrites, wrongfully accused 'A'ishah رضي الله عنها, all of Madinah seemed to have been gripped by a gigantic tremor and a wave of confusion swept through the Believers. How could they reconcile themselves to their Prophet's wife having committed a cardinal sin?

The whole of Madinah was flooded by this slanderous gossip, which reached 'A'ishah رضي الله عنها inadvertently from the mouth of Umm Mistah herself, whose son was the originator of this scandal. 'A'ishah رضي الله عنها was heartbroken and appalled at the sheer spite of the man. She took the permission of the Prophet ﷺ and went to her parents. They also corroborated the story she had heard and she could not stop the flood of tears. Her sympathetic and loving mother was also an image of grief.

Then the Prophet ﷺ, who was himself very upset, came to see her. When he saw her weeping he told her that if she had sinned she should ask Allâh for His forgiveness, because he is Merciful; if she had not sinned she should not grieve, for Allâh ﷻ would surely absolve her and forgive her. 'A'ishah رضي الله عنها asked her mother to respond to him, but her mother remained quiet. She then appealed to her father, Abu Bakr Siddeeq ؓ, to give a convincing reply to the Prophet ﷺ but he too remained silent. Finally she said that if she denied that she was guilty – and Allâh ﷻ knew she was innocent – Muhammad ﷺ would not believe her; if she admitted the guilt, may be he would be satisfied, but then her admission of guilt would be contrary to facts. The best answer would be the answer of the father of Yûsuf ﷺ, when he was helpless before his sons:

> "So patience is most fitting. And it is Allâh Whose help can be sought against that (lie) which you describe." (12:18)

Fâtimah bint Asad رضي الله عنها

Later, 'A'ishah رضي الله عنها recounted that she was so disturbed that day that even though she tried hard, she just could not remember the name of Ya`qub ﷺ, the father of Yûsuf ﷺ. Even as this conversation was being carried on the *Âyât* of clarification were revealed to the Prophet ﷺ. When the revelation was over he was covered in beads of perspiration; he then turned to 'A'ishah رضي الله عنها with a happy smile and recited the *Âyât*.

Her parents were proud and relieved; and they asked their daughter to thank her husband, but 'A'ishah رضي الله عنها replied that she was grateful to Allâh ﷻ for He exonerated her. This relief, with the specially revealed *Âyât* of Allâh ﷻ, increased her worth in the heart of her husband.

Umm Rummân رضي الله عنها was a lady who spent her nights and days in prayer, meditation and supplications to Allâh ﷻ. Her earnest desire was to win the pleasure of Allâh ﷻ and His Messenger ﷺ. She was a dutiful wife who stood by her husband at all times. She noted what her husband had to say about prayers. Once when he entered the house he found her praying and told her that the body should express an attitude of calmness and tranquility. A calm and still posture helped to perfect concentration in prayer, he said.

'Ali bin Bulbân Muqaddasi in his book *Tufah As-Siddeeq fi Fadhâ'il Abi Bakr Siddeeq* and Imâm Dhahabi in his book *Siyar A'lâm an-Nubalâ'* says that one day both Abu Bakr Siddeeq ؓ and his wife, Umm Rummân رضي الله عنها, went to visit the Prophet ﷺ. He asked them the purpose of the visit. They both simultaneously requested him to offer supplications to Allâh ﷻ for 'A'ishah رضي الله عنها.

Then he prayed to Allâh ﷻ to forgive 'A'ishah رضي الله عنها bint Abu Bakr for all her hidden and apparent shortcomings, such a forgiveness that would leave no sin. Both her parents looked very happy with this perfect supplication.

Then he told them that this was his prayer for all those who accepted Islâm after his being named Messenger of Allâh, and remained steadfast in their belief.

The Prophet ﷺ respected Umm Rummân رضي الله عنها very much, and she in turn tried her utmost to do things that pleased him. One day the Prophet ﷺ praised Khadîjah رضي الله عنها at great length by extolling her many virtues. 'A'ishah رضي الله عنها felt a very strong twinge of feminine jealousy; involuntarily she said that he was talking of Khadîjah رضي الله عنها as if there was no other woman on earth. The Prophet ﷺ did not like this at all, and his face reddened with displeasure. When Umm Rummân رضي الله عنها heard of this she went to the Prophet ﷺ and tried to apologise for 'A'ishah رضي الله عنها telling him that she was still very young that he should not take her seriously. Very curtly, addressing 'A'ishah رضي الله عنها, he asked her if she had not said that there was no other woman on the face of the earth besides Khadîjah رضي الله عنها? He swore by Allâh ﷻ that this great lady had believed him when the tribe of 'A'ishah رضي الله عنها had denied that he was the Messenger and Prophet of Allâh. She gave him the great gift of children, which was not the case with 'A'ishah رضي الله عنها.

Umm Rummân رضي الله عنها listened in complete silence because she knew that all that he spoke was by the command and revelation of Allâh ﷻ. He did not speak of his own accord, his words were always based on revelations of Allâh.

❖∞❖∞❖∞❖

Tradition has it that Umm Rummân رضي الله عنها passed away in the sixth year after *Hijrah*. During her burial, the Prophet ﷺ asked Allâh ﷻ to forgive her. Doubtless this was a great honor for her. It was on this occasion that he said that if any person wanted to see a beautiful celestial maiden of Paradise, he could see Umm Rummân رضي الله عنها. Thus these words are an indication that she will, Allâh Willing, be in Paradise in the hereafter. May Allâh ﷻ fill her grave with radiance. Another tradition regarding the death of Umm Rummân رضي الله عنها is however more reliable. It says that she died after the passing away of the Prophet ﷺ.

Indeed the words of Allâh ﷻ are true:

> "*Verily, those who believe and do righteous deeds, and humble themselves before their Lord, they will be dwellers of Paradise to dwell therein forever.*" (11:23)

Sumayyah bint Khabbât رضي الله عنها

> The Prophet ﷺ said:
> "*O family of Yâsir! Be patient because your destination is Paradise.*"

Sumayyah bint Khabbât رضي الله عنها

Three brothers set out from Yemen to go to Makkah. They had heard about this city and wanted to experience its culture and to partake of its various social activities. One was named Yâsir and the other two were named Hârith and Mâlik. The latter two left to return home to Yemen after some time, but Yâsir liked to live there so much, that he decided to stay on permanently. According to the custom of the time he got the sponsorship and support of Abu Hudhaifah bin 'Abdullâh Makhzoomi, and became his companion and partner. As they got to know each other better, they took a liking to each other. Abu Hudhaifah had a very intelligent and sensible slave girl called Sumayyah. In due course of time she got married to Yâsir.

It was a happy marriage and soon they had a son whom they named 'Ammâr. Abu Hudhaifah was a very kind, loving and generous man, and he liberated the family from his bondage; but he continued to keep good terms with them and very often helped them with money as well. Yâsir had two more sons, whom he named 'Abdullâh and Hareeth. The latter was murdered before the advent of Islâm, and with this tragedy it seemed as if ill fortune started to haunt the family.

Sumayyah bint Khabbât رضي الله عنها was one of the first seven people to be enlightened by Islâm and swear allegiance to the Prophet ﷺ. She is among the foremost of the greatest women Companions. Islâm is unique in the sense that a person's value does not depend on color, race, language, sex or nationality. The norms are purity of heart and goodwill towards all. As Allâh The Almighty says:

"Verily, the most honorable of you with Allâh is that (believer) who is most pious." (49:13)

Thus, a person who wishes for his fellow human beings what he wishes for himself, who is kind to his fellow human beings for the sake of Allâh ﷻ, is the one who fulfills the conditions of the test set by Him.

The seven people who first accepted Islâm were the following:

1. Abu Bakr Siddeeq ﷺ.
2. 'Ali bin Abi Tâlib ﷺ.
3. Khadîjah رضي الله عنها.
4. Zaid bin Hârithah ﷺ.
5. Sumayyah bint Khabbât رضي الله عنها.
6. 'Ammâr bin Yâsir ﷺ.
7. Bilâl bin Abi Rabâh ﷺ.

The Quraish of Makkah could not harm the Prophet ﷺ because of the power and position of his uncle Abu Tâlib. Abu Bakr Siddeeq ﷺ was also a very powerful man because of the wealth of his tribe and his own personal influence. But the common Muslim -- whether man or woman -- was not spared any imaginable torture or torment by them.

❖∞❖∞❖∞❖∞❖

Sumayyah bint Khabbât رضي الله عنها, her husband and her son 'Ammâr were very often the targets for the cruelty of the Quraish. On one occasion as the Prophet ﷺ was passing by the marketplace he saw all three members of the family being put through the most excruciating form of torture possible. But he was so helpless, that there was no way he could rescue them. He could only console them and said:

'Be patient O family of Yâsir!, for your final destination is Paradise.'

'Uthmân ﷺ also narrated that the Prophet ﷺ used to say these words to comfort the family. Once 'Ammâr managed to escape and reach the Prophet ﷺ. He then asked him when this persecution of the innocent Muslims would end, and when would they would be able to live peacefully. The Prophet ﷺ then comforted him with a prayer to Allâh ﷻ to protect and save the family of Yâsir from the fire of Hell.

Abu Jahl subjected Sumayyah bint Khabbât رضي الله عنها to the worst kind of torture, but she did not waver even for a second and remained as steady as a rock. He tried to pressure her, cajole her and threaten her to recant, but she bluntly refused. He could not accept the fact that she could resist him so stubbornly, and in a rage thrust a spear into her. This proved to be a fatal blow, and she died. Thus, Sumayyah bint Khabbât رضي الله عنها had the distinction of being the first woman martyr of Islâm. This incident took place seven years before the *Hijrah*. Then her husband also fell victim to the torture of the Quraish, and he too was martyred. After the martyrdom of both his parents, 'Ammâr took a special place in the affections of the Prophet ﷺ. He used to address him lovingly as Ibn Sumayyah رضي الله عنها. He often spoke of the family of Yâsir in the highest terms of praise.

'Abdullâh bin Mas'ood ؓ says the Prophet ﷺ once said that when dissensions and disputes appeared among the people Ibn Sumayyah would always stand by the right and just.

This family sacrificed their lives, all in order to nourish the truth, and to earn rewards for the hereafter. It is about people like these that Allâh the Almighty says:

> *"Verily, Allâh has purchased of the believers their lives and their properties for (the price) that theirs shall be the Paradise. They fight in Allâh's cause, so they kill (others) and are killed. It is promise in truth which is binding on Him in the Taurât and the Injîl and the Qur'ân. And who is truer to His covenant than Allâh? Then rejoice in the bargain that you have concluded. That is the supreme success."* (9:111)

Umm Harâm bint Milhân رضي الله عنها

> The Prophet ﷺ once said:
>
> *"From among my Ummah (followers) an army will sail on the sea as a king sits on his throne."*
>
> Umm Harâm asked him if she would be one among them. He answered that she would be one of the foremost among them.

Umm Harâm bint Milhân رضي الله عنها

Umm Harâm رضي الله عنها came from a noble family. Her sister was the mother of Anas bin Mâlik ﷺ. Her two brothers, Harâm bin Milhân and Saleem bin Milhân, took part in the Battles of Badr and Uhud. She was also related by marriage to Abu Talhah ﷺ, another distinguished Companion. Her husband was 'Amr bin Qais bin Zaid ﷺ, and her son was Qais bin 'Amr bin Qais ﷺ – these were two eminent Companions of the Prophet ﷺ who were martyred at the Battle of Badr. After her husband's death she married 'Ubâdah bin Sâmit ﷺ, a distinguished General of the Muslim army. She had a son by this marriage, Muhammad bin 'Ubâdah bin Sâmit.

'Ubâdah bin Sâmit ﷺ was a member of all the three delegations which had the honor of going to Makkah before the migration to personally pledge allegiance to Allâh ﷻ and His Messenger. The first delegation had six members; the second had twelve and the third had seventy-two members.

'Ubâdah bin Sâmit ﷺ was an exemplary husband and a loving father — not just to his own children, but also to 'Abdullâh bin 'Amr who had been born to Umm Harâm رضي الله عنها by her first husband. Muhammad bin 'Ubâdah ﷺ was a member of the congregation when the Âyah to change the direction (Qiblah) for prayers to the Ka'bah from Masjid Al-Aqsâ was revealed. Thus he had the privilege of facing both the 'Qiblahs' in this one prayer.

Generosity, benevolence and the spirit of sacrifice were an innate part of Umm Harâm's nature. Her ambition was to be martyred in the cause of Islâm, and in pursuit of this consuming desire she left no stone unturned. She lived on the outskirts of Madinah, in the small town of Qubâ. When the Prophet ﷺ migrated to Madinah, he stopped at Qubâ to rest before proceeding. She was the first among the *Ansâr* women to not only accept Islâm, but also announce it; and she did so before the migration of the Prophet ﷺ. Umm Harâm رضي الله عنها was a very wise and balanced person, God-fearing, just and pious. She held a very high position among the women of the *Ansâr*. The Prophet ﷺ would often visit her house and rest there if he was tired. Whenever the Prophet ﷺ stopped at her place she felt grateful for his presence and she considered serving him to be the greatest honor.

Anas bin Mâlik ؓ narrated that once he was at his house when the Prophet ﷺ came there. His mother and her sister were also there. He told them to rise and he would lead them in a special prayer; it was not the time for one of the obligatory prayers. After prayers he made a supplication to Allâh ﷻ to bless the family both in this world and the hereafter.

Traditions attributed to Umm Harâm رضي الله عنها have been quoted by such noteworthy Companions of the Prophet ﷺ such as 'Ubâdah bin Sâmit, Anas bin Mâlik, 'Umair bin Aswad, 'Atâ bin Yasâr and Ya'li bin Shaddâd bin Aws رضي الله عنهم. The feelings of love, respect and reverence for the Prophet ﷺ almost reached the peak of perfection in the heart of Umm Harâm رضي الله عنها. Whenever he visited either her house or the house of her sister Umm Sulaim رضي الله عنها, their happiness knew no bounds. She would prepare special delicacies for him and arrange a comfortable bed for him to rest. The atmosphere was such that the Prophet ﷺ too would feel a real sense of peace and joy when he called on her. When he was asked if there was a special reason why he visited her house so often, he replied that he felt a great sense of pity for the family ever since he saw two of her brothers being martyred in the Battle of Bi'r Ma'oonah. Ever since then, he said that he visited her to see to her needs and comfort her.

Umm Harâm bint Milhân رضي الله عنها

The *Ansâr* were noted for their spirit of sacrifice, generosity and hospitality, and Umm Harâm رضي الله عنها was an embodiment of this spirit. This spirit is glorified in the Words of the Noble Qur'ân:

> "And those who, before them (emigrants), had homes (in Madinah) and had adopted the Faith, love those who emigrate to them, and have no jealousy in their breasts for that which they have been given, and give them (emigrants) preference over themselves even though they were in need of that. And whosoever is saved from his own covetousness, such are they who will be the successful." (59:9)

Allâh The Almighty was so pleased with the sympathy, generosity and sacrifice displayed by the *Ansâr* for the migrants of Makkah that He immortalized their selfless character in His Qur'ân. There was no difference between men or women in this display of selflessness. And it seemed Umm Harâm رضي الله عنها was blessed in more than ample measure with this typical generosity of spirit. The family was fortunate to have the blessings and goodwill of the Prophet ﷺ. What more can one ask for in this world? When he passed away he was very happy with her for the exceptional services she rendered.

During the caliphate of 'Uthmân bin 'Affân, in the year 27AH, Mu'âwiyah bin Abu Sufyân ؓ was given permission to conquer the Island of Cyprus. To reach there a naval force was readied. This was the first time in Islâmic history that such a measure was taken. 'Ubâdah bin Sâmit ؓ was accompanied by his wife Umm Harâm رضي الله عنها, accompanying Mu'âwiyâh with his wife Fâkhtah bint Qurdhah رضي الله عنهما.

'Umair bin Aswad 'Ansi writes that he visited 'Ubâdah ؓ who was staying in the coastal area of Hamas. He met Umm Harâm رضي الله عنها who told him that she had heard the Prophet ﷺ say that some of his people would journey on the sea for the purpose of *Jihâd* (war in the cause of Allâh). She asked him if she would be one among them, and he replied in the affirmative. She was really elated at this because it had been her earnest desire to take part in *Jihâd*. By the grace of Allâh ﷻ the Muslims were victorious. After her journey by sea Umm Harâm رضي الله عنها got on to a mule to travel on land, but unfortunately the mule bacame frightened of something and she fell down. She sustained a serious neck injury that cost her her life. Thus she attained the martyrdom which she always desired. She was buried in Cyprus.

Thus, Umm Harâm was the fortunate woman Companion who took part in this naval venture and attained martyrdom, and proved herself worthy of the blessed tidings of the Prophet ﷺ about her place in Paradise.

May Allâh be pleased with them and they with Him.

Asmâ' bint Abu Bakr Siddeeq رضي الله عنها

> The Prophet ﷺ said:
> "*You will be bestowed two waist collars in exchange of one.*"

Asmâ' bint Abu Bakr Siddeeq رضي الله عنها

She was related to the Prophet ﷺ by his marriage to her sister 'A'ishah رضي الله عنها. Her father, Abu Bakr Siddeeq ؓ, was the closest Companion and trusted friend of Muhammad ﷺ. Her grand- mother was Umm Al-Khair Salmâ bint Sakhr. Her father's sisters were such eminent women Companions as Fardah, Qareebah and Umm 'Amer رضي الله عنهن. Her paternal grandfather was Abu Quhâfah. Her husband, Zubair bin 'Awwâm ؓ, was a Companion of the Prophet ﷺ. Her son, 'Abdullâh bin Zubair ؓ, was another eminent Companion of the Prophet ﷺ. She was the lady who bravely and calmly carried the burden of the Prophet's secret migration to Madinah in the dead of night with her father. She was the one who packed up their food and other little items necessary for that historic journey. On that occasion the Prophet ﷺ blessed her with the auspicious news of Paradise in the hereafter. When the enemy came to question her, she remained calm and did not betray any nervousness or fear by so much as the blinking of an eye. Her life is worthy of study, coming as she did from a background where each and every member of the family was a trusted confidant and Companion of the Prophet ﷺ.

Asmâ' رضي الله عنها was born twenty-seven years before the migration of the Prophet ﷺ to Madinah. Her mother's name was Qateelah bint Abdul 'Uzzâ and her father, Abu Bakr ؓ, married her before the advent of Islâm; Asmâ' رضي الله عنها was born when he was only twenty-one years old. Asmâ' رضي الله عنها and 'Abdullâh ﷺ were born of this marriage. For a long time her mother did not accept Islâm; finally after the conquest of Makkah she pledged allegiance to the Prophet ﷺ. Asmâ' رضي الله عنها entered the fold of Islâm because of the influence and teachings of her father.

Piety, farsightedness, intelligence, courage and integrity, generosity – all the qualities praised by Islâm could be found in this one person. When her father and the Prophet ﷺ took refuge in the Cave of Thawr after leaving Makkah to migrate to Madinah, it was she who went in the wilderness to deliver fresh food to them. As soon as they left on their journey, Abu Jahl came to the house of Abu Bakr Siddeeq ﷺ looking for them, breathing fire and fury. He asked her where her father was? She answered that she did not know. He gave proof of his barbaric nature by slapping her hard; but so as not to betray her secret she faced him with steadfastness, courage and tolerance.

Asmâ' رضي الله عنها came to be known by the title *Dhât An-Natâqayn*. There is an interesting little episode about how she got this name. In Arabic the belt, or girdle worn by women around the waist is called a *Natâq*. When the Prophet ﷺ and Abu Bakr Siddeeq ﷺ prepared to set off for Madinah, Asmâ' رضي الله عنها packed the eatables into a leather bag, but there was no rope with which she could tie up the mouth of the bag. So she divided her girdle into two and used one part to tie up the leather bag. The Prophet ﷺ blessed her and said that in place of this one girdle that she sacrificed, she would get two in Paradise. So, he implied that she would go to Paradise. In this manner the Prophet ﷺ gave the news of a glorious hereafter to his faithful Companions.

After her father and the Prophet ﷺ left, Asmâ' رضي الله عنها was left with her blind and aged grandfather, Abu Quhâfah. When he realized that his son had migrated he was sad and worried whether he had left any money to meet his family's expenses. Asma' رضي الله عنها narrated that they had about four or five thousand Dinârs in the house and her father had taken it all for the expenses of the journey. But she comforted the old man saying there was plenty in the house, and

Asmâ' bint Abu Bakr Siddeeq رضي الله عنها

nothing was lacking. In order to convince him she collected some pebbles that were of the size of Dinârs; these she put in a pot and spread a cloth over them. Then she guided his old hands over the cloth; Abu Quhâfah was very pleased that his son had not neglected them. Asmâ' رضي الله عنها had done this for the old man's peace of mind; but in truth Abu Bakr Siddeeq ؓ with a strong faith in Allâh, had taken all that he owned to spend in the way of Allâh and His Messenger ﷺ.

Her husband, Zubair bin 'Awwâm ؓ, the Prophet's friend and Companion was the son of Safiyyah bint 'Abdul Muttalib. When he migrated to Madinah, he owned a house in which he lived, a sword and a horse. It was the duty of Asmâ' رضي الله عنها to tend to the horse and feed him. One day she was walking home with a bundle of hay on her head when the Prophet ﷺ saw her. He immediately made his camel sit down so that he could let her ride. But she was embarrassed and thought it would displease her husband who was a very proud man. So she refused the offer and preferred to walk. When she told her husband about it, he said she should have got on to the camel, it would have been less troublesome than walking with a bundle of hay.

When Asmâ' رضي الله عنها was migrating to Madinah, near the valley of Qubâ she went into labor, and gave birth to a son 'Abdullâh bin Zubair. This was a very special occasion for the Muslims. For a very long time no sons had been born among their people. The disbelievers were very happy and they used to gossip among themselves that now the Muslims would be rooted out. All the Muslims were excited, as was the Prophet ﷺ. He picked up the baby in his arms and congratulated the family. Then he bit off a little piece of a date, softened it in his mouth and gave it to the baby. This was an honor that made the family feel very proud.

When 'Abdullâh bin Zubair ؓ grew up he was the personification of learning, understanding and courage. Later his mother came to live with him and when he moved to Makkah she also accompanied him. He did not accept right of the Banu Umayyah to the caliphate and succeeded in winning the support of most people since they acknowledged him to be a powerful, learned and brave man. However, when 'Abdul Malik bin Marwân ascended the throne, he took over some of the provinces. He sent Hajjâj bin Yûsuf as his representative to Hijâz. Hajjâj took command of the Syrian forces and besieged Makkah, attacking it from all sides; following which an intense battle ensued between the two forces.

At this critical juncture, 'Abdullâh bin Zubair ﷺ went to see his mother. When she told him that she was sick, he replied that human beings could find peace and rest after death. She smilingly asked him if he wished her to die. She said she wanted him to live and wanted to live herself, because she had to see the end of his struggle. If he were martyred she would accept it with patience and fortitude, and if he routed his enemy in this battle she would be happy.

A desperate battle was waged in Makkah and 'Abdullâh bin Zubair's army was facing defeat. He went to see his mother who was at the mosque and asked her if he should surrender. She replied that if he was in the right he should not worry about dying. He said he feared that the enemy would mutilate his body after death. She answered it was irrelevant what they did with the body. Once a goat is slaughtered the skinning cannot cause it any pain. She added that fear of death should not stand in the way of a truly courageous man. Death with honor was better than a life of peace with dishonor. A peace based on humiliation did not suit a young hero like him. So 'Abdullâh bin Zubair ﷺ returned to the battlefield with renewed ardour and advanced through the ranks fighting courageously; but since his army was outnumbered he died the death of a martyr. The cruel Hajjâj bin Yûsuf hung up his body for all to see, and did not take it down even after three days. On the third day the aged mother went to try and recover the body of her valiant and noble son. Since she had lost her eyesight due to age she could only feel her way around. Sighing, she asked, if the time had not yet come for her son to get down from his horse. She faced this great torture with characteristic strength and fortitude.

When Hajjâj saw the mother standing near the son's body he sent a messenger to bring her to him. She answered with scornful hatred that she would not go to see her son's murderer. When Hajjâj bin Yûsuf got the message, he was filled with rage and told the messenger to go and tell her that if she did not come by herself, she would be dragged into his presence by her hair. She answered him with supreme indifference that she would not go to see the despicable ignoble man; this was her final decision, and he could do anything he wished. When Hajjâj saw his threats were ineffective he went to see her. He asked her if she had seen what he had made of her son. She replied that he had ruined her son's life in this world, but her son had ruined him for eternity. She added that she had heard the Prophet ﷺ saying that a man would appear from the tribe of Banu Thaqeef who would be a liar and a cruel and ignoble barbarian. Today she had seen him for herself. Hajjâj bin Yûsuf left silently.

One day when she went to the Haram (sanctuary) in Makkah, she heard Hajjâj bin Yûsuf addressing the gathering from the pulpit. Even in her extreme old age she had not lost her spirit; boldly she went and stood next to him. When he saw her he said her son had spread disbelief and atheism in the House of Allâh ﷻ and so He gave him a terrible punishment. Asmâ' رضي الله عنها promptly answered that her son was never an atheist; he was a pious, learned man who always prayed to Allâh ﷻ, worked for the welfare of the Muslim *Ummah* and was a standard bearer of integrity and honesty. *"You, on the other hand, are known to be a liar, a hypocrite and a treacherous man,"* she said, adding that he should fear the wrath of Allâh ﷻ, for it hit man when he was least expecting it to strike. Hajjâj, pretending he had not heard her, continued his speech and said,

> *"I admit that 'Abdullâh bin Zubair was an excellent member of the Ummah, but he had a burning desire for power. Thus he created differences among the people and caused trouble right there in the House of Allâh ﷻ, so he met a terrible end. You know Adam ﷺ was much greater and more highly respected as a Prophet of Allâh than 'Abdullâh bin Zubair. Allâh ﷻ gave him a tranquil and peaceful life in Paradise. But when he disobeyed the Command of Allâh and ate the fruit of the forbidden tree he was thrown out of Paradise. Doubtlessly Paradise is a far better place than the sanctuary of the Ka'bah."*

Then in a thundering voice he asked the people to rise up and get ready for prayers. 'Abdullâh bin 'Umar ؓ was present and he said in a loud voice,

"O Hajjâj! if I call you a hypocrite and a liar it will not be contrary to facts. I swear by the Majesty and the Wrath of Allâh ﷻ that 'Abdullâh bin Zubair ؓ never took any step in his entire life that went contrary to the injunctions of Allâh ﷻ. I now testify in public that 'Abdullâh bin Zubair ؓ was a Muttaqi (Allâh-fearing man) who fasted and prayed at nights. He always stood by what was right and stood by it."

Then he went to the body of 'Abdullâh bin Zubair ؓ that was still hanging there and in a grief-stricken trembling voice said,

"Peace be upon you O Abu Khubaib, Peace be upon you O Abu Khabeeb."

Khabaib was the family name of 'Abdullâh bin Zubair ؓ. Then looking at the body he said that he warned 'Abdullâh bin Zubair ؓ not to get involved in a struggle for power. The most respected people often lost their prestige struggling for power. Then he prayed to Allâh ﷻ to grant him a place in His Merciful Paradise.

After a few days Hajjâj threw the body into the graveyard on the instructions of 'Abdul Malik bin Marwân. When Asmâ' رضي الله عنها heard this news she sent for the body, had it bathed and had the congregational prayer for the dead conducted. Finally, she buried her beloved son's body.

Hajjâj bin Yûsuf received a message from the court of Syria saying that he should personally visit Asmâ' رضي الله عنها and ask her if she needed anything. The government would be happy to oblige her. Hajjâj went to her house to pass on the message of the governor of 'Abdul Malik bin Marwân. Asmâ' رضي الله عنها flew into a terrible rage; she told him in a thundering voice that she did not need anything and shouted at him to get out of her house; she said she kicked his offer in his face. She asked if the shameless scoundrel had come to prick her wounds. She said he was a burden on this earth, and she considered him an unfortunate and impious man.

Asmâ' bint Abu Bakr Siddeeq رضي الله عنها

Asmâ' رضي الله عنها would pray with full concentration. Zubair bin 'Awwâm ؓ relates that when he came home one day he saw her praying and weeping; she kept on repeating these words from the Qur'ân again and again:

"*Allâh has blessed us and saved us from the torture of the burning winds."* (52:27)

When he saw her thus lost in the presence of Allâh ﷻ, he left the house and went to the market. He came back much later and still found her still lost in prayer.

Asmâ' رضي الله عنها had a very sharp memory. If she heard anything even once she would never forget it. Like 'A'ishah, Umm Salamah and Asmâ' bint Yazîd bin Sakan Ansâriyah رضي الله عنهن, she also has many *Ahâdîth* attributed to her. Many Companions and successors would come to her for guidance and verification of *Ahâdîth*. 'Abdullâh bin Zubair, 'Urwah bin Zubair, 'Abdullâh bin 'Abbâs, Fâtimah bint Manthar bin Zubair and 'Abdullâh bin Keesân رضي الله عنهم are some of the noteworthy ones.

Asmâ' bint Abu Bakr Siddeeq رضي الله عنها died in the year 73 after *Hijrah*. She was almost a hundred years old, but even at that age she had a full set of teeth and a sharp memory.

May Allâh be pleased with them and they with Him.

Umm Sulaim bint Milhân Al-Ansâriyah رضي الله عنها

> The Prophet ﷺ said:
>
> "When I entered Paradise, I heard someone's footsteps – it was explained to me that she was Ghameesâ bint Milhân."
>
> Ghameesâ is the name of Umm Sulaim Al-Ansâriyah رضي الله عنها. She is also called Rumaysâh', Sahlah, and Ramlah but her nickname overcame the name.

Umm Sulaim bint Milhân Al-Ansâriyah رضي الله عنها

Learning, courage, patience and fortitude, steadfastness of purpose and generosity of heart and mind – these are the qualities common to all the women Companions who are the subject of this book.

Umm Sulaim رضي الله عنها is no exception. She too came from an illustrious family who sacrificed its all for Islâm. Her son was the famous Companion Anas bin Mâlik ؓ and her brother was the eminent Companion Harâm bin Milhân ؓ.

Her first marriage was unhappy and there were constant quarrels between husband and wife because she became a Muslim. Her husband, Mâlik bin Nadhr, tried his very best to make her recant and give up the new religion to which she had vowed allegiance, but he failed and she remained loyal to her new faith. On the other hand she started persuading her son, Anas ؓ, as well to convert to Islâm, under the most trying circumstances. Mâlik bin Nadhr accused her of spoiling his son. However, Umm Sulaim replied that far from spoiling him, she was teaching him the path to true and everlasting success in the Hereafter. Her persistence finally paid off, and Anas read the words signifying acceptance of Allâh as the only Deity worthy of being worshipped and Muhammad ﷺ as His Messenger.

There were frequent violent scenes in the house, but Umm Sulaim stood her ground, patiently and calmly. She told him that he just could not perceive the nature of the treasure she found. She said that it was a treasure for all time, a light that illuminated her heart. Her husband said she was without any religion, and she replied courageously that by accepting Islâm she had accepted the True religion and hence she would be successful even in the Hereafter.

Finally her husband left her and migrated to Syria where he was murdered. Dedicating her son to the service of the Prophet ﷺ, she requested him to pray for her son. The Prophet ﷺ then prayed for Anas ؓ for increase in knowledge and riches. The *Ansâri* ladies used to call her Sahlah, Ghameesâ', Rumaysâh' and Ramlah, but finally she came to be known only as Umm Sulaim.

In Madinah there was a handsome young man called Abu Talhah, who was also the leader of his tribe. He had not yet converted to Islâm, though many people were influenced by the teachings of Mus'ab bin 'Umair ؓ. Abu Talhah knew that the widow, Umm Sulaim رضي الله عنها, had many admirable qualities. Her integrity, loyalty and courage – all these appealed to him, and he sent her a proposal of marriage. She said it was not possible because she was a Muslim and he was a disbeliever. When he insisted she asked him what kind of a man was he: sometimes he worshipped trees growing in the earth, at other times he worshipped stone idols which other people carved out. She asked him if he had ever considered how these things could solve his problems when they were themselves helpless.

When Abu Talhah heard these arguments he had no answer. He tried his best to persuade her, but she was adamant. She told him that normally a proposal from a man of his stature would not be rejected, but she was helpless. She had dedicated her life to Islâm and he was, up to that time, deprived of this great blessing. Finally, he asked her if she would marry him if he converted to Islâm. She was very happy at this; she said the *Mahr* (dowry) for her would be his acceptance of Islâm.

Umm Sulaim رضي الله عنها then told Anas ؓ to arrange for her marriage. Thâbit bin Aslam Bannâni, the famous successor and scholar says this was an excellent *Mahr* and unique in the history of Islâm. The Prophet ﷺ often used to visit her and prayed for prosperity and the blessings of Allâh for her.

After her husband's murder in Syria she dedicated her son, Anas ؓ to the service of the Prophet ﷺ. Anas ؓ lived the next ten years of his life in his service, and these were the best years of his life. Umm Sulaim رضي الله عنها requested the Prophet ﷺ to supplicate to Allâh ﷻ for an increase in knowledge and for his prosperity, both in this world and the next. And Allâh ﷻ answered his prayers in ample measure. Anas ؓ

Umm Sulaim bint Milhân Al-Ansâriyah رضي الله عنها

lived to the age of a hundred and three and had eighty children. He had a magnificent palace in Basrah and huge beautiful gardens. He was a fastidious man who loved to dress well and dye his hair with henna. Among his sons, many became learned scholars. After his death he became an heir to the gardens of Paradise.

Umm Sulaim رضي الله عنها had a happy second marriage and soon the couple was blessed with a son, Abu 'Umair. One day the Prophet ﷺ visited the house and found Abu 'Umair looking very dejected. He asked why the little boy was upset. Umm Sulaim رضي الله عنها told him that his pet bird, which he loved to play with, had died. The Prophet ﷺ caressed him and tried to console him lovingly.

After some time Abu 'Umair fell sick, and one night his temperature shot up very high and he passed away. Umm Sulaim رضي الله عنها displayed exemplary patience and control. She did not inform anyone or scream and shout in her grief. She did not want to upset her husband when he came home after a hard day's work. On his return home, he asked her how the child was and she told him he was better than before. Then she served him dinner and chatted with him. When he had enjoyed himself in her company in peace and tranquility, late in the night she brought up the topic. She said she wanted to ask him a question. He asked her what she wanted to know. She asked him whether if a person entrusted one with something, and then came to claim it, should one return it? He answered that certainly one should return it gladly. Then she took him to the room where the son was lying in a peaceful eternal sleep. She removed the sheet from his face and said in a trembling voice that Allâh ﷻ had taken back the son He had entrusted to their care.

Abu Talhah ؓ was shocked and asked her why she had not informed him as soon as he had come home. In the morning they went to see the Prophet ﷺ and told him what happened the previous night. He prayed for Allâh's blessings and prosperity for the couple. And soon another son was born to them. Anas ؓ carried him in his lap to the Prophet ﷺ; he softened a piece of a date and gave it to the newborn, and named him 'Abdullâh. He prayed that Allâh ﷻ grant him prosperity. And by the grace of Allâh ﷻ when he grew up and married he had nine sons; all of them were memorizers of the Qur'ân.

Anas ﷺ narrates that his mother had a goat. One day she made *ghee* (clarified butter) from milk and collected it in a little leather bowl. When it was full she sent it as a gift for the Prophet ﷺ with her adopted daughter. The Prophet ﷺ told his family to empty the bowl and return it with the little girl. She brought back the empty bowl and hung it by a nail on the kitchen wall.

Umm Sulaim رضي الله عنها saw that the bowl was still hanging and it was full – in fact it was overflowing and dripping. She asked her daughter why she did not carry out her instructions. The little girl said that she had taken the *ghee* to the Prophet's house as instructed and brought back the empty bowl and hung it. Umm Sulaim رضي الله عنها was amazed by this mystery.

She went to the Prophet's house and told him about this strange incident. He said the little girl brought the gift which he accepted. And she left his place with an empty bowl.

Umm Sulaim رضي الله عنها swore by Allâh ﷻ Who sent him as a Messenger of the one True Religion that the bowl was full and dripping even then. The Prophet ﷺ then told her that she should not be amazed; she had sent a gift for Allâh's Prophet ﷺ, so He in turn had sent a gift for her. She should eat it and feed others also with it. Umm Sulaim رضي الله عنها says she emptied this bowl of *ghee* into a larger vessel. It lasted them for two months and others also ate from it.

Anas ﷺ narrates that one day Abu Talhah ﷺ came home and told Umm Sulaim رضي الله عنها that the Prophet ﷺ sounded very weak, possibly he was hungry. If there was some food in the house they could have the honor of having him over for a meal. She answered that she had some bread wrapped up in cloth. Abu Talhah ﷺ went to the mosque and invited the Prophet ﷺ to join him.

He accepted and invited the people sitting there to join him at the house of Abu Talhah ﷺ. All of them rose to go with the Prophet ﷺ. When Abu Talhah ﷺ saw this he became nervous, because he did not have enough food for so many people. When he went home he expressed this fear to his wife Umm Sulaim رضي الله عنها. She smiled and told him not to worry; they would just put out all the food they had in the house. And this was what she did. The Prophet ﷺ came in and

Umm Sulaim bint Milhân Al-Ansâriyah رضي الله عنها

made a supplication to Allâh ﷻ for plenitude. Then he asked Abu Talhah ؓ to call in ten people from outside. So ten people came in to a satisfying meal. After they finished he asked Abu Talhah ؓ to call in ten more. And so it went on till about seventy or eighty had taken their fill of the food. And there was some still left over!

When the Prophet got married to Zainab bint Jahsh رضي الله عنها, Umm Sulaim رضي الله عنها made a special dish of dates and *ghee* and sent it to him as a gift. And after the Battle of Khaybar when he married Safiyyah رضي الله عنها it was Umm Sulaim رضي الله عنها who dressed her up as a bride. She also played a very active role in the battlefields of Islâm. Anas ؓ says that in the Battle of Uhud his mother and 'A'ishah رضي الله عنها used to fill leather bottles with water and give it to the thirsty wounded soldiers. Umm Sulaim رضي الله عنها was pregnant at the time but that did not deter her in any way. She took an active part in the Battle of Hunain as well. She carried a spear and when Abu Talhah ؓ saw this he told the Prophet ﷺ about it. He asked her why she was carrying a spear. She answered that if any enemy soldier came before her she would slit his belly. The Prophet ﷺ smiled at her spirit.

Anas ؓ narrated that once the Prophet ﷺ came to visit them when his mother, her sister and he was at home. He told them that he would lead the prayer in their house that day. After praying he made special supplications to Allâh ﷻ to bless them, both in this world and in the hereafter.

Anas ؓ reported that the Prophet ﷺ used to visit them often. When someone asked him for the reason, he said he felt pity for Umm Sulaim and her sister ever since he saw her brother, Harâm bin Milhân ؓ killed before his eyes. He participated in the two crucial battles of Badr and Uhud. In the year 4 after *Hijrah* he was fighting in the Battle of B'ir Ma'oonah, when the enemy took an opportune moment to trap him and hit him from the back with a spear which pierced through his heart. His last words have become immortal in Islâmic history. He said,

" *I swear by the Sustainer of the Ka'bah I have become successful.*"

His brother Sulaim bin Milhân ؓ was also martyred in the same battle.

In *Sahîh Muslim,* the *Book of Fadhâ'il* talks about the beads of perspiration of the Prophet ﷺ. One afternoon the Prophet ﷺ went to visit Umm Sulaim رضي الله عنها; she was out and he dropped off to sleep while waiting for her. When she came home she found him sleeping and in the heat his perspiration was dripping on a small piece of leather. She was very happy to see him in her house and started collecting the beads of perspiration in a small bottle to preserve them. The Prophet ﷺ woke up to find her doing this. He asked her what she was doing. She replied she was collecting the drops of his perspiration to put them into some perfume. If the Prophet ﷺ passed on a road or street he left a trail of perfume in the atmosphere and people would sense that he had passed that way. When Anas ؓ realized he was dying he made a will that some of these drops should be added to the water with which his body would be bathed.

On the occasion of the final pilgrimage, when the Prophet ﷺ shaved his head, Abu Talhah ؓ collected his hair and took it back to Madinah. There he gave it to Umm Sulaim رضي الله عنها to preserve it. She put it away safely as a memento.

Anas ؓ mentioned that one day when the Prophet ﷺ visited their house he took a drink of water from a leather bowl kept in the courtyard. His mother cut out the section that his lips had touched and preserved it as well.

On another occasion when he visited them Umm Sulaim offered him dates and *ghee*. He said she should put them away as he was fasting that day. He stood in a corner of the room to pray, then he spent a long time making supplications to Allâh ﷻ to bless the members of the family both in this world and the next. Umm Sulaim رضي الله عنها then requested him to pray for her son. He prayed so long for his welfare both here and in the Hereafter that Anas ؓ felt he must have asked Allâh ﷻ for the best possible good for him in both this world and the next.

Once the Prophet ﷺ told them that when he entered Paradise, he could hear someone's footsteps ahead of him. When he asked who it was, he was told that was Ghameesâ' bint Milhân, or Umm Sulaim رضي الله عنها. So she heard directly from the Prophet ﷺ the joyful tidings of Paradise which awaited her after this earthly life.

May Allâh be pleased with them and they with Him.

Umm 'Ammârah Nusaybah رضي الله عنها

> The Prophet ﷺ said:
> "*O Allâh! Make this family my friends in Paradise.*"

Umm 'Ammârah Nusaybah رضي الله عنها

Umm 'Ammârah رضي الله عنها was also a woman from the *Ansâr*. She was from the famous Banu Najjâr tribe, that was an offshoot of the Khazraj tribe. Her two sons had been martyred and her brother 'Abdullâh bin Ka'b ﷺ was a Companion of the Prophet ﷺ in the Battle of Badr. She was renowned for her courageous exploits in the battlefields. She was a faithful and loyal wife, and a loving mother, also remarkable for her patience and forbearance. She was very learned in the Qur'ân and *Hadîth*. Her life makes pleasurable and instructive reading for the growth and development of one's faith.

The fortunate *Ansâr* in Madinah who were converted to Islâm by the teachings of Mus'ab bin 'Umair ﷺ went to a particular mountain pass near Makkah to pledge allegiance to Allâh ﷻ and His Messenger ﷺ for the second time. There were about seventy-two men and two women, and the Prophet ﷺ had also reached there. One of the women was Umm 'Ammârah رضي الله عنها and the other was Umm Munee' Asmâ' bint 'Amr bin 'Adi. The former narrates that her husband, Ghazyah bin 'Amr, told the Prophet ﷺ that these two women also wanted to swear allegiance on his palm. He said it was all right, but for these women too the terms would be the same as for the men. He said that the only difference would be that he took the men's palms in his palm, but he did not shake hands with women. This incident of the swearing of allegiance is called *Bai'at-al-'Aqabah ath-Thaniyah* (Second Pledge at al-'Aqabah) in Islâmic history. When Umm 'Ammârah رضي الله عنها returned to Madinah after taking this oath of allegiance, she devoted herself to the education and training of women in accordance with the teachings of Islâm.

Umm 'Ammârah رضي الله عنها was married the first time to Zaid bin 'Asim Mâzini. She had two sons by him - 'Abdullâh and Habîb رضي الله عنهما. Both were among the Companions of the Prophet ﷺ. A boy Tameem, and a girl Khawlah, were born from her second marriage which was to Ghazyah bin 'Amr Mâzini.

In his book *Siyar A'lâm An-Nubalâ'*, Imâm Dhahabi writes that Umm 'Ammârah رضي الله عنها took part in the Second *Bai'at-al-'Aqabah*, the Battle of Uhud, the Battle of Hunain, the Battle of Yamâmah, and the Treaty of Hudaibiyah. Her skill with the sword in the Battle of Uhud astonished those who saw her. The Prophet ﷺ said that in whichever direction he turned in the battlefield he could see her defending and protecting him.

She herself describes a very critical stage in the Battle of Uhud. The *Mujâhideen* of Islâm were on the verge of defeat and they were scattering. She, along with her two sons and husband tried to surround the Prophet ﷺ in order to ward off and repel any attack on him. She had a sword in one hand and a shield in the other. If the enemy had been on foot and not on horseback, they would have slain all of them. When one of the enemies attacked her she warded off the attack with her shield; she then pulled at the bridle of the horse to turn it around. Taking this opportunity, she plunged her sword into the horse's back. The wounded horse fell, taking the rider with him. Seeing this, the Prophet ﷺ called out to 'Abdullâh bin Umm 'Ammârah ؓ to help his mother. And together she and her son finished off the enemy soldier.

'Abdullâh bin Umm 'Ammârah ؓ relates how during the Battle of Uhud the enemy made a forceful thrust against them. The *Mujâhideen* scattered before them and he and his mother moved close to the Prophet ﷺ to defend him from all quarters. The Prophet ﷺ called out to him to attack the enemy. He threw a stone at the disbeliever; it hit the eye of the horse he was riding. The horse fell to the ground somersaulting. He threw another heavy stone and the enemy died. The Prophet ﷺ looked pleased, and then he noticed that Umm 'Ammârah رضي الله عنها was bleeding from the shoulder; he asked 'Abdullâh ؓ to bandage his mother's wound and said that they were a truly great family.

He invoked Allâh's blessings on them, and prayed that they should be his friends in Paradise as well.

Both Umm 'Ammârah رضي الله عنها and 'Abdullâh ؓ were overjoyed when they heard these auspicious words from the lips of the Prophet ﷺ. At the same time they were inspired to greater heights of heroism and returned to the attack with renewed vigour. His next victim injured him on the left arm with his sword, and a fountain of blood gushed out. The Prophet ﷺ told him to immediately bandage his wound. When Umm 'Ammârah رضي الله عنها saw her son bleeding profusely, she bandaged his arm and told him not to lose courage but continue with his attack on the enemy. The Prophet ﷺ smiled when he saw the heroism and courage of both mother and son, and said:

> 'From where can anyone get courage like you, O Umm 'Ammârah رضي الله عنها?'

Umm 'Ammârah رضي الله عنها was standing in front of the Prophet ﷺ with a naked sword when the same man came before them. The Prophet ﷺ pointed out to her that this was the man who injured her son. She struck a powerful blow cutting off his leg. The man fell face down; a few other *Mujâhideen* leapt on him and killed him.

The Prophet ﷺ was very impressed with this display of strength and courage by Umm 'Ammârah رضي الله عنها. He smiled and thanked Allâh ﷻ who gave her that success and had soothed her grief and avenged her by the death of the enemy before her very eyes.

'Umar bin al-Khattâb ؓ says that the Prophet ﷺ once told him that in the Battle of Uhud wherever he turned, whether to the right or to the left, he saw Umm 'Ammârah رضي الله عنها fighting to defend him.

During this battle she sustained at least twelve major wounds; the deepest one, the one on her shoulder being inflicted by a disbeliever named Ibn Qamiah. It was so deep that she fainted; and it took a year for it to heal. When she regained consciousness her first question was about the well being of the Prophet ﷺ, rather than about her own sons or husband. When she learned that he was fine, she thanked Allâh ﷻ. Besides the Battle of Hunain and the conquest of Makkah, Umm 'Ammârah رضي الله عنها fought valiantly in the battle against Musailamah al-Kaththâb. She sustained eleven wounds and her arm was cut. Her son, Habîb bin Zaid al-Ansâri was martyred in this battle, slain by Musailamah himself.

Her other son, 'Abdullâh bin Zaid ؓ was martyred in the Battle of Harrat. This war was fought in the year 63 after *Hijrah*, on stony black ground to the east of Madinah. Stony black ground is called *Harrah* in Arabic, and it is to be found on three sides of Madinah. 'Abdullâh bin Zaid ؓ was that great Companion who took part in many wars and the one, who killed Musailamah al-Kaththâb with his sword. Wahshi bin Harb, who martyred Hamzah bin 'Abdul Muttalib ؓ was also among those who inflicted mortal wounds on Musailamah al-Kaththâb. After the battle of Uhud when the Muslim troops returned to Madinah under the leadership of the Prophet ﷺ, he announced that they should get ready to march to a place called, Hamrâ' Al-Asad, to chase the pagans. The *Mujâhideen* spent just one night in Madinah. Umm 'Ammârah رضي الله عنها also got up to join them, energized as she was by her ardor to fight the pagans, but weakened by her serious injuries she could not make it. As soon as the Prophet ﷺ returned he asked her brother, 'Abdullâh bin Ka'b Mâzini about her sister's welfare. When he heard that her wounds were healing he breathed a sigh of relief and thanked Allâh ﷻ for His Divine Mercy.

Umm 'Ammârah رضي الله عنها and some other women also took part in a war with the Banu Quraidhah. The Prophet ﷺ gave them part of the booty taken during this war. These were the terms of equality practised by the Prophet ﷺ. She was also active during the Treaty of Hudaibiyah. She related how they set out from Madinah to perform *'Umrah* under the leadership of the Prophet ﷺ. They were stopped at Hudaibiyah because the Quraish did not want the Muslims to enter Makkah. 'Uthmân bin 'Affân ؓ was appointed ambassador and sent to Makkah to negotiate. Since his return was delayed, rumors spread that he had been martyred. At the command of Allâh the Prophet ﷺ sat under a tree and people started swearing allegiance to Allâh ﷻ and His Messenger.

Those who were armed took hold of their weapons. Most people came unarmed as they had set out for *'Umrah*. Umm 'Ammârah رضي الله عنها says she had a stick and she stuck a knife in her belt, to defend herself

Umm 'Ammârah Nusaybah رضي الله عنها

in case of an enemy attack. As it turned out the news about the death of 'Uthmân bin 'Affân ﷺ but turned out to be a false rumor. And a pact was made with the enemy that came to be known as the Treaty of Hudaibiyah. This treaty is mentioned in the Qur'ân in the following words:

> "Indeed, Allâh was pleased with the believers when they gave the pledge to you under the tree: He knew what was in their hearts, and He sent down calmness and tranquility upon them, and He rewarded them with a near victory. And abundant spoils that they will capture. And Allâh is Ever All-Mighty, All-Wise." (48:18-19)

Twenty women took part in the Battle of Khaybar; one of them was Umm 'Ammârah رضي الله عنها. Once again when the Muslim army triumphed women were given a share of the booty of war. Umm 'Ammârah رضي الله عنها got expensive dresses and jewelry and two dinars. In the Battle of Hunain as well she had fought valiantly and received some part of the booty. A man of the tribe of Banu Huwâzin entered the battlefield on camel back, waving a flag. She hit the camel from the back so violently that it stumbled and fell; the rider also fell, she attacked him so that he never recovered.

The Prophet ﷺ sent Umm 'Ammârah's son, Habîb bin Zaid ﷺ, as his representative to Musailamah al-Kaththâb, in order to bring him to the right path. Breaking all norms of diplomacy, this villain captured Habîb ﷺ and tied him to a pillar. He then asked him,

> "Do you testify that Muhammad is the Messenger of Allâh?" When he answered in the affirmative, he asked him if he also testified that he, Musailamah, was also the messenger of Allâh ﷺ.

Habib ﷺ replied that he was deaf and could not hear him. He kept on repeating the question again and again. And Habib ﷺ kept on repeating the same answer. Then this cruel man cut off each part of his body, one by one, and gradually martyred him. When Umm 'Ammârah رضي الله عنها got this news about her son she displayed exemplary patience. The Prophet ﷺ consoled the family and prayed for them.

During his caliphate, Abu Bakr Siddeeq ﷺ sent the army to test the challenge of the army of Musailamah. Umm 'Ammârah رضي الله عنها was also in the army. She was about sixty years old at the time, and her son 'Abdullâh bin Zaid ﷺ was also with her; he was one of those who finally killed this man. During this battle her arm was cut off and she sustained eleven injuries. Khâlid bin Waleed ؓ, the General of the army boiled some oil and immersed her arm in it to cure her wounded arm; but for Umm 'Ammârah رضي الله عنها her happiness at the death of Musailamah, was much greater than her grief at the loss of her arm.

During the caliphate of 'Umar bin al-Khattâb ؓ, some beautiful and exclusive sheets were sent to him. One of these sheets was exceptionally beautiful and large as well. Some of the companions suggested that it should be sent as a gift to Safiyyah bint 'Ubaid, the wife of 'Abdullâh bin 'Umar رضي الله عنهما. But 'Umar bin al-Khattâb ؓ said that he knew of someone even better than her and praised by no less a person than the Prophet ﷺ. He then sent it to Umm 'Ammârah رضي الله عنها.

Once Umm 'Ammârah رضي الله عنها told the Prophet ﷺ that in the Noble Qur'ân only men were mentioned and women were often deprived of any importance. Then this *Âyah* was revealed.

> *"Verily, the Muslims men and women, the believers men and women, the men and the women who are obedient (to Allâh), the men and women who are truthful, the men and the women who are patient, the men and the women who are humble, the men and the women who give Sadaqât (i.e. Zakât and alms), the men and the women who observe fast, the men and the women who guard their chastity (from illegal sexual acts) and the men and the women who remember Allâh much with their hearts and tongues, Allâh has prepared for them forgiveness and a great reward (i.e. Paradise)."* (33:35)

Umm 'Ammârah رضي الله عنها held a very special place among the women Companions. When the Prophet ﷺ saw the valor and spirit of sacrifice of the whole family – husband, wife, and sons – in the most intense part of the Battle of Uhud he prayed that Allâh ﷻ might have Mercy on that family.

Umm 'Ammârah رضي الله عنها requested him to pray that they should have the good fortune to be with him in Paradise. It was then that he prayed that they should be his friends in Paradise.

May Allâh be pleased with them and they with Him.

Ar-Rubai' bint Mu'awwith رضي الله عنها

The Prophet ﷺ said:
"*Whosoever participated in the Pledge of Ridhwân, are the holders of Paradise.*"

Ar-Rubai' رضي الله عنها participated in the Pledge of Ridhwân so she is a lady of Paradise.

Ar-Rubai' bint Mu'awwith رضي الله عنها

Rubai' رضي الله عنها was the daughter of Mu'awwith bin 'Afrâ' and her uncles (her father's brothers) were Mu'âdh bin 'Afrâ' and 'Awf bin 'Afrâ' رضي الله عنهم. All the three sons of 'Afrâ' were at the Battle of Badr. In the Noble Qur'ân, Allâh has said:

> The Prophet's Companions were granted forgiveness at the Battle of Badr.

In the battlefield at Badr, 'Utbah bin Rabee'ah, Shaibah bin Rabee'ah, and Waleed bin 'Utbah had come forward from the pagans to challenge the forces of the Muslims. From among the Muslims the three sons of 'Afrâ' رضي الله عنهم came forward to meet the challenge. The Makkan champions said arrogantly that people worthy of them and chieftains of tribes should be sent to oppose them. The Prophet ﷺ called these three brothers back and sent his uncle, Hamzah bin 'Abdul Muttalib, 'Ali bin Abi Tâlib and 'Ubaidah bin Hârith رضي الله عنهم to face these arrogant men. These three riders launched such a powerful attack that the three heroes of the pagans were shattered. In a second the pride of these Makkans was laid low in the dust. Licking their wounds they were dispatched to death and their place in Hell.

'Abdur-Rahmân bin 'Awf ﷺ relates that in the battlefield of Badr the son of 'Afrâ' Mu`awwith ﷺ, came to him and asked him in a whisper which one of the pagans was Abu Jahl and where he was. He had barely answered him when his brother came running to him and asked the same question.

'Abdur-Rahmân bin 'Awf ﷺ asked them why they were looking for Abu Jahl. They replied that they had heard that he always cursed the Prophet ﷺ; they were determined that on this day they would either chop off his head or be martyred themselves. On hearing this 'Abdur-Rahmân bin 'Awf ﷺ was very happy. As they were speaking they saw Abu Jahl riding up in all his pride and glory. Pointing out to him 'Abdur-Rahmân ﷺ told them that this was their target. They both leapt and made such a powerful attack that he fell from his horse. They struck at him again so that he could not rise up. Then 'Abdullâh bin Mas'ood ﷺ reached there and prepared to lop off his head. Even at this stage his pride was such that he requested them to cut him off lower in the neck, so it would look like the head of a chieftain. He said that he wished he had been slain by a strong young person rather than by these "lowly farmers". The Prophet ﷺ prayed for Mu'awwith bin 'Afrâ' and Mu'âdh bin 'Afrâ'. All the three sons of 'Afrâ' ﷺ were present at the *Bai'at-al-'Aqabah ath-Thaniyah*.

'Afrâ's daughter, Ar-Rubai' رضي الله عنها was married to a prominent businessman, Ayâs bin Bakeer. She had a son by this marriage, Muhammad bin Ayâs.

Rubai' bint Mu`awwith رضي الله عنها was the daughter of a well-known family. The Prophet ﷺ used to visit her house sometimes, and always gladly accepted any gift she offered him. She was justifiably proud of this great honor. She relates that on the day she was married the Prophet ﷺ visited her house and sat on the bed. Young girls were singing to the accompaniment of the *Daf*[1] and the Prophet ﷺ enjoyed their singing.

When they started saying that a Prophet who knew things about the future was sitting in their midst, the Prophet ﷺ stopped them, and gently told them that no one had knowledge about the unknown, except Allâh ﷻ. Leaving out this phrase they could continue with their singing, he said.

---

[1] Similar to a tambourine without cymbals or bells.

This shows that there is no harm for young girls of a family to get together and sing on a joyous occasion like a marriage to express their happiness.

Rubai' bint Mu`awwith رضي الله عنها used to serve the Prophet's favorite dishes when he visited her house. Once she served him ripe dates that he relished. On that day he gave her some gold and silver ornaments he received from Bahrain. He asked her to accept them and wear them.

Rubai' bint Mu`awwith رضي الله عنها, a lady who had been assured a place in Paradise, was indeed fortunate to receive such a gift from the Prophet ﷺ himself. It was a *Sunnah* (tradition) of the Prophet ﷺ to exchange gifts, which increase affection and pleasant feelings of mutual regard between the people exchanging them.

She was also fortunate in that the Prophet ﷺ often used to come to her house to make the ablution, offer prayers, have a meal and then rest for a while. In this way, Rubai' bint Mu`awwith رضي الله عنها used to acquire knowledge about many points of religion. Many Companions used to value her and often request her to relate *Ahâdîth* and the knowledge she had gained from her experiences. Rubai' bint Mu'awwith رضي الله عنها relates that when the Prophet ﷺ visited her, he would ask her to get some water. She would arrange for it and then help him to perform the ablution for prayer. She describes the correct procedure that she learnt from watching him: 'He would wash his hands three times, then wash his face three times. He would rinse his mouth once and clean his nose by drawing in water. Next he washed his arms up to the elbows three times. Then he would wipe his head by drawing his palms over from the front of his forehead to the back of the nape of his neck, then back to the forehead. Then he would insert his fingers into the outer and inner parts of his ears. Then he washed each foot three times.'

Abu 'Ubaidah bin Hamd bin 'Ammâr bin Yâsir ؓ says that he once asked Rubai' bint Mu`awwith رضي الله عنها to describe how the Prophet ﷺ looked.

She said that he looked as bright as the sun.

She compared his face to the sun, because it shone like the sun and also because sunshine reached every corner of the earth, like the message of the Prophet ﷺ.

During the days of the Prophet ﷺ women had the privilege of taking part in wars as well. They would nurse the wounded and quench the thirst of the soldiers in the battlefields. It is mentioned in *Sahîh Al-Bukhâri* that Khâlid bin Thakwân narrated from Rubai' bint Mu'awwith رضي الله عنها that she took part in the wars. She would bandage and nurse the wounded, give water to the *Mujâhideen*, carry the wounded and the dead and convey them to Madinah. She was part of the congregation which swore the oath of allegiance in the sixth year after *Hijrah* which became famous in Islâmic history as *Bai'at Ridhwân*. Thus she heard of her succession to Paradise in the hereafter from the lips of the Prophet ﷺ himself. This is a greater distinction than any other in this world.

Rubai' bint Mu'awwith رضي الله عنها was a woman of mature understanding, farsighted and quick-witted. One day Abu Rabee'ah's wife, Umm 'Ayâsh came to her door selling perfumes. During the course of the conversation she said she would not sell any perfumes to her because she was the daughter of the man who killed the leader of her tribe. Rubai'bint Mu'awwith رضي الله عنها was enraged and asked the woman to get out of her sight and her house, saying her perfume was worse than any stink.

Later in life, during the caliphate of 'Uthmân bin 'Affân ﷺ, Rubai'bint Mu`awwith رضي الله عنها and her husband developed some differences. She asked him to take everything she had and give her *Khula'*[1], as she did not want to remain his wife any longer. He agreed and left taking everything with him. It is said he did not leave even a sheet in the house. When the complaint went to 'Uthmân bin 'Affân ﷺ he said

---

[1] The release from the marriage tie obtained by a wife upon the return of the dowry.

nothing could be done as he was within his rights according to the *Shari'ah*. Nothing could be taken back from him. Even people of the highest caliber sometimes have to face such unexpected critical times in their life.

People of modern times who talk so loudly about "women's liberation" and "women's rights" should remember this law of Islâm. If a woman cannot bear life with her husband, she can demand separation or divorce. She can settle the matter trough mutual agreement or go to a court of law. Only in this case, in the language of *Sharî'ah*, it is called *Khula'*, and not *Talâq*, or divorce. Just as a man has the right to *Talâq*, so a woman has the right to *Khula'*. These two possibilities are there for both the partners in a marriage to ease the tension caused by conflicts in family life. Separation, it is said in the Noble Qur'ân, is not the ideal way but it is permitted. It is the least desirable, yet best possible way under the worst marital circumstances. If this escape route had not been there, both partners would live life as if it were a war. And that is not the best environment, either for them or their children. Thus, such rules of the *Sharî'ah* (Islâmic legislation) are a blessing for the common problems of society.

There are twenty-one *Ahâdîth* associated with Rubai' bint Mu`awwith رضي الله عنها. 'A'ishah bint Anas bin Mâlik, Sulaimân bin Yassar, Khâlid bin Thakwân, 'Abdullâh bin Muhammad bin Aqeel, Abu 'Ubaidah Muhammad bin 'Ammâr bin Yassir رضي الله عنهم — some of the most famous followers of Islâmic *Sharî'ah* (Islâmic legislation) — are some of those who have narrated her words.

After living a long eventful life, Rubai' bint Mu`awwith رضي الله عنها passed away in the year 45 after *Hijrah* during the caliphate of Mu'âwiyah bin Sufyân ﷺ.

May Allâh be pleased with them and they with Him.

Faree'ah bint Mâlik رضي الله عنها

The Prophet ﷺ said:

"*Whosoever participated in the Pledge of Ridhwân, are the dwellers of Paradise.*"

Faree'ah رضي الله عنها participated in the Pledge of Ridhwân, so she is a lady of Paradise.

Faree'ah bint Mâlik رضي الله عنها

She was the daughter of the great Companion, Mâlik bin Sinân bin 'Ubaid Ansâri al-Khudri ﷺ. It was about him that the Prophet ﷺ said:

"Whosoever wants to see a person of Paradise, then they should look at him."

Her brother was Abu Sa'eed al-Khudri ﷺ, the *Mufti* (scholar) of the Grand Mosque at Madinah. He was an extremely learned man, and an authority on *Hadîth*, with 1,170 *Ahâdîth* attributed to him. He was also a *Mujâhid* and General of the Muslim army and had been a ruler of a province. Her half brother on her mother's side was also a General. He was Qatâdah bin Nu'mân Ansâri ﷺ, who had taken part in the battles of Badr and Uhud.

On one occasion his eye was injured by the enemy and came out of its socket. When the Prophet ﷺ saw this, he thrust it back with his hand; it went back to its original position and his vision became sharper than before.

The father of Faree'ah bint Mâlik رضي الله عنها, Mâlik bin Sinân bin 'Ubaid Ansâri al-Khudri ﷺ was one of the greatest and foremost Companions, and a personality who, the Prophet ﷺ said, was among the dwellers of Paradise. He could not take part in the Battle of Badr, but in Uhud he was martyred defending the life of the Prophet ﷺ. When he went to the Prophet ﷺ to volunteer for the Battle of Uhud he was accompanied by his son, Sa'd, that is, Abu Sa'eed al-Khudri ﷺ. He was very young and the Prophet ﷺ did not give him permission to go to war. He started to weep and his sister, Faree'ah bint Mâlik رضي الله عنها, embraced him affectionately, and wiping his tears asked him to be patient and wait for the right time. Abu Sa'eed al-Khudri ﷺ grew up to shine in the world of knowledge and learning and occupy the post of *Mufti* (deliverer of formal legal verdicts) of Madinah.

When Mâlik bin Sinân bin 'Ubaid Ansâri al-Khudri ﷺ met the Prophet ﷺ he spoke to him in a very eloquent manner and said that they were setting out to test their strength against the disbelievers. They would either triumph by the Grace of Allâh ﷻ or be martyred. Both the likely alternatives were good for a true Muslim as both would bring victory to him. At the time when the fighting was at its most intense, he earnestly adopted the best defensive position to protect the Prophet ﷺ. Finally, he lost his life in the way of Allâh ﷻ, fulfilling this most demanding duty. At this critical juncture in the battle the world saw the Prophet ﷺ injured on his face and bleeding from his wounds. Mâlik bin Sinân bin 'Ubaid Ansâri al-Khudri ﷺ sucked the blood from the wound. Thus the blood of the Prophet ﷺ mingled with his own.

As soon as the Prophet ﷺ reached Madinah after the Battle of Uhud he was met by Abu Sa'eed al-Khudri ﷺ. He immediately recognized him and asked if he was Sa'd bin Mâlik. When the latter noticed the encouraging and affectionate tone of the Prophet's greeting, he drew nearer to him. The Prophet ﷺ condoled with him and told him to be patient and brave. He said his father's martyrdom would earn blessings for him.

When he returned home, Abu Sa'eed al-Khudri ﷺ gave his sister, Faree'ah bint Mâlik رضي الله عنها, the news regarding their father, and the injunctions of the Prophet ﷺ about how to accept his loss. She accepted her father's martyrdom with equanimity, courage and patience as advised by the Prophet ﷺ, taking it as a matter of pride to be addressed by the Prophet ﷺ. She expressed happiness that the Prophet ﷺ had returned safe and sound.

After her father's martyrdom, the family lost their sole means of sustenance. Despite this, the children displayed exemplary patience as advised by the Prophet ﷺ, and did not ask anyone for aid. They had heard him say that a person who is content and trusts in Allâh is made wealthy by Him; one who wishes to be pure and chaste, Allâh ﷻ makes him pure; one who restrains himself, is granted patience and fortitude by Allâh ﷻ. As a result of following the injunctions and teachings of the Prophet ﷺ the family became wealthy and prosperous beyond their greatest expectations.

Faree'ah bint Mâlik رضي الله عنها was married to Sahl bin Râfi' bin Bashir Khazraji. He was killed by some of his slaves near Madinah. This tragedy left her grief-stricken. After the murder of her husband she wanted to go back to her parents' house. She consulted the Prophet ﷺ as to what course of action was permitted by the *Sharî'ah* (Islâmic legislation), and what she could do so. He said that she should continue to stay in her house till she completed the prescribed waiting period. It should be noted that when a woman's husband dies she should observe a period of mourning for four months and ten days (*'Iddah*). Faree'ah bint Mâlik رضي الله عنها says that she obeyed the Prophet ﷺ and stayed in her house for the prescribed period, and after that she devoted the rest of her life to the service and propagation of Islâm.

She was one of those who took part in the *Bai'at Ridhwân* (Pledge of Ridhwan), which took place in the year 6 AH, when 1400 people went to perform *'Umrah* (Lesser Pilgrimage) and were stopped by the Quraish at Hudaibiyah. They gathered under a tree to swear allegiance to Allâh ﷻ and His Messenger ﷺ. They also swore to take revenge for the death of their emissary, 'Uthmân bin 'Affân ؓ, who was sent by the Prophet ﷺ to Makkah to negotiate with the enemy. Rumor had it that he was killed by the Quraish. The ardour and spirit of sacrifice of these people appealed so much to Allâh ﷻ that He promised Paradise for all of them. It was an honor of which they could be truly jubilant and proud. Surely such a promise is given to only the very fortunate, and Faree'ah bint Mâlik رضي الله عنها was one of them.

The Prophet ﷺ said about these people that none of them would be cast into Hell. In other words, they would all go to Paradise.

During the caliphate of 'Uthmân bin 'Affân ﷺ a lady's husband died. The matter of her place of residence during the period of her *'Iddah* came under consideration. Faree'ah bint Mâlik رضي الله عنها was summoned to the court of the Caliph. She was asked what the Prophet ﷺ had told her when she was in a similar situation regarding the place where she should pass the period of *'Iddah*. What she said was accepted in the court and applied to the lady in question.

Faree'ah bint Mâlik رضي الله عنها, had a very good memory. If she heard a command of the Prophet ﷺ even once, she would immediately learn it and retain it in her memory. In their study of narrations and *Ahâdîth* (Prophetic narrations), many great scholars would approach her for authentication or reference. Especially in the matter of observance of *'Iddah*; she has the distinction of being the predominant authority regarding the rules to be observed.

Those learned in *Fiqh* (Islâmic jurisprudence) in Madinah, Syria, Iraq and Egypt gave their *Fatâwâ* (religious verdicts) on *'Iddah* based on what she said. Ibn al-Qayyim in his famous book, *Zâd Al-M'âd*, has written that the famous interpreter of the *Sharî'ah* , Muhammad bin Sireen, writes that a woman was sick when her husband died. People moved her from her husband's place to her parents' house. When the learned people of the community came to know of this, they all said she should be moved back to her husband's house and pass the days of her *'Iddah* there. So she moved back. This was done based on the life and experience of Faree'ah bint Mâlik رضي الله عنها.

May Allâh be pleased with them and they with Him.

Umm Hishâm bint Hârithah bin Nu'mân رضي الله عنها

> Jâbir bin 'Abdullâh ؓ narrated that Allâh's Messenger ﷺ said:
>
> "*Those who participated in the Pledge of Ridhwân will never be cast into Hell.*"
>
> Umm Hishâm bint Hârithah participated in the Pledge of Ridhwân, therefore, she is a lady of Paradise.

Umm Hishâm bint Hârithah bin Nu'mân رضي الله عنها

She was one of the woman Companions who participated in the *Bai'at ar Ridhwân*, and so she was ensured of a place in Paradise for her spirit of sacrifice and selflessness. Loyal and faithful, learned and knowledgeable in matters of religion, she was pious and very particular about cleanliness – especially with regard to ablution and prayer. She had the good fortune to be the neighbor of the Prophet ﷺ in Madinah. She was the daughter of another noteworthy Companion, Hârithah bin Nu'mân ؓ. He was a very wealthy man and one of the leading and well-known personalities of the city. Her father had given away several houses as gifts for the use of the Prophet ﷺ. In fact, in praise of this Companion the Prophet ﷺ said:

"*He had given me so many houses that I felt embarrassed to ask him for a new one.*"

Umm Hishâm bint Hârithah رضي الله عنها was, like her father, a great personality, and an exemplary character.

When the Prophet ﷺ came to Madinah after his migration from Makkah he enjoyed the hospitality of Abu Ayyûb Ansâri ؓ for almost six months. Their next door neighbor was Hârithah bin Nu'mân ؓ. His daughter, Umm Hishâm bint Hârithah رضي الله عنها, often used to cook and send food for the esteemed guest, the Prophet ﷺ. Whenever the Prophet ﷺ contracted a marriage he needed a new house. And it was Hârithah bin Nu'mân ؓ who gave him his own house and moved on to another house himself. The Prophet ﷺ felt ashamed that he was put to so much trouble and had to move so often.

'Allamah Yâqut al-Hamawi in his book, *Mu'jam Al-Buldân*, writes that Hârithah bin Nu'mân ؓ was the first Companion to be fortunate enough to offer so many houses to the Prophet ﷺ. He was also extremely obedient to his mother, hence Allâh ﷻ gave him such a high status in life. 'A'ishah رضي الله عنها narrated that the Prophet ﷺ once said that when he entered Paradise he heard someone reciting the Noble Qur'ân beautifully. He asked who this might be and he was told it was Hârithah bin Nu'mân ؓ. He then said that thus were the good people, who were obedient to their mothers.

Hârithah bin Nu'mân ؓ was so exalted that he actually had the good fortune to see the Angel Jibrîl ؑ twice. When the Prophet ﷺ left for the battle with Banu Quraidhah he saw him in the guise of another Companion of the Prophet ﷺ, Dihyah al-Kalbi ؓ. This was in *Jannatul Baqi'*. The second time he saw him in the battlefield, during the Battle of Hunain when he was busy talking to the Prophet ﷺ. When he passed by the two of them silently, the Angel Jibrîl ؑ asked the Prophet ﷺ who he was. He replied that it was Hârithah bin Nu'mân ؓ. Then he said he was one among the hundred persons who, Allâh ﷻ had said, would be blessed with the food of Paradise. *"If he had greeted me today, I would have returned his greetings,"* said the Angel. This noble Companion also had the honor of taking part in the Battle of Badr.

Umm Hishâm bint Hârithah رضي الله عنها was a descendant of noble families from both sides. Her mother, Umm Khâlid bint Khâlid bin Ya'eesh was from the Banu Mâlik tribe. She had the privilege of swearing allegiance to Islâm with the Prophet ﷺ. She was married to Hârithah bin Nu'mân ؓ. She had five children by him – 'Abdullâh, 'Abdur-Rahmân, Saudah, 'Umrah and Umm Hishâm – who filled the house with love and liveliness. All of them had the good fortune of accepting Islâm. This entire family served the Prophet ﷺ in a remarkable manner. Umm Hishâm bint Hârithah رضي الله عنها visited the Prophet's house very often; thus she had the golden opportunity of meeting and mixing with the Mothers of the Believers and observing them from close quarters on many an occasion. And the close social contact with these ladies of noble character deeply influenced her.

Umm Hishâm bint Hârithah bin Nu'mân رضي الله عنها

On the days of *'Eid* and on Fridays, the Prophet ﷺ would recite *Surah Qâf* of the Noble Qur'ân. Umm Hisham رضي الله عنها had learned it by heart by listening to him. She had a very sharp mind and a remarkable memory. She also remembered many *Ahâdîth* by heart. Her sister, 'Umrah, Muhammad bin 'Abdur-Rahmân bin As'ad bin Zurâh, Yahyâ bin 'Abdullâh and Habîb bin 'Abdur-Rahmân have narrated *Ahâdîth* from her.

In the sixth year after *Hijrah* when the Prophet ﷺ announced his intention to set out for Makkah for *'Umrah*, 1,400 Companions – both men and women -- prepared to accompany him. This group of pure-minded people set out on this sacred journey, but they were stopped at Hudaibiyah by the Quraish, who restricted their entry into Makkah. The Prophet ﷺ sent 'Uthmân bin 'Affân as his emissary to negotiate with the Quraish. They did not send him back for a long time and rumors spread that he had been killed by them.

When this news reached the Prophet ﷺ he was very sorrowful and upset. He said that they could not return to Madinah without avenging the murder of 'Uthmân bin 'Affân ؓ. He sat down under a tree; all his Companions – men and women – gathered around him and swore the oath of allegiance; they also swore to battle with the Quraish to avenge the murder of their delegate. *Bai'at Ridhwân* was the name given to this historic event. Allâh ﷻ gave his approval to this convention and also foretold for them victory in the future.

As He says in *Surat Al-Fath*:

"Indeed, Allâh was pleased with the believers when they gave the pledge to you (O Muhammad ﷺ) under the Tree: He knew what was in their hearts, and He sent down calmness and tranquility upon them, and He rewarded them with a near victory." (48:18)

The Companions and woman Companions present there on this occasion of historic and religious significance are also remembered in Islâmic history as the 'Companions of the Tree'. As it turned out 'Uthmân bin 'Affân ؓ did not have to stay there for very long, and the Quraish sent Abu Yazîd Suhail bin 'Amr as their representative to Hudaibiyah where the Prophet ﷺ was encamped with his Companions. On the basis of some terms, a peace treaty was concluded here. This came to be known as the Peace Treaty of Hudaibiyah. When Makkah was taken by the Muslims he converted to Islâm and became a devout Muslim, zealous with prayers,

Zakât, sacrifice and charity. When he recited the Noble Qur'ân he would start weeping and sobbing. When the Prophet ﷺ passed away there was an upheaval; many of the people in Makkah started to recant and return to their old ways. At this critical point in time, Abu Yazîd Suhail bin 'Amr ؓ stood up and addressed the Quraish in a thundering voice:

"O Quraish! You should be ashamed. You were the last to enter into the fold of Islâm, and you are the first to leave this strong circle? Remember Islâm will ultimately triumph. Its light will spread as far and wide as the light of the sun and the moon, taking the whole world in its embrace.

Stop, O Quraish! And do not become unfaithful apostates. You will ruin yourself both in this world and the next."

Listening to his sincere and moving advice, the people of Makkah then held on firmly to Islâm.

Abu Yazîd Suhail bin 'Amr ؓ took part in the Battle of Yarmook and died as a martyr.

The Prophet ﷺ gave the good news of eternal life in Paradise for all of the 1,400 people, who were the 'Companions of the Tree'. The Prophet ﷺ said that those who took part in the Bai'at ar-Ridhwân were promised that not one of them would go to Jahannum (Hell). Thus, Umm Hishâm bint Hârithah رضي الله عنها was also given the glad tidings of Paradise.

There was one misguided hypocrite Jadd bin Qais among these 'Companions of the Tree', who owned a very expensive red camel. According to a narration in Sahîh Al-Bukhâri, this man was separated from the pure-hearted members of this group. The words of the Hadîth are:

"All those people who swore allegiance under the tree will certainly go to Paradise, except the man with the red camel."

This promise of Paradise in the Hereafter is the greatest reward, the parallel of which cannot be found in this world. Fortunate are those who received this promise from Allâh ﷻ and His Messenger ﷺ. And when Umm Hishâm bint Hârithah رضي الله عنها left this world, this is the treasure she carried with her.

May Allâh be pleased with them and they with Him.

Umm Salamah Asmâ' bint Yazîd bin Sakan Al-Ansâriyah رضي الله عنها

The Prophet ﷺ said:

"*Whosoever participated in the Pledge of Ridhwân will never be cast into Hell.*"

Asmâ bint Yazîd رضي الله عنها got the honor of participating in the Pledge of Ridhwân.

Umm Salamah Asmâ' bint Yazîd bin Sakan Al-Ansâriyah رضي الله عنها

Patient, with complete faith in Allâh, pious, wise and God fearing – these were some of the qualities of Umm Salamah Asmâ' bint Yazîd al-Ansâriyah رضي الله عنها. But, above all, it was her courage that inspires a reader of the biographies of these women Companions. Daring in the extreme, she was so brave that with the pole of her tent she killed nine Roman soldiers in the Battle of Yarmook. Her statements were well considered, therefore she was always eloquent and convincing. It was almost as if she was casting a spell when she spoke. Her phrases were in beautiful sequence like a string of pearls, and her tone was well modulated and sweet sounding. On one occasion she appeared before the Prophet ﷺ as a representative, rather as an attorney to plead for the cause of women. She addressed him very respectfully and said,

> "Today I have come into your presence to plead the case for women. Allâh ﷻ sent you as His Prophet for all mankind – men and women. We women also have had the privilege and honor of swearing allegiance to Allâh ﷻ and to you. We also follow your teachings and your Sunnah (traditions). We women live within our houses and fulfill our duties. We are absorbed in looking after our husbands and fulfilling their needs. We see to the upbringing of our children and to the daily function of the household. Men, however have more opportunities for earning rewards from Allâh ﷻ because they can do things which we, as women, cannot do. Men attend the congregational prayers in the mosques and special Friday prayers.

They participate in the special prayers for the dead; they also have the privilege of taking part in the Jihâd. When they go for Jihâd we are left at home to protect their property and look after the family. Are we not also equally deserving of reward from Allâh?"

The Prophet ﷺ was very moved and impressed by her eloquently presented and rational plea. He turned around to his Companions and asked them if they had ever heard anyone else express a better question regarding religion.

Simultaneously they all answered that she was truly excellent. The Prophet ﷺ then turned around to the lady and answered her:

'Please go and tell the ladies whom you represent that by doing your duty to your spouses in a pleasant manner, keeping in mind what will make them happy, and following them faithfully, you will greatly please Allâh ﷻ and He will give you the same rewards as have been promised to men.'

She was so happy on hearing this good news that she rose from the meeting, reciting the words *'Lâ ilâha illallâh, Allâhu-Akbar'*. She rushed to give her friends the good news she had just received from Allâh's Messenger ﷺ.

She narrated that once she was sitting with her friends when the Prophet ﷺ passed by. When he saw them he addressed them saying they should not be ungrateful to their benefactors. Since she was bolder than the rest of her friends she asked him to be more specific and clarify what he meant by his statement. He said:

'A woman lives with her parents, then she gets married and Allâh ﷻ blesses her with children. At times when she gets annoyed with her husband she says that she never got any happiness in his house. This is a display of sheer ingratitude to her husband. Every Muslim woman should try to avoid saying such things.'

Talking about the status and position of a husband he said:

'If I were to order a person to prostrate before another human being, I would ask a wife to prostrate before her husband.'

Umm Salamah Asmâ' bint Yazîd bin Sakan Al-Ansâriyah رضي الله عنها

'Amr bin Qatâdah ؓ relates that among the ladies of the *Ansâr*, the first to pledge allegiance to Allâh ﷻ and His Messenger and recite the testimony of faith were Umm Sa'd bin Mu'âdh, Kabthah bint Râfi', Umm Salamah Asmâ' bint Yazîd, and her sister Hawâ' bint Yazîd al-Ansâriyah رضي الله عنهن. And they all had the privilege of doing this personally with the Prophet ﷺ. This was not a trifling matter. One who gains this opportunity is very fortunate indeed, and he or she should be justifiably proud.

Umm Salamah Asmâ' bint Yazîd al-Ansâriyah رضي الله عنها narrates that when the Prophet ﷺ got married to 'A'ishah رضي الله عنها, she was the one who helped to get the bride ready. When the Prophet ﷺ arrived she offered him a glass of milk. He had some of it and then gave the rest to 'A'ishah رضي الله عنها; she was feeling very shy and did not take the glass. So Umm Salamah رضي الله عنها told her this was a golden opportunity which did not come every day; she should accept it and not feel bashful.

'A'ishah رضي الله عنها narrated that she was so nervous and shy that her hands were trembling. She took the glass and started drinking the milk.

The Prophet ﷺ told her to give some to her friends as well, meaning to the other ladies who were present. All of them started laughing and said that they had no desire to have the milk.

> He joked with them saying that lies and hunger should not be joined together.

Umm Salamah Asmâ' رضي الله عنها says that one day the Prophet ﷺ came to their house when it was the time for *Maghrib* prayers. In the courtyard of their house they made a small mosque and he prayed there. Then she offered him some bread and some soup she had cooked. She said that she swears by Allâh ﷻ in whose Hand is her soul, that there were about forty people who sat down for the meal; there was just a little bread and the soup was in a small leather bowl, but everyone had a hearty meal and there was still a lot of food left over. Then the family too ate their fill. She said that she cleaned the bowl and put it away in a safe place and whenever anyone in the family fell sick, she would give them water in that bowl and they would be cured. Sometimes for plenitude they would use the bowl to drink water and their needs would be fulfilled.

During the Battle of the Trench Umm Salamah Asmâ' bint Yazîd رضي الله عنها sent his favorite dish of dates and clarified butter to the Prophet ﷺ. At the time he was with the Mother of the Believers Umm Salamah رضي الله عنها. She took as much as she wanted and then she sent a general invitation to the *Mujâhideen* who were taking part in the war to come and partake of it. Everyone had their fill, but there was still the same quantity of food left over.

Jâbir bin 'Abdullâh رضي الله عنهما had also given a dinner; there too the same thing happened. Another such incident of plenitude and blessings of Allâh ﷻ took place when Umm Sulaim رضي الله عنها served a meal to the Prophet ﷺ.

Umm Salamah Asmâ' bint Yazîd رضي الله عنها narrated that in the lifetime of the Prophet ﷺ she was divorced. There was no precedent for the *'Iddah* of a divorced woman before this. When she got divorced the following Verse of the Noble Qur'ân was revealed:

> "And divorced women shall wait for three menstrual periods." (2:228)

In the field of knowledge and learning Umm Salamah Asmâ' رضي الله عنها occupied a very high position. Among the women Companions her position was after that of the Mother of the Believers 'A'ishah رضي الله عنها and the Mother of the Believers Umm Salamah رضي الله عنها. There are eighty-one *Ahâdîth* associated with her name. One of the *Ahâdîth* narrated by her says:

> 'The Prophet ﷺ said: 'Verily, Allâh forgives all the sins and it does not bother Him.'

Umm Salamah Asmâ' bint Yazîd رضي الله عنها was a very patient person and thankful to her Lord under all circumstances. During the Battle of Uhud her father, Yazîd bin Sakan, her brother, 'Amir bin Yazîd bin Sakan, and her uncle رضي الله عنهم were all martyred. When she was told about it, she asked for news about the Prophet ﷺ. After she herself saw him arriving, she, Ziyâd bin Sakan رضي الله عنهما thanked Allâh ﷻ, and said,

Umm Salamah Asmâ' bint Yazîd bin Sakan Al-Ansâriyah رضي الله عنها

"As long as he was all right and well, all other troubles faded into insignificance, and the greatest of difficulties were of minor consequence."

In short, looking at the various events of her life, one realises her greatness. The food she served in the Battle of Uhud became the occasion of one of the miracles of the Prophet ﷺ. She had the distinction and honor of being a member at the signing of the Peace Treaty of Hudaibiyah. She was among the Companions of the Tree at the *Bai'at Ridhwân*. She took part in the Battle of Khaybar. At the Battle of Yarmook she killed nine enemy soldiers with just the pole of her tent. At the Battle of Uhud she was given the good news of eternal life in the Hereafter in Paradise for the tribe Banu 'Abdul-Ashahal. Among those martyred was her father as well. About these people, the Prophet ﷺ had said that the whole family will meet together in Paradise, and intercession was accepted for all of them. In the light of this statement it can be said that she too would go to Paradise.

She lived to a ripe old age, and died during the caliphate of Yazîd bin Mu'âwiyah. She had moved to Damascus in the latter part of her life. It was there that she died. She was buried near the Saghir Gate of Damascus.

May Allâh be pleased with them and they with Him.

Umm Sa'd Kabshah bint Râfi' Al-Ansâriyah رضي الله عنها

> The Prophet ﷺ said:
> "O Umm Sa'd! Be happy and give the good news to your family that all their martyrs have entered Paradise and their intercession has been accepted for their family."

Umm Sa'd Kabshah bint Râfi' Al-Ansâriyah رضي الله عنها

Her name was Kabshah bint Râfi' al-Ansâriyah and she was the mother of a great *Sahâbi*, Sa'd bin Mu'âdh ﷺ. When Abu Sa'eed al-Khudri ﷺ started digging his grave he said that the earth gave out perfumed air as of saffron or musk. The Prophet ﷺ said that the very throne of Allâh ﷻ was elated at his arrival in Paradise. He was the chieftain of the Banu 'Abdul-Ashahal tribe, and when he accepted Islâm the whole tribe did so too, because he was held in such high esteem for his learning and knowledge.

Usaid bin Hudhair, the leader of the 'Aws tribe, came to know that a young man, Mus'ab bin 'Umair ﷺ, had come from Makkah and he was attracting people to himself with his magical eloquence. Once a person heard him, he became his constant companion. One day Usaid came to know that Mus'ab bin 'Umair was sitting in a garden and people had gathered around him. Also present there was As'ad bin Zurârah. He went there in full pride and arrogance, holding a small spear in his hand. Glorying in his power and position, he spoke in a haughty tone to Mus'ab bin 'Umair ﷺ, asking who had given him permission to spread trouble in their peaceful city. He said that if Mus'ab dared to enter his neighborhood, he would be the worst person to deal with and Mus'ab himself would be responsible for the consequences.

Mus'ab bin 'Umair ﷺ, was a dignified and patient man, with steadfast faith in Allâh ﷻ. He addressed him politely and patiently, calling him 'brother', and requested that he should just spend a few minutes with him and listen to what he had to say. If he liked what he heard he could accept it; on the other hand if what he heard did not appeal to him he could reject it. This sounded reasonable to Usaid bin Hudhair and he agreed. After all, the world accepted him as a learned man, and he was also a poet whose mastery over his language was well-known. He thrust his spear in the ground and sat down next to Mus'ab ﷺ to listen to what he had to say.

Mus'ab bin 'Umair ﷺ started by reciting the first *Surah* of the Noble Qur'ân, *Surat Al-Fâtihah*. He did so in such a moving and appealing tone that Usaid bin Hudhair, for whom the meaning and content were completely new, could not help but exclaim,

> *"These are not the words of a human being. These are surely Divine and True Words. If you have brought this message and these Verses for the people of Madinah, please address them openly. No one will prevent you from spreading the Message. Please also do me the favor of accepting me into the fold of Islâm."*

As soon as he swore his pledge of allegiance to Islâm, his way of thinking changed. He went back and sent Sa'd bin Mu'âdh on some pretext to listen to Mus'ab bin 'Umair ﷺ. In the very same manner, arrogantly and angrily, he also went one day to meet Mus'ab ﷺ. The cousin of Sa'd bin Mu'âdh ﷺ happened to be sitting there, and softly he whispered to him the identity of the person approaching them; he then asked him to talk to him, as he was a very influential leader of his tribe. If he accepted Islâm, then so would the whole tribe of Banu 'Abdul-Ashahal. As they were speaking, Sa'd bin Mu'âdh, strode up angrily. Mus'ab bin 'Umair ﷺ again spoke very politely and humbly to him, appealing to him to at least patiently listen to him. If he did not like what he heard then he would leave. After all it was not his land, and he was a stranger there without any power.

When Sa'd ﷺ heard this refined and cultured man appealing to him so politely, he calmed down, and sat next to him to listen to what he had to say. Mus'ab bin 'Umair ﷺ spoke first about the principles of Islâm

Umm Sa'd Kabshah bint Râfi' Al-Ansâriyah رضي الله عنها

that made it a great religion. Then he recited various Verses of the Noble Qur'ân. Sa'd bin Mu'âdh ؓ was also overcome by this new approach to life and its values. He immediately swore the oath of allegiance and converted to Islâm. That very evening he gathered the members of his tribe and asked them,

"O Banu Abdul-Ashahal, do you accept me as your leader?"

They all answered in the affirmative, saying he was a leader who was loved by them. They acknowledged him to be a highly learned man. Then, becoming intensely emotional he appealed to them that if they did not swear allegiance to Allâh ﷻ and His Messenger ﷺ he would not talk to any one of them.

All the members of his tribe, men and women, had pledged allegiance to Islâm by the evening. When such a large number of people entered the fold of Islâm the whole of Madinah, echoed with the cries of *Allâhu-Akbar* (Allâh is the Greatest). The mother of Sa'd bin Mu'âdh ؓ was the first to accept Islâm and the city experienced its first spring season, as it were, with the advent of this great religion. The emissary of the Prophet ﷺ moved from the house of As'ad bin Zurârah ؓ to that of Sa'd bin Mu'âdh ؓ. And his house was filled with the blessings of Islâm.

The eloquence, hard work and sincere efforts of Mus'ab bin 'Umair ؓ bore fruit and the Islâmic revolution took over the city of Madinah. At this stage Allâh ﷻ commanded His Messenger, Muhammad ﷺ to migrate from Makkah to Madinah, which today is known as the Prophet's City. When the new converts to Islâm heard that the Prophet ﷺ was going to settle there in their midst, they could not contain their joy. The ladies of the two most prominent tribes of the city, 'Aws and Khazraj, started looking forward to his arrival excitedly. Umm Sa'd رضي الله عنها was the foremost among the ladies. She earnestly wished the Prophet ﷺ would stay at her house, just as his emissary, Mus'ab bin 'Umair ؓ had.

Anas bin Mâlik ؓ narrates that the display, by both the *Ansâr* men and women, of such love, respect and sincere happiness moved the Prophet ﷺ deeply. He repeated emotionally three times:

'By Allâh you people are dearer to me than any others.'

Prophet ﷺ stayed at the house of Abu Ayyûb al-Ansâri ﷺ. But he said about the houses in Madinah that among the houses of the *Ansâr*, the best were those of Banu Najjâr. Then those of Banu 'Abdul-Ashahal; then those of Banu Hârith bin Khazraj, then those of Banu Sâ'dah; in other words, all the houses of the *Ansâr* were the best.

Sa'd bin Mu'âdh ﷺ says that when the Prophet ﷺ reached Madinah and started accepting the oath of allegiance from the people of the city, his mother, Umm Sa'd رضي الله عنها was the first among the *Ansâri* women to do so. With her were Umm 'Âmir bint Yazîd bin Sakan and Hawâ bint Yazîd bin Sakan رضي الله عنهما.

Umm Sa'd رضي الله عنها was a very dignified, forbearing, courageous, God-fearing and pious lady. Her two sons, Sa'd bin Mu'âdh and 'Amr bin Mu'âdh رضي الله عنهما took part in the Battle of Badr. She nursed the wounded *Mujâhideen* and carried around the battlefield large water bags made of leather to quench their thirst. She took an active part in the Battle of Uhud. When she heard that her son, 'Amr bin Mu'âdh ﷺ, had been martyred she went swiftly to the area where intense fighting was going on. She thanked Allâh ﷻ for protecting the Prophet ﷺ, and said her grief for her son was lessened when she saw him safe and sound.

Prophet ﷺ condoled with her on her son's death and tried to console her. 'Amr bin Mu'âdh ﷺ, had thrust himself into the enemy ranks, moved by the spirit of *Jihâd* and also killed Dharâr bin Khattâb by his sword. In the Battle of Uhud twelve people from Umm Sa'd's tribe, Banu 'Abdul-Ashahal were killed, and thirty were injured.

In the Battle of Trench the Prophet ﷺ had taken safety precautions for the ladies and they stayed in the fort of Banu Hârithah. 'A'ishah رضي الله عنها narrated that Umm Sa'd رضي الله عنها was also with them. When she looked outside she saw Sa'd bin Mu'âdh ﷺ wearing very little armor, carrying a spear, reciting war poetry and advancing triumphantly. She pointed out to his mother, Umm Sa'd رضي الله عنها, that he was wearing very little armor; it would have been better if he had worn a larger one. His arms were outside it and unprotected. The enemy could injure him. And it happened exactly as she feared. Habbân bin 'Arqah let loose an arrow which pierced the main artery in his arm and blood

Umm Sa'd Kabshah bint Râfi' Al-Ansâriyah رضي الله عنها

gushed out. Seeing this, Habbân bin 'Arqah guffawed happily and said that it was a gift from him. Sa'd bin Mu'âdh ؓ cursed him saying his face would burn in *Jahannum*.

Since it was a very deep wound it was very painful. The Prophet ﷺ had the tent of Sa'd ؓ pitched inside the sanctuary at Madinah so that he could be nursed and attended to more easily. When he saw that the blood had not stopped flowing, he had the wound branded with a hot iron. This stopped the bleeding completely, but it became swollen. One day after the Battle of Banu Quraidhah was over, a goat happened to walk across his wound. This reopened the wound that burst with blood gushing out. He became very weak, and finally died with his head in the lap of the Prophet ﷺ.

Asmâ' bint Yazîd bin Sakan ؓ says that when Sa'd bin Mu'âdh ؓ died his mother broke into uncontrollable tears. The Prophet ﷺ condoled with her and asked her to be patient. Her son was such a great person, he said, that Allâh ﷻ smiled when he saw him and His '*Arsh* (Throne) welcomed him gladly.

When all the forts of the Banu Quraidhah were finally conquered the booty of war was distributed equally among all the soldiers – men and women – who fought in the war. Among them was the Prophet's aunt, Safiyyah bint 'Abdul Muttalib, Umm Sa'd bin Mu'âdh, Umm 'Ammârah, Umm Saleet, Sameerah bint Qais and Umm-ul-'Alâ رضي الله عنهن.

Umm Sa'd رضي الله عنها is that fortunate lady who heard from the Prophet ﷺ himself that she would go to Paradise. A *Hadîth* narrated by Anas bin Mâlik ؓ says that the Prophet ﷺ said:

> "If a person lost three sons or daughters and remained patient, and made the intention of earning reward from Allâh ﷻ, then he or she would enter Paradise."

A woman rose up and asked about a person who lost two sons or daughters, and he answered in the affirmative.

She later wished that she had asked about one child also. Umm Sa'd bin Mu'âdh رضي الله عنها is that lady who bore patiently the loss of two sons in the cause of Allâh.

In the Battle of Uhud she saw the Prophet ﷺ on horseback and moved swiftly towards him. Her son, Sa'd bin Mu'âdh ؓ, was holding the reins of the horse and he pointed out to the Prophet ﷺ that his mother was approaching. The Prophet ﷺ reined in his horse and greeted her warmly and said:

"O Umm Sa'd رضي الله عنها! be pleased and pass on the glad tidings to your family that the martyred members of your family are gathered in Paradise, and intercession for them had been accepted."

When she heard this, Umm Sa'd was very happy. Who could possibly weep and mourn for the dead after hearing that they were already in Paradise? Then she requested the Prophet ﷺ to pray for those of the family left behind. The Prophet ﷺ offered the supplication to Allâh to remove grief and sorrow from their hearts and make their troubles pass away.

After her two sons were martyred Umm Sa'd رضي الله عنها spent most of her time in prayer and remembrance of Allâh and she continued to earn this reward till the end of her life.

May Allâh be pleased with them and they with Him.

Umm Munthir Salamâ bint Qais رضي الله عنها

> The Prophet ﷺ said:
>
> "*Those who participated in the Pledge of Ridhwân are the dwellers of Paradise.*"
>
> Umm Al-Munthir Salamâ رضي الله عنها participated in the Pledge of Ridhwân, so she is the dweller of Paradise.

Umm Munthir Salamâ bint Qais رضي الله عنها

Umm Munthir رضي الله عنها was an eminent daughter of the tribe of Banu Najjâr. She was the sister of a prominent Companion, Saleet bin Qais ؓ, who participated in the Battle of Badr. She had the privilege of being a member of the congregation, when the verse regarding the change of *Qiblah* or direction of prayer, was revealed during the middle of prayer. She was also a distant aunt of the Prophet ﷺ, who had great regard for her tribe. Whenever a member of the tribe fell ill he would visit them.

One of the men of the Banu Najjâr tribe was sick. The Prophet ﷺ went to see him and addressing him as maternal uncle, asked him to recite the words:

'None has the right to be worshipped except Allâh.'

The man said that he was not his maternal uncle, but his paternal uncle.

The Prophet ﷺ smiled and said all he had to do was to recite the *Shahadah* (testimony of faith) once.

He asked if it would be better and more beneficial for him. The Prophet ﷺ said that it would be not just better but the best possible action, after which his life would be better both in this world and in the Hereafter.

Umm Munthir Salamâ bint Qais رضي الله عنها was the great lady who had accepted the invitation of Mus'ab bin 'Umair ؓ to accept Islâm. She came to be known by her son's name as Umm Munthir رضي الله عنها. Her original name was Salamâ bint Qais رضي الله عنها. Her two sisters, Umm Sulaim bint Qais and 'Umairah bint Qais also accepted Islâm and swore allegiance to it in the presence of the Prophet ﷺ.

In no time the women of Madinah were accepting Islâm and pledging allegiance personally to the Prophet ﷺ. When the women requested that they wanted to do so in the Prophet's presence, he agreed, though he did not touch their palms, when swearing them in. But he made some conditions before swearing them in. He told the women that they should abstain completely from the following six things:

- They should not accept any other but Allâh as worthy of worship.
- They should not steal.
- They should not commit adultery.
- They should not kill their children.
- They should not slander or accuse a person falsely.
- They should not be disobedient to the commands of Allâh.

Umm Munthir رضي الله عنها relates that when the *Ansâri* women gathered to take the pledge, she was among them. They repeated all the six points with the Prophet ﷺ when they swore allegiance to Islâm.

The Prophet ﷺ also told them they should not deceive their husbands.

Umm Munthir Salamâ bint Qais رضي الله عنها was married to Qais bin Sa'sa' bin Wahab; so her father's name was Qais and so was her husband's. But she came to be known by her son's name as Umm Munthir رضي الله عنها.

After the Battle of Ahzâb, the Battle of Banu Quraidhah took place. In this battle the *Mujâhideen* besieged Banu Quraidhah for twenty-five[1] days. Since they were allies of the 'Aws, the Jews of Banu Quraidhah

---

[1] By some accounts the siege lasted fifteen days.

Umm Munthir Salamâ bint Qais رضي الله عنها

appealed to their leader, Sa'd bin Mu'âdh ؓ, for his judgment on the egoistic and arrogant Banu Quraidhah and how they should be punished. Sa'd bin Mu'âdh ؓ declared that the warmongers among them should be beheaded, their children should be taken prisoner and their property should be confiscated. The sentence meted out by him was carried out. At the time he gave his judgment he was lying injured in the tent which had been put up in the courtyard of the Prophet's Mosque.

Realising that the situation was critical, Rafâ'ah bin Samwâl Qurdhi appealed to Umm Munthir Salamâ رضي الله عنها to give him refuge, and appeal to the Prophet ﷺ for his safety. He said that he would not forget this favor for the rest of his life. Feeling sorry for him, Umm Munthir Salamâ رضي الله عنها gave him shelter and requested the Prophet ﷺ to accept him since she had given him refuge. He agreed and fixed a bail for Rafâ'ah. Thus he was saved from certain death. One day Umm Munthir Salamâ رضي الله عنها told the Prophet ﷺ that her refugee prayed regularly and also ate camel meat. He smiled and answered that if the prisoner said his prayers it would be beneficial to him; but if he remained loyal to his own faith and did not accept Islâm it would be of no use. Sometime later Rafâ'ah converted to Islâm, swearing the oath of allegiance.

This great act of goodness would certainly be recorded among her other good deeds. If she had not given him refuge and if she had not appealed for his life to the Prophet ﷺ, he might have died as a disbeliever and gone to the eternal Fire of Hell in the Hereafter.

Among Banu Quraidhah there was a lady, Raihânah bint Zaid bin 'Amr, whom the Prophet ﷺ took as a slave for his household. According to some accounts he married her and she became one of the Mothers of the Believers. The wedding ceremony took place in the house of Umm Munthir رضي الله عنها. When the Prophet ﷺ came back from his Farewell Pilgrimage, she passed away and had been buried in *Jannatul Baqi'*.

The Prophet ﷺ sometimes used to visit Umm Munthir Salamâ bint Qais رضي الله عنها. He would have his lunch and rest for a while there. She used to cook very well and the Prophet ﷺ enjoyed eating at her place.

She would make special dishes on Fridays because he would drop in with some of the Companions for a meal.

Umm Munthir رضي الله عنها was one of those fortunate fourteen hundred Companions of the Tree at the *Bai'at Ridhwân* to whom Allâh ﷺ promised Paradise. As the *Hadîth* in *Sahîh Muslim* says:

> 'No one among them, who swore allegiance under the tree will go to Jahannum.'

Umm Munthir رضي الله عنها left this world when both Allâh and His Prophet Muhammad ﷺ were well pleased with her.

May Allâh be pleased with them and they with Him.

Umm Waraqah bint 'Abdullâh bin Hârith Al-Ansâriyah رضي الله عنها

The Prophet ﷺ said:
"*Umm Waraqah! Dwell in your house, Allâh will grant you the death of a martyr.*"

Umm Waraqah bint 'Abdullâh bin Hârith al-Ansâriyah رضي الله عنها

The *Ansâr* of Madinah were standing on the outskirts of their city, looking with impatient eyes towards the road approaching from Makkah.

Men, women, girls and boys, the young and the old were waiting for the arrival of their beloved Prophet ﷺ who was migrating from his city to theirs at their invitation and at the command of Allâh ﷻ. Suddenly someone shouted, *"Here they come!"* And all the young girls and women burst into a song of praise of Allâh ﷻ and a welcome to His Messenger ﷺ.

Among these *Ansâri* women was Umm Waraqah bint 'Abdullâh رضي الله عنها. She was a learned, scholarly, pious and modest lady, who was well known among the women Companions as one who spent her nights and days in prayer and meditation. She used to recite the Noble Qur'ân beautifully; it was second nature for her to spend a lot of time meditating on the meaning of its verses.

The Prophet ﷺ valued her highly and he told her to lead her family in congregational prayers. The courtyard of the house was converted into a mosque; with the permission of the Prophet ﷺ they had a *Mu'adhdhin* to give the call to prayers. 'Abdur-Rahmân bin Khallad says that he saw the *Mu'adhdhin*, who was a very aged man. Thus Umm Waraqah bint 'Abdullâh رضي الله عنها was appointed by the Prophet ﷺ to be an *Imâm* and lead the prayer for women.

Besides her thirst for knowledge of the Qur'ân, *Sharî'ah* (Islâmic laws) and *Ahâdîth*, Umm Waraqah رضي الله عنها had a burning desire to die as a martyr in the cause of Islâm. When it was announced that the army should prepare to leave for the Battle of Badr, Umm Waraqah رضي الله عنها went to the Prophet ﷺ and volunteered her services to tend to the wounded in the battlefield. She told him that it was her earnest desire to die in the cause of Islâm. The Prophet ﷺ could see her enthusiasm and ardor, but he told her to stay at home and she would attain martyrdom there. She went back happily because it was her duty to yield to the command of the Messenger of Allâh ﷺ.

The Prophet ﷺ, would sometimes take along some of his Companions and visit the house of Umm Waraqah رضي الله عنها. He would tell them to accompany him to the house of the lady who was a living martyr. He would ask about her welfare, rest for a while and then offer supplications to Allâh ﷻ for her well being. Allâh ﷻ revealed to his beloved Messenger ﷺ that Umm Waraqah رضي الله عنها would die the death of a martyr in her own home. Nobody could understand how this would take place with her sitting in her house, but they were sure it would definitely happen, as this news had been given to them by their Truthful Prophet ﷺ.

Umm Waraqah رضي الله عنها herself was waiting every moment to see how this auspicious event would take place, which would be the fulfillment of her greatest dream. She waited patiently, for it would give her eternal life and a place in Paradise. *When would it take place? How exactly would it take place? What shape would it take? How would it be possible to become a martyr sitting in the house?* Lost in these thoughts she passed her nights and days. The Prophet ﷺ passed away. Abu Bakr Siddeeq ؓ succeeded him and he too passed away; 'Umar Farooq ؓ became the Caliph.

Umm Waraqah رضي الله عنها had two slaves working for her, a girl and a man. She told them that after her death they would be free. One day they got together and decided that they were tired of waiting for this old lady to die. They planned that they would kill her while she lay asleep and escape to freedom. They were so tempted by the thought of freedom that they forgot to consider their future as well as life in the hereafter.

Umm Waraqah bint 'Abdullâh bin Hârith Al-Ansâriyah رضي الله عنها

In the dead of night as Umm Waraqah رضي الله عنها lay in a deep sleep, they killed her, covered her body with a sheet and crept away from the house silently. As day broke and the sun came up, the neighbors missed the sound of the beautiful recitation of the Noble Qur'ân by Umm Waraqah رضي الله عنها which used to fill the air early at dawn. When they entered the house they were shocked to see her lying in the sleep of death. Then they saw that both the slaves – the man and the girl – were missing. They realised that they must be the criminals. 'Umar bin al-Khattâb ﷺ ordered that people should be sent out to search for them. Finally they were found hiding. When they were brought before the Caliph in the court, they admitted their guilt and were put to death.

Thus the Prophet ﷺ was proved right, that Umm Waraqah رضي الله عنها would die a martyr's death in her own home, and attain Paradise.

"Verily, the pious will be in the midst of Gardens and Rivers. In a seat of truth, near the Omnipotent King (Allâh, the One, the All-Blessed, the Most High, the Owner of Majesty and Honor)." (54:54-55)

Umm Aiman bint Tha'labah رضي الله عنها

The Prophet ﷺ said:

"*Whosoever wishes to marry a lady of Paradise, then he should marry Umm Aiman رضي الله عنها.*"

Umm Aiman bint Tha'labah رضي الله عنها

Her real name was Barakah bint Tha'labah, but she came to be known by her son Aiman's name as Umm Aiman رضي الله عنها. She was the lady who played the role of mother and took care of the young boy, Muhammad ﷺ when his mother Âminah bint Wahb passed away while traveling from Makkah to Madinah. The Prophet ﷺ used to address Umm Aiman as *'Mother'* and said she would go to Paradise in the hereafter. She was a lady who was like a member of the Prophet's family over the years. When Khadîjah رضي الله عنها passed away, she was deeply affected and wept for her. She was the one who bathed and shrouded her, and prepared her body for burial. When the Prophet's daughter, Zainab رضي الله عنها passed away, again she was as grief-stricken as any member of the family. She also prepared her body for burial, with the help of Mothers of the Believers Saudah رضي الله عنها and Umm Salamâh رضي الله عنها. She took part in the Battles of Uhud, Khaybar and Hunain. She also had the distinction of migrating twice – once to Abyssinia and again to Madinah.

She had been a slave of the Prophet's father, 'Abdullâh bin 'Abdul Muttalib. She was originally from Abyssinia. According to the tribal customs prevailing in the Arabia of the time, the Prophet ﷺ spent his early years with the tribe Banu Sa'd. He was nursed by Haleemah Sa'diyah, and was brought up by her. When he was five years old he was returned to Makkah to his mother. When he was six years old his mother decided to take him to Yathrib to meet his maternal relatives who were from the tribe of Banu Najjâr. Her bondswoman Barakah bint Tha'labah also accompanied them. On the way back when they reached Abwâ', the Prophet's mother suddenly fell ill and died. They then buried her there.

Barakah bint Tha'labah consoled the little boy, and tried her best to fill the gap of his mother.

When the Prophet ﷺ grew up to be a young man he freed her and married her to 'Ubaid bin Zaid al-Khazraji. When Umm Aiman converted to Islâm, differences developed between them. He was not willing to swear the oath of allegiance and accept Allâh ﷻ and His Messenger; and so they separated.

By her first husband, 'Ubaid, she had a son, Aiman. Thus she became known as Umm Aiman. He grew up to be a very prominent Companion and was martyred in the Battle of Hunain. Her second marriage was to Zaid bin Hârithah ؓ. He was the General of the Muslim army and was martyred in the Battle of Mu'tah. They had a son, Usâmah bin Zaid ؓ, who was another great General of the Muslim army.

The Prophet ﷺ was aware of her exemplary character, noble manners and purity of heart and said that whosoever wished to marry a lady of Paradise should marry Umm Aiman رضي الله عنها.

When Zaid bin Hârithah ؓ heard this statement of the Prophet ﷺ, based not on her looks, but on her character, he developed a liking for her and was only too happy to marry her. Their son, Usâmah bin Zaid ؓ, because of his praiseworthy character was loved deeply by the Prophet ﷺ. Zaid bin Hârithah ؓ became famous because of the Prophet's love for him; as did his son, Usâmah bin Zaid ؓ, who became famous as the Prophet's favorite.

The Prophet ﷺ had great respect for Umm Aiman رضي الله عنها, and regarded her as his mother. Sometimes because of her simple nature, she would become insistent and stubborn. The Prophet ﷺ would then be very respectful and patient and try his utmost to please her.

Umm Aiman رضي الله عنها

Anas bin Mâlik ﷺ says that the *Ansâr* of Madinah gave their date orchards to the Prophet ﷺ; he in turn distributed them among the *Muhâjirs* (Emigrants) from Makkah. When the Muslims triumphed over Banu Quraidhah and Banu Nadheer, the Prophet ﷺ started returning their property to the generous *Ansâr* owners. Anas bin Mâlik ﷺ relates that when he went to take back his orchards from Umm Aiman رضي الله عنها, she refused point blank. Not only that, she tied a cloth around his neck, jerked him and said that it was out of the question, that she would return the orchards to him under any circumstances.

When the Prophet ﷺ saw this he tried to persuade her to return the orchards. He said he would give her something of the same value in exchange, but she did not agree. Then he offered her something double the value; still she refused. Then he went on to offer three times the value and so on. At last, he offered her something ten times the value of the orchards, and she finally agreed. And thus, Anas bin Mâlik ﷺ got his date orchards back.

The Prophet ﷺ often visited her. As soon as he saw her he would say that she was a reminder of his family and she was his mother who deserved respect.

'A'ishah رضي الله عنها narrates that one day when all of them were seated together, the Prophet ﷺ drank some water. Umm Aiman رضي الله عنها asked him to fetch some water for her too.

'Aishah رضي الله عنها asked in a rather shocked tone if she was asking the Messenger of Allâh ﷺ to get some water for her.

She said, "Why not? I have served him often." He fetched the water for her and offered it to her in a very respectful manner.

Anas bin Mâlik ﷺ narrates that he would sometimes visit Umm Aiman رضي الله عنها with the Prophet ﷺ. She would express great pleasure on their arrival and serve delicious food and drinks. If the Prophet ﷺ refused to partake of it for some reason, she would be very angry and offended. She would ask him why he did not eat or drink. The Prophet ﷺ would smile at her getting upset in this manner. Sometimes it would so happen that he was fasting.

Anas bin Mâlik ؓ said that one day, she started kneading dough to make some bread. He asked her what she was doing. She answered she was making some bread for him as was the custom in her country, Ethiopia. Usâmah ؓ, resembled his mother rather than his father. So the Hypocrites used to taunt him, saying that he was not really the son of Zaid bin Hârithah ؓ. This used to upset the Prophet ﷺ very much. 'A'ishah said that once, the Prophet ﷺ entered the house looking very happy and smiling. She asked him if there was any special reason for this. He answered that something strange had happened. He said Zaid bin Hârithah and Usâmah bin Zaid رضي الله عنهما were lying asleep with their faces covered, but their feet could be seen from under the sheet. Majzaz Madalji, an expert in physiognomy saw them sleeping and said,

"*Looking at the bone structure of the feet, it seems that father and son are sleeping.*"

The Prophet ﷺ said he was very pleased to hear this.

Some miracles associated with Umm Aiman رضي الله عنها are to be found in books of history. In *Tabaqât Ibn Sa'd* it is mentioned that during her migration from Makkah to Madînah, she experienced such severe thirst that she thought she would die. There was no sign of water in the vicinity. Suddenly she saw a bowl of water tied with an extremely beautiful pure white rope, descending gradually towards her from the sky. It came near her face and stopped. She put her lips to it and drank her fill to her heart's content. This cool water from the heavens was enough to ward off hunger, thirst and disease for the rest of her life. After that, she says she never experienced thirst for the rest of her life. Though she fasted during the hottest months possible she never experienced a desire for water. Abu Nu'aym Asbahâni, a noted biographer and historian, has mentioned this incident in his book *Hilyat-ul-Awliya'*. He says Umm Aiman رضي الله عنها was an Allâh-fearing, good-hearted, pious woman of pure character who fasted during the day and spent her nights in prayer.

Umm Aiman رضي الله عنها

Under the guidance of the Prophet ﷺ she played an active role in *Jihâd*. She was active in various battles. In the Battle of Uhud she gave herself up completely to nursing the wounded and providing water to the thirsty *Mujâhideen* in the battlefield. In the Battle of Khaybar she was one of the twenty women who fought against the enemy. When her son did not take part in this war because his horse was sick she called him a coward.

A devotee of the Prophet ﷺ and a poet of Islâm, Hassân bin Thâbit ؓ wrote poetry on this occasion, and elaborated on this point. The horse of Aiman ؓ had eaten poisoned grain and he could not take part in the battle because he had to tend to it.

In the Battle of Hunain this same courageous and fearless warrior Aiman ؓ was martyred, proving his valor as a warrior of Islâm. When the Muslim army was losing ground, a few of the Companions – Abu Bakr Siddeeq, 'Umar Farooq, 'Ali bin Abi Tâlib, 'Abbâs bin 'Abdul Muttalib, Abu Sufyân, Hârithah bin Nu'mân, Usâmah bin Zaid and Aiman bin 'Ubaid رضي الله عنهم were those noteworthy Companions who stood their ground with the Prophet ﷺ. They did not falter and displayed unmatched loyalty and bravery.

During the Battle of Hunain the Muslim army faced a very critical situation, the army panicked and scattered and the *Mujâhideen* were on the verge of running away from the battlefield. It seemed that the earth that was spread out so wide was now closing in on them. At this stage when all seemed lost, the Prophet ﷺ displayed extraordinary courage and said:

'I am the Prophet no lie.
I am the son of 'Abdul Muttalib.'

He meant that he was standing steadfast in the field of battle and at that critical stage it was no trivial matter.

Umm Aiman رضي الله عنها lost her son Aiman ؓ in this battle, but she was a role model in patience and acceptance of the Will of Allâh.

During the Battle of Mu'tah, Zaid bin Hârithah ؓ was appointed General of the Muslim army. The Prophet ﷺ said if Zaid bin Hârithah ؓ was martyred, then Ja'far bin 'Ali Tâlib ؓ should be made General. If he too was martyred, then 'Abdullâh bin Rawâhah ؓ should take his place, and if he was martyred then the *Mujâhideen* should choose anyone they thought suitable. And it was Allâh's Will that all three of them were martyred one by one. Umm Aiman رضي الله عنها bore the loss of her husband with great fortitude and asked her son Usâmah ؓ to bear the loss of his father bravely.

Umm Aiman رضي الله عنها sometimes pronounced some words in the Ethiopian dialect. When the Prophet ﷺ heard her pronunciation of certain words he would just smile pleasantly and correct her. She could not say *Assalâm-u-Alaikum* and would invariably say *Assalâm la Alaikum*. He told her gently one day to just say *Salâm*, as the meaning became the opposite the way she said it. In the same way she mispronounced certain expressions in supplications to Allâh ﷻ; so he told her to keep silent.

She was a very straightforward person with absolutely no malice; she was very soft-hearted, sincere and sympathetic. On returning from the Battle of Bani Mustaliq when the Hypocrites spread slanderous gossip regarding the character of 'A'ishah رضي الله عنها, she vouched unhesitatingly for the purity of her character. This endeared her and increased her worth in the eyes of 'A'ishah رضي الله عنها. It is recorded in history books that 'A'ishah رضي الله عنها said about Umm Aiman رضي الله عنها.

"*My eyes and my ears have the best impressions about her.*"

The Prophet ﷺ prepared an army to crush the power and might of the Romans in Palestine; Usâmah bin Zaid bin Hârithah ؓ was appointed General of the Army. Companions like Abu Bakr Siddeeq and 'Umar Farooq رضي الله عنهما were also asked to serve under him. Some of the *Mujâhideen* were not happy with this appointment. But the Prophet ﷺ remained very firm about his decision and said that Usâmah bin Zaid ؓ would retain that position as he deserved it. He sent for Usâmah bin Zaid ؓ and told him to start on his journey in the Name of Allâh. The army had hardly reached Jaraf near Madinah when Umm Aiman رضي الله عنها sent a messenger to say that the Prophet ﷺ was very ill. The army stopped and camped at Jaraf. When Usâmah ؓ reached Madinah, the Prophet ﷺ passed away. It seemed that Umm Aiman رضي الله عنها could not withstand this sorrow.

Umm Aiman رضي الله عنها

Involuntarily, plunged in grief, she burst into tears. The people there were taken by total surprise; they had never heard anything like it before. She had nurtured him in his childhood and held him in her arms; she had seen him grow into a fine young man – a young man who then wore the mantle of the Prophet of Allâh ﷺ. She witnessed him as a young bridegroom, when he wed Khadîjah رضي الله عنها. She also underwent the tortures and cruelties inflicted by the Quraish and the polytheists of Makkah against him and the new converts. She experienced the days when Makkah was like the Final Day of Judgment. She saw those historic days when he ruled over the newly founded Islâmic state. And best of all she saw the miraculous revelations of Allâh's radiance. All the golden pages of his life seemed to pass before her eyes.

A few days after the death of the Prophet ﷺ Abu Bakr Siddeeq and 'Umar Farooq رضي الله عنهما went to visit Umm Aiman رضي الله عنها to condole with her. She started to cry remembering the Prophet ﷺ. They asked her why she was crying though she knew very well that he was in a far better world than this one, with Allâh ﷻ. She said that although she indeed knew this, she was crying because the revelations from Allâh ﷻ had come to an end with his passing away. Hearing this they also started weeping.

One day Mu'âwiyah bin Abi Sufyân ؓ talking to Usâmah bin Zaid ؓ praised his mother highly. Usâmah bin Zaid ؓ agreed saying that she was more blessed than even his mother, Hind. Mu'âwiyah bin Abi Sufyân ؓ accepted the truth of this statement and said he was right. Then he said Allâh ﷻ also said so and quoted the following:

> "Verily, the most honorable of you with Allâh is the most pious among you." (49:13)

❖☙❖☙❖☙❖☙❖

She had looked after the Prophet ﷺ from his childhood and given him a mother's love and care after Âminah bint Wahab's death. The Prophet ﷺ loved and regarded her highly; his Companions also treated her with great respect.

Sahîh Muslim records that Umm Aiman died just six months after the passing away of the Prophet ﷺ. But some others disagree and say that she died during the caliphate of 'Uthmân bin 'Affân ؓ. She lived to a ripe old age.

May Allâh be pleased with them and they with Him.

© Maktaba Dar-us-Salam, 2003
King Fahd National Library Cataloging-in-Publication Data
Ghadanfar , Mahmmod Ahmad
Great Women of Islam/ Mahmood Ahmad Ghadanfar.
Riyadh 2003
272 p : 14cm X 21 cm
ISBN: 978-9960-897-27-3
1-Women in Islam   2-Prophet, companions and successors
I.Title
239.6 DC   1424/5178

L.D. no. 1424 / 5178
ISBN: 978-9960-897-27-3